THE THISTLE AND THE BRIER

CONTRIBUTIONS TO SOUTHERN APPALACHIAN STUDIES

1. *Memoirs of Grassy Creek:
Growing Up in the Mountains on the Virginia–North Carolina Line.*
Zetta Barker Hamby. 1997

2. *The Pond Mountain Chronicle:
Self-Portrait of a Southern Appalachian Community.*
Leland R. Cooper and Mary Lee Cooper. 1997

3. *Traditional Musicians of the Central Blue Ridge:
Old Time, Early Country, Folk and
Bluegrass Label Recording Artists, with Discographies.*
Marty McGee. 2000

4. *W.R. Trivett, Appalachian Pictureman:
Photographs of a Bygone Time.*
Ralph E. Lentz. 2001

5. *The People of the New River:
Oral Histories from the Ashe, Alleghany and
Watauga Counties of North Carolina.*
Leland R. Cooper and Mary Lee Cooper. 2001

6. *John Fox, Jr., Appalachian Author.*
Bill York. 2003

7. *The Thistle and the Brier:
Historical Links and Cultural Parallels Between Scotland and Appalachia.*
Richard Blaustein. 2003

8. *Tales from Sacred Wind:
Coming of Age in Appalachia. The Cratis Williams Chronicles.*
Cratis Williams. 2003

9. *Willard Gayheart, Appalachian Artist.*
Willard Gayheart and Donia S. Eley. 2003

THE THISTLE AND THE BRIER

Historical Links and Cultural Parallels Between Scotland and Appalachia

BY RICHARD BLAUSTEIN

CONTRIBUTIONS TO SOUTHERN APPALACHIAN STUDIES, 7

McFarland & Company, Inc., Publishers
Jefferson, North Carolina, and London

Library of Congress Cataloguing-in-Publication Data

Blaustein, Richard.
    The thistle and the brier : historical links and cultural parallels
between Scotland and Appalachia / by Richard Blaustein.
        p.   cm. — (Contributions to southern Appalachian studies ; 7)
    Includes bibliographical references and index.

    ISBN 0-7864-1452-9 (softcover : 50# alkaline paper) ∞

    1. Appalachian Region, Southern — Relations — Scotland.
2. Scotland — Relations — Appalachian Region, Southern.   3. Appalachian
Region, Southern — Civilization.   4. Scotland — Civilization.
5. Ethnicity — Appalachian Region, Southern.   6. Ethnicity — Scotland.
7. Group identity — Appalachian Region, Southern.   8. Group identity —
Scotland.   I. Title.   II. Series.
F217.A65B58   2003
303.48'2750411 — dc21   2002154977

British Library cataloguing data are available

On the cover: photograph by the author

Manufactured in the United States of America

McFarland & Company, Inc., Publishers
  Box 611, Jefferson, North Carolina 28640
    www.mcfarlandpub.com

To the memory of Michael Barr (1936–2000)

Born the same year as Appalachian poet/cultural activist Jim Wayne Miller, my sister Carole's late husband personified tenacity in the face of adversity. He would have been glad to know that I finally finished this book.

Table of Contents

Preface   1

Introduction   7

1. Tracing Scottish Allusions in American Discourse
   on Appalachia   19

2. Appalachia Studies Comes of Age   47

3. Scottish Cultural Revivals: A Sketch and a Theory   72

4. Conversation with a Cultural Missionary:
   Flora MacDonald Gammon, Waynesville,
   North Carolina, 17 January 1994   76

5. Core and Periphery: A Critique of the Internal
   Colonialism Model in Scotland and Appalachia   98

6. The Thistle and the Brier: Poetics and Identity Politics
   in Scotland and Appalachia   104

7. Self Portrait of a Cultural Activist: A Conversation
   with Hamish Henderson, Edinburgh, 13 June 1996   110

8. Folk-Bashing and Cultural Self-Determination in
   Scotland, Nova Scotia and Appalachia: Looking for
   Constructive Alternatives to Deconstructionism   124

9. Dinna Say Dinna: Teachers As Agents of Linguistic
   Colonialism in Scotland and Appalachia   132

10. Poems Make the People: A Conversation with Joy Hendry, Edinburgh, 1 July 1996   146

11. The Beginning of a New Song: Some Reflections Upon the Opening of the New Scottish Parliament   160

Conclusion: Thinking Ocean to Ocean   162

Bibliography   165
Index   171

Preface

𝒯he process of writing this book, which took five years to complete, brings to mind images of vision quests in which initiates endure mortifying ordeals, figuratively wandering through trackless thickets of thistles and briers, until they happen to experience a unifying vision that inspires them to complete their missions.

Long before the title of this book came to me in May of 1996, I began exploring connections and parallels between Scotland and Appalachia, especially regarding cultural revivals and identity politics. This book brings together my published and unpublished research and writing on these subjects dating back to 1990, including lecture notes originally prepared for my seminar in Appalachian Studies at East Tennessee State University, papers written for academic conferences, as well as articles and book reviews published in regional journals. I also include edited transcriptions of recorded conversations with three extraordinarily eloquent and insightful cultural activists, Hamish Henderson and Joy Hendry of Edinburgh, Scotland, and Flora MacDonald Gammon of Waynesville, North Carolina. I want to thank all three for their patience and generosity, particularly for granting permission to quote them at length in this book.

Chapter One enlarges upon lecture notes from my Appalachian Studies seminar dating back to fall 1992 concerning the etymology, geology and history of human habitation of Appalachia. This chapter also includes excerpts from a public lecture at the School of Scottish Studies in Edinburgh during July of 1991 on connections between Scotland, Northern Ireland and Appalachia. It also includes portions of a paper on "Religion, Regionalism and Radical Politics in Colonial Appalachia," presented at the 1992 Appalachian Studies Conference in Asheville, North Carolina, and excerpts of "Conflicting Scottish Traditions in American Folk Culture," presented at the 1994 American Folklore Society meeting in Milwaukee, Wisconsin, culminating

1

with an expanded discussion of Scottish allusions in the writings of early commentators on Appalachia first published in my review of Bill Best's 1997 anthology *One Hundred Years of Appalachian Visions*, in the winter 1998 edition of the *Appalachian Journal*.

Chapter Two draws upon lecture notes from my Appalachian Studies seminar also dating back to 1992, outlining the ideas of major figures in the Appalachian Studies movement from the late 1960s and early seventies to the early 1990s regarding Appalachia's marginal relationship to mainstream America including Helen Lewis, Cratis Williams, Wilma Dykeman, Henry Shapiro, Jim Wayne Miller, Frank Einstein, Bob Snyder, David Whisnant, Allen Batteau, Archie Green, and Rodger Cunningham. My criticism of David Whisnant's deconstruction of Scottish romantic nationalism in this chapter first appeared in a letter to the editor in the spring 1995 *Appalachian Journal* challenging Whisnant's misrepresentation of my article "Rethinking Folk Revivalism" in his generally favorable fall 1994 *AppalJ* review of *Transforming Tradition: Folk Music Revivals Examined* (University of Illinois Press, 1993) edited by Neil V. Rosenberg. This chapter concludes with quotes from my 1991 *Journal of the Appalachian Studies Association* article, "Hegemony, Marginality and Identity Reformulation: Further Thoughts Regarding a Comparative Approach to Appalachian Studies," originally presented at the 1990 Appalachian Studies Conference in Helen, Georgia.

Chapter Three, "Scottish Cultural Revivals: A Sketch and a Theory," was originally presented as a lecture during the Scottish-Appalachian program jointly offered by the ETSU Center for Appalachian Studies and Services and Edinburgh University's School of Scottish Studies during July of 1990 in Johnson City, Tennessee.

Chapter Four is based upon the transcription of a taped conversation with Flora MacDonald Gammon recorded at her home in Waynesville, North Carolina, on January 17, 1994.

Chapter Five builds upon a paper, "Scotland, Appalachia, and the Politics of Post-Modern Culture," originally presented at the 1994 Appalachian Studies Conference in Blacksburg, Virginia, and published in the 1994 edition of the *Journal of the Appalachian Studies Association*, now the *Journal of Appalachian Studies*.

Chapter Six, "The Thistle and the Brier: Poetics and Identity Politics in Scotland and Appalachia," was originally presented as a memorial tribute to Jim Wayne Miller at the 1997 Appalachian Studies Conference in Fort Mitchell, Kentucky.

Chapter Seven is based upon the transcription of a recorded conversation with Hamish Henderson, recorded at the School of Scottish Studies in Edinburgh on June 13, 1996.

Chapter Eight expands upon a paper presented at the 1997 American

Folklore Society meeting in Austin, Texas, "Folk Revivalism and Cultural Self-Determination in Contemporary Scotland and Appalachia," including excerpts of an earlier paper, "Nativistic and Transnational Folk Revivals in Global Perspective," presented at the 1992 AFS meeting in Jacksonville, Florida.

Chapter Nine expands upon my discussion of linguistic colonialism in Scotland and Appalachia in my winter 1998 *AppalJ* review of Bill Best's *One Hundred Years of Appalachian Visions*. I read an early version of "Dinna Say Dinna: Teachers As Agents of Linguistic Colonialism in Scotland and Appalachia" at the 1998 meeting of the Tennessee Folklore Society at Middle Tennessee State University in Murfreesboro, Tennessee.

Chapter Ten is based upon the transcript of a conversation with Joy Hendry, recorded in her home in Edinburgh, Scotland, on the first of July, 1996, exactly three years to the day before the inauguration of the new Scottish parliament in 1999.

Many generous people on both sides of the Atlantic have helped to bring this project to fruition. First of all, endless thanks to my longtime friend and recently retired colleague Dr. Jean Haskell. She succeeded me as director of the ETSU Center for Appalachian Studies and Services in 1992, whereupon I became the center's first senior research fellow and coordinator of a newly established undergraduate minor in Appalachian Studies. She and other old friends and colleagues in the Department of Sociology and Anthropology, including Drs. Scott Beck, Anthony P. Cavender, Judith Hammond, and Robert G. Leger, provided enthusiastic support and generous funding which enabled me to spend May through July of 1996 as a visiting scholar at the School of Scottish Studies and also at the International Social Sciences Institute.

I also want to thank Dr. Paul Stanton, President of East Tennessee State University, Dr. Bert C. Bach, Provost and Vice President of Academic Affairs, Dr. Don Johnson, Dean of the College of Arts and Sciences, Dr. Michael Woodruff, Vice President for Research, and Dr. Henry Antkiewicz, Director of International Studies, for generously providing funds that enabled me to do research in Edinburgh in 1996 and also for approving non-instructional leave in the spring of 1997 when I began writing the first draft of this book. Special thanks also to Professors Jim Odom and Colin Baxter of the ETSU History Department for being such patient listeners and good friends.

I especially want to thank another longtime friend, Dr. Margaret A. Mackay, Director of the School of Scottish Studies, for her continual support for my work. Many thanks likewise to her University of Edinburgh colleagues including Professor Anthony P. Cohen of the Department of Social Anthropology and Provost of the Faculty Group of Law and Social Sciences and Dean of Social Sciences, Professor David McCrone of the Department of

Sociology and Unit for the Study of the Government of Scotland, Professor Ged Martin, Director of the Centre for Canadian Studies and former Deputy Director of the Visitor's Programme of the International Social Sciences Institute, and his successor as Deputy Director of the Visitor's Programme, ISSI's senior research fellow Dr. Eberhard Bort, for their unstinting generosity and hospitality. Many thanks also to Owen Dudley Edwards of the Department of History, and also to Ian Fraser, John Shaw, Emily Lyle, Gary West, Catherine Campbell, Peter Cooke, Mark Trewin and Morag Macleod of the School of Scottish Studies. I also must express my deepest thanks to Hamish Henderson, Joy Hendry and Ian Montgomery, John Greig and Helga Rhein, Margaret Bennett, Frances Fisher, Ewan McVicar, Billy Kay, Nancy Nicolson, John Knox, Ailie Munro, John MacGregor, Angus Calder, Kevin Docherty and Janet Lachlan, Willie Haynes, Ian and Talitha McKenzie, Iain MacLachlan, Colin McKinnon, Charlie Woolley, Ian Grant, Herman Rodriques, Sheila Douglas, Tony McManus, Keith Whyte, and other friends in Scotland too numerous to mention.

I also wish to thank old friends in the Scottish American heritage community including David Farquharson, Larry and Catherine Long, Scott and Jane MacMorran, Flora MacDonald Gammon and her husband John Dall, and also Wayne and Jean Bean for their unwavering good wishes and moral support.

Also, my heartfelt thanks to North American academic colleagues including Philis Alvic, Patricia Beaver, Bill Best, Thomas G. Burton, Keith and Kathy Cunningham, Rodger Cunningham, Angus Gillespie, Jim Griffith, Loyal Jones, Bill Lighfoot, Michael Lofaro, Howard W. Marshall, Judith McCulloh, Michael Montgomery, Ted Olson, Neil V. Rosenberg, Catherine Shoupe, Hamish Thompson, Allison Webster, Patricia and Paul Wells, John R. Williams and Charles K. Wolfe for their expert advice and good wishes. They and everybody named above inspired me to persevere in bringing this rambling, brambly opus to something like a clear-cut conclusion. Any errors of style and fact still remaining in this book are purely mine.

Finally, thanks to all the individuals and publishing organizations listed below for providing permission to reprint copyrighted material:

Gordon McKinney and Susan Lewis on behalf of the Appalachian Studies Association for permission to reprint excerpts from two of my articles, "Hegemony, Marginality and Identity Reformulation: Further Thoughts Regarding a Comparative Approach to Appalachian Studies," *JASA*, Vol. 1, 1991, and also "Scotland, Appalachia, and the Politics of Postmodern Culture," *JASA*, Vol. 4, 1994.

Sandra Ballard, *Appalachian Journal*, excerpts of my review of Bill Best's *One Hundred Years of Appalachian Visions* in *Appalachian Journal*, vol. 25, no. 2, winter 1998.

Bill Best for excerpts from his anthology *One Hundred Years of Appalachian Visions,* Berea: Appalachian Imprints, 1999 [1997].

Mike Epley, Appalachian Consortium Press, for excerpts of Jim Wayne Miller's "The Brier Sermon" in *The Mountains Have Come Closer* and David Cratis Williams' and Patricia Beaver's introduction to *The Cratis Williams Chronicle: I Come to Boone.*

Michael Schmidt and Joyce Nield, Carcanet Press, Manchester, England, for excerpts of poems of Hugh MacDiarmid, "A Drunk Man Looks at the Thistle" and "Empty Vessel," included in Michael Grieve and Alan Riach, eds. *Hugh MacDiarmid: Selected Poems,* London: Penguin Books, 1994.

Michelle Kass of Michelle Kass Associates, London, England, for excerpts from Gordon Williams' novel *From Scenes Like These,* originally published by Magna Print Books, Edinburgh, 1986.

Ruth Hussey, University of Tennessee Press, for excerpts from Emma Bell Miles' *The Spirit of the Mountains,* Knoxville: University of Tennessee Press, 1975 (1905), and Horace Kephart's *Our Southern Highlanders: A Narrative of Adventure in the Southern Appalachians and a Study of Life Among the Mountaineers,* 1976 (1913).

Craig Wilkie, the University of Kentucky Press, for excerpts from John C. Campbell's *The Southern Highlander and His Homeland,* 1969 (1921).

Hugh Morton, Linville, North Carolina, for photographs of the Grandfather Mountain Highland Games.

Jim Thompson, West Jefferson, North Carolina, and Kent Hay Atkins, Santa Barbara, California, for photographs of Flora MacDonald Gammon.

Fred Hay, Director of the W.L. Eury Appalachian Collection, and Patricia Beaver, Director of Appalachian Studies, Appalachian State University, for photographs of Cratis Williams.

David Cratis Williams, for photographs of his father Cratis Williams.

Mary Ellen Miller, Bowling Green, Kentucky, for photographs of Jim Wayne Miller.

Norma Myers, Director, Archives of Appalachia, ETSU, for photographs of the MacDonald Family and Cratis Williams.

Ian McKenzie, School of Scottish Studies, Edinburgh University, for photographs of Hamish Henderson.

And lastly but definitely not least, thanks to Nancy Nicolson of Edinburgh, Scotland, for permission to reproduce photographs of herself and the lyrics of her song "Listen tae the Teacher."

Richard Blaustein
Johnson City, Tennessee
Fall 2002

Introduction

Through the wet and waving forest with an age-old sorrow laden
Singing of the world's regret wanders wild the faerie maiden,
Through the thistle and the brier, through the tangles of the thorn,
Till her eyes be dim with weeping and her homeless feet are torn.

*Clive Hamilton [C. S. Lewis], excerpt from
"World's Desire," in* Spirits in Bondage. *ed. Mike W. Perry
(London: William Heineman: 1919, 1999), pages 102–04*

*P*rickly plants stubbornly clinging to the stony slopes of marginal uplands, the thistle and the brier are living embodiments of tenacity in the face of adversity.

The thistle is the ancient national symbol of Scotland, whose motto, translated from the Latin *nemo me impune lacessit* into English declares, "None Touch Me with Impunity, " or more emphatically in braid Scots, "Wha Daur Meddle Wi' Me!" Down through the centuries, the thistle has been an enduring symbol of the tenacity of Scottish national identity.

Appalachian people share that prickly mixture of pride and defensiveness embodied in the Scottish thistle. Many present-day inhabitants of the Appalachian region of the United States of America proudly claim Scottish ancestry and strongly identify with Scotland to this day. For roughly a hundred years, the Scottish Connection has been a central theme of American discourse concerning Appalachia.

Unlike the thistle, the brier is neither a national nor even a regional identity symbol, not in any widespread or positive sense. What then inspired the late Jim Wayne Miller (1936–1996), a leading contemporary Southern Appalachian poet-scholar-cultural activist, to invent the poetic persona he named The Brier?

The Brier stems from "brierhopper," a contemptuous synonym for "hillbilly." Miller poetically converted a badge of prickly shame into an emblem of blossoming pride — the first stage in healing the fragmented, internally divided identities of subordinated national or regional minorities like Scots or Appalachians. Many notable creative artists and scholars, particularly poets and folklorists beginning with W.J. Thoms, the Englishman who coined the term folklore in 1846, have initiated their life's work as leaders of cultural revival movements by re-naming themselves.

Jim Wayne Miller's best-known and most frequently quoted poem, "The Brier Sermon: You Must Be Born Again" (1980), outlines a process of identity reformulation following the phases of a heroic quest or rite of passage. This archetypal progression of separation, marginality, and return is characteristic of the careers of leaders of cultural revitalization movements throughout recorded history, not only in late twentieth century Scotland and Appalachia. The Paiute founder of the pan-tribal Ghost Dance Movement that spread across the late nineteenth century American West discarded the white man's name he had been given, Jim Wilson, and reclaimed his native appellation, Wovoka.

Since the early eighties Miller's "Brier Sermon" has become a primary reference point for Appalachian Studies, comparable to Hugh MacDiarmid's celebrated poem "A Drunk Man Looks at the Thistle" (1926) in the discourse of twentieth century Scottish cultural nationalism. Though outwardly different in cadence and accent, "The Brier Sermon" and "A Drunk Man Looks at the Thistle" express the same basic human desire for self-definition. Hugh MacDiarmid was in actuality the pen-name of the late Christopher Murray Grieve (1892–1978), who wrote critically acclaimed modern poetry in innovative revitalized twentieth century Scots yet linked himself to the Celtic heartland with a Gaelic appellation, emotionally distancing himself from the ambiguous Borders where he was born and raised.

I can only speculate about Grieve's personal reasons for reinventing himself as MacDiarmid. I have only read about and heard my Scottish friends talk about Hugh MacDiarmid, but I did get to know Jim Wayne Miller personally. I literally sat at his feet and listened to him expound upon the need to develop a comparative vision of Appalachia and other peripheral parts of the world. I heard him recite sections of "The Brier Sermon" before it appeared in print. More than once I played the fiddle at impromptu Saturday night hoedowns during the early Appalachian Studies Conferences. I vividly recall leading lights of the movement including Jim Wayne Miller and Cratis Williams doffing their professorial coats and ties and rolling up their sleeves, dancing the old Southern Appalachian flatfoot and clog steps, drinking moonshine and store-bought corn liquor with equal gusto, singing, joking, telling tales and carrying on until we reluctantly stumbled off to bed with old tunes and new songs tumbling around in our heads.

MacDiarmid's Drunk Man would have felt right at home at some of those pioneer era Appalachian Studies Conferences, when there were still giants in the earth who partied all night instead of going to bed early in order to get up bright-eyed and bushy-tailed to network with the right people about nominations and committees over breakfast the next morning. Of course, Jim Wayne and Cratis might have lived longer if they had partied less, gone to bed earlier and taken better care of themselves. The same is true of Robert Burns. I learned a lot from these two charismatic Appalachian cultural leaders, and I'm forever thankful that I got to know them personally.

In the fall of 1970 I began teaching cultural anthropology, sociology, and folklore at East Tennessee State University in Johnson City, Tennessee, and became actively involved with Appalachian Studies as soon I arrived there. I am grateful that so many people in this part of the country have accepted and befriended me. Nonetheless, I will always be an exotic outsider here in "the buckle of the Bible Belt" because of my Jewishness, not to mention where I was born and raised, perhaps the very last place on earth you might expect to find someone developing an avid interest in Appalachian history and culture — Brooklyn, New York.

My active interest in Appalachia dates back to the fall of 1959, when I took up the five-string banjo (and fiddle two years later) and started reading everything I could find about southern mountain people. At the age of fifteen, I was a banjo-toting citybilly, one of the hordes of Brooklyn folkniks who took the subway to Manhattan to play around the fountain in Washington Square and check out what was happening in Greenwich Village. I remember first encountering Cratis Williams's name and photograph in a copy of *Mountain Life and Work* I picked up at Israel G. Young's Folklore Center in Greenwich Village. The urban folk revival was beginning to take off just about the time Cratis was completing his exhaustive dissertation on *The Southern Mountaineer in Fact and Fiction* at NYU, located in the Village. I didn't meet Cratis Williams at that time. Now I wonder if he might not have taken an occasional break from his dissertation research on a sunny Sunday afternoon to enjoy the impromptu open-air hootenannies around the fountain in Washington Square. That's only one of many questions I wish I had thought to ask Cratis, but that's the way life is, especially when you're young and expect people to be around forever.

Cratis became one of my first Appalachian mentors, along with Helen Lewis, who left ETSU to set up the first college level course in Appalachian Studies at Clinch Valley College in 1970. Cratis and Dr. Joe Smiddy, then chancellor of Clinch Valley College in Wise, Virginia, another native born musician and early advocate of Appalachian Studies, didn't hold my origins and background against me when they awarded me first prize at a local fiddle contest they were judging at Emory and Henry College in Emory, Virginia, in the summer of 1971. My fiddling rang true for these open-minded, warm-hearted people who had grown up with authentic old time Appalachian music. Where I came from didn't matter to them. They knew where I was coming from. I will always appreciate the support and encouragement they gave me.

Not everybody in the southern mountains has been so welcoming to New York citybillies like myself. During the early fifties, Bascom Lamar Lunsford refused to let urban folkies perform at the Asheville Mountain Dance and Music Festival, including Roger Sprung, one of New York's first bluegrass banjo players, who taught me how to play in the old-time frailing style he used to accompany Jean Ritchie on one of her early albums "Saturday Night and Sunday Morning." For about a year I used to take the subway from my home in the Gravesend section of Brooklyn to Roger Sprung's studio on the Upper West Side of Manhattan to take banjo lessons every week. Then I would go back home and sit on the steps of our two family brick house within window-rattling distance of the elevated line and try to frail the old East Kentucky banjo tunes Roger had learned from Rufus Crisp and Buell Kazee by way of Stu Jamison and Margot Mayo. I read and re-read Harry Caudill's *Night Comes to the Cumberlands* after it came out in 1962; I still have the dog-eared paperback copy I bought when I was an undergraduate at Brooklyn College. Even then I wanted to know more about the backgrounds and lives of the people who played this music that had become my consuming interest, much to the consternation of my long-suffering parents Rose and Elliott Blaustein, who would have been much happier if I had devoted a fraction of the energy I put into learning fiddle and banjo into subjects like mathematics and chemistry.

The way I saw it back then, studying for chemistry and math exams took away precious time from playing the fiddle and banjo. I was only sixteen when I entered college in the fall of 1960, intellectually precocious in some ways but temperamentally disinclined to study required subjects that weren't personally rewarding or fulfilling. Though it took six years, I finally managed to graduate from Brooklyn College in 1966 with a bachelor's degree in sociology and anthropology and minor in Mandarin Chinese and the desire to pursue an advanced degree in folklore. Another of my mentors, Lee Haring, who played banjo and taught a folklore course in the English department, wrote a glowing letter of recommendation that convinced Richard M. Dorson to admit me to the Folklore Institute at Indiana University in the fall of 1967.

Moving to Southern Indiana proved to be an excellent preparation for settling in the Southern Appalachians for my wife Rosemary Brookman and myself, whereas moving directly from Brooklyn to East Tennessee could well have induced severe cultural shock akin to the bends. Like the local people we later got to know in East Tennessee, Hoosiers, at least down in the southern end of the state, informally addressed grandparents as Mamaw and Papaw, ate biscuits and gravy for breakfast, said "you'uns" when Brooklynites would have said "youse" (a linguistic link between Brooklyn and Glasgow) and in many other ways, some not so trivial or innocuous, perpetuated the cultural traditions of the Upland South in the Midwest. Three years in southern Indiana, settled in the early nineteenth century by migrants from south of the Ohio River with a substantial contingent of recent Appalachian arrivals looking for work in the area's industrial plants and limestone quarries, enabled me to actually get to know some of these people and develop an appreciation of their lives extending beyond their music, visiting in their homes, listening to them talk about why they had left the mountains.

Moving to East Tennessee was the next step in my personal exploration of Appalachia, where the Appalachian Studies movement was beginning to blossom. I happily recall chatting with Cratis Williams at the very first meeting of the Appalachian Consortium not long after I moved to East Tennessee in the fall of 1970. I first met Jim Wayne Miller in the mid 1970s when he was serving as senior academic consultant to a proposed public television series on Appalachia that was never funded for various reasons. It was keenly disappointing at that time (about twenty-five years ago) to take part in drafting a lengthy, detailed scenario only to have it rejected. Nonetheless I learned a great deal about Appalachia from Jim Wayne Miller, who combined encyclopedic breadth of scholarly knowledge with intense depth of feeling for his native place and its misunderstood, often derided people. Not only did Jim Wayne Miller write terse, witty, moving poetry, he had seemingly read and thoroughly digested everything ever written about Appalachia up to that point in time. Beyond that, he was fluent in a number of languages. For thirty-three years, he taught German language and literature at Western Kentucky University in Bowling Green, Kentucky, where he died in August of 1996.

It was during the summer of 1996 that the seed of *The Thistle and The Brier* first germinated, largely as the result of reading Scottish cultural historian Christopher Harvie's discussion of MacDiarmid and the Scottish Renascence of the 1920s and long late night conversations with Scottish friends in Edinburgh, particularly my banjo-playing pal John Greig. Comparing Miller's "Brier Sermon" (1980) with MacDiarmid's "A Drunk Man Looks at the Thistle" (1926) led me to consider how vernacular language, literature, and folk arts all serve to liberate suppressed native voices, empowering subordinated peoples to define themselves in their own terms.

I was eager to discuss my budding ideas concerning the convergence of poetry and identity politics with my old friend and mentor, with Jim Wayne Miller when I returned to the United States. To my great disappointment and sadness, I learned that he had succumbed to lung cancer at the age of sixty.

Instead, I found myself presenting a memorial essay titled "The Thistle and the Brier: Poetics and Identity Politics in Scotland and Appalachia" at the 20th Annual Appalachian Studies Conference on a panel chaired by Rodger Cunningham, whose award-winning book *Apples on the Flood* (1987), a highly original and challenging exploration of the Celtic Question in Appalachia, has yet to reach the wider trans–Atlantic audience it deserves.

All of us who had personally known him talked about Jim Wayne Miller throughout that clear, chilly weekend in March of 1997 at Fort Mitchell, Kentucky. One of the high points of that Sunday morning's memorial service was pioneer Appalachian Studies advocate Bill Best's vivid description of his Berea College classmate Jim Wayne Miller, a fellow native of the mountains of Western North Carolina, refining a wicked curve ball under the tutelage of an old school varsity baseball coach who quoted Homer and Virgil in the original Greek and Latin.

Bill Best's anecdote captured the essence of the Jim Wayne Miller we had known and loved, the very model of an Appalachian renaissance man; a real life culture hero; a homegrown visionary cultural leader who played a key role in inspiring and sustaining Appalachian Studies in the region's schools and universities. He played a major part in directly inspiring and sustaining my personal interest in Appalachia. I hope this book does credit to Jim Wayne Miller's memory and serves to make his work and thought better known inside and outside the Appalachian region.

This book has been a long time in the making, and I do not claim that it is or will be the final word on this subject. Instead, it is an exploratory excursion into uncharted territory, with all of the attendant virtues and flaws of pioneering efforts. References to Scotland abound in the primary literature of Appalachian Studies, but until I took on this task no one else had taken the time to systematically review the foundation documents of this field to locate, identify and comment upon these Scottish allusions. In Chapter One, I define Appalachia in geological terms, discuss the impact of European colonization on the aboriginal inhabitants of Southern Appalachia, and then proceed to glean the writings of major American commentators on Appalachia published between 1899 and 1936 for Scottish references. The American idea of Appalachia is to a substantial extent grounded in comparisons to Scotland derived from selective, romantic readings of Scottish history and literature by such influential commentators as William Goodell Frost, John Fox, Jr., Emma Bell Miles and Horace Kephart. Though largely the descendants of Scottish lowlanders, the people of the Southern Appalachians have been equated with Scottish highlanders in popular and scholarly literature. The romantic haze of the Celtic Twilight continues to confuse perceptions of Appalachian and Scottish highlanders to the present day, despite the best efforts of revisionist regional historians, beginning with John C. Campbell, himself the American-born son of a Scottish highlander. Chapter One ends with a summary of a concise history of Southern Appalachia with a strongly Scots-Irish emphasis written by Paul Doran, a Presbyterian minister from East Tennessee, published in *Mountain Life and Work* in 1936, the same year Jim Wayne Miller was born.

Chapter Two continues with a brief survey of the rise of the present-day Appalachian Studies movement as it has developed in the wake of the War on Poverty initiated during John F. Kennedy's 1960 presidential campaign. Kennedy's successor Lyndon B. Johnson established the Appalachian Regional Commission in 1965, including 406 counties in the Appalachian Highland sections of thirteen states from southwestern New York down to northeastern Mississippi, taking in all of West Virginia along with parts of Pennsylvania, Ohio, Maryland, Virginia, North Carolina, South Carolina, Kentucky, Tennessee, Georgia and Alabama. An uneasy and volatile aggregation of scholars and activists drawn from diverse backgrounds, participants in the Appalachian Studies movement have nonetheless found common cause in working to better the lives of the people of a region long seen as out-of-step and out-of-line with the American national mainstream.

To acquaint my readers with the ideas of some of the leading scholar-activists in Appalachian Studies since the early nineteen seventies concerning Appalachian otherness, the assumption that Southern mountaineers are a people apart from other Americans, I review a set of selected critical essays beginning with founding figures like Helen Lewis, Cratis Williams and Wilma Dykeman, and culminating with a detailed survey of Rodger Cunningham's controversial, award-winning book *Apples on the Flood* (1987). In his ambitious psychohistory of the Scottish people and their Appalachian descendants, Cunningham proposes that the internal division of the contemporary Appalachian psyche can be traced back to waves of invaders subordinating native inhabitants of the Western fringe of Atlantic Europe, culminating in the imposition of English upon Gaelic-speakers in Scotland in the fourteenth century. Some scholars might challenge Cunningham's chronology, arguing that this process of linguistic domination and subordination was already underway in Scotland by the twelfth century. Nevertheless, the external imposition of official language and the suppression of native speech ways in culturally depriving schools has undeniably been part of the common experience of Scottish and Appalachian schoolchildren within living memory. Much of the creative activity in Scotland and Appalachia today helps to bring about "healing of the divided self," through reviving and reinventing indigenous language and literature along with various folk traditions including instrumental music, song, dance and crafts.

The rest of this book explores diverse aspects of cultural revivalism and identity politics in Scotland and Appalachia. It was largely inspired by re-

reading Cunningham's *Apples on the Flood* after visiting Scotland for the first time in 1989 and again in the summer of 1991. I was an active participant in the first seminars and field trips of a newly initiated Scottish-Appalachian summer program linking the School of Scottish Studies of the University of Edinburgh and East Tennessee State University's Center for Appalachian Studies and Services, which I directed from its inception in 1983 until 1992.

I must confess that I really did not begin to appreciate or understand Rodger Cunningham's *Apples on the Flood* the first time I read it, or the second time, for that matter. Cunningham was using terms and concepts that were frankly foreign to me. Nonetheless I had a nagging sense that this book had important implications for understanding what the people of Scotland and Appalachia shared in common, if only I could understand its basic premises. Only after I encountered Scottish intellectuals and artists actively engaged in revivals of folk arts, vernacular language and literature did I finally began to connect with what Cunningham was saying. Actually getting to know Cunningham and discuss the issues raised in his book gave me a greater appreciation of the trans–Atlantic significance of his ideas concerning the divided self and the role of literary, linguistic and cultural revivals in the process of its healing. Reading some of the writers who had inspired Cunningham, particularly Malcolm Chapman's *The Gaelic Vision in Highland Scotland* (1978), made me rethink some of my earlier ideas concerning cultural revival movements.

I first visited Scotland in 1989 with my wife Rosemary and our two daughters Rachel and Jessica, who were then twelve and ten. We flew to London a week before the ETSU Scottish-Appalachian program was scheduled to commence. Rosemary had traveled to Europe and Israel when she was thirteen, but the girls and I had never been outside of the United States. We arrived in London in the midst of a scorching heat wave, staying in an old hotel on Piccadilly Circle where we kept as cool as we could by taking frequent baths in the long porcelain tubs in the communal bathrooms down the hall. We dressed lightly, drank lots of water, and enjoyed as many of the sights of the British capital as we could take in, including visiting Westminster Cathedral, Buckingham Palace and the Tower of London, where we saw the ravens at the Traitor's Gate, gawked at the stiff, blank-eyed Grenadier Guards, and then were briskly herded past the royal jewels by pike-wielding Beefeaters.

One day we took a coach tour to Oxford. I chatted with the tour guide as we waited for other passengers to arrive. He asked me what we were doing in London. I told him that we were seeing the sights in and around London before going up to Edinburgh for three weeks. His upper lip curled. "Oh really, what could you possibly do in Edinburgh for three weeks?" I didn't appreciate his supercilious attitude, and when our coach tour returned to London from Oxford, I didn't bother to tip him even though his hand was outstretched.

We stayed in a guest house just north of the Meadows in the center of the old town of Edinburgh, handy walking distance to the School of Scottish Studies on George Square and Sandy Bell's, a lively little pub on Forrest Road where the folk music revival that flourished in Scotland following World War II was still going full blast. The faculty and students of the School of Scottish Studies jokingly called Sandy Bell's their unofficial seminar room, but it really was that and a whole lot more.

Sandy Bell's instantly became my local pub. It was there that I first talked and shared ballads with the late Hamish Henderson, the venerable poet/folklorist/songwriter who played such a prominent role in contemporary Scottish politics and culture. A major radical intellectual who had translated *The Letters from Prison* of Sardinian/Italian Communist theorist Antonio Gramsci, Hamish also found time to collect folksongs and also write brilliant original songs and poetry in braid Scots. It was also in Sandy Bell's that I met Scottish people of my own generation including John Greig and Harry Lawson who had fallen in love with Appalachian fiddle and banjo music and played it with skill and verve. I quickly felt very much at home in Edinburgh.

So did my family. The people in Edinburgh were very much like our neighbors back in East Tennessee: warm, open and friendly. The girls remarked upon the difference between the kilted Scottish guards at the portal of Edinburgh Castle, who rocked on their heels and smiled at us as we passed by, unlike the haughty, rigid guards at the Tower of London where we had seen the royal jewels.

We made our way down the Royal Mile that runs down the red volcanic spine of Edinburgh to Holyrood Palace situated at the foot of the spectacular flat-topped crag called Arthur's Seat.

While we were exploring the ruined abbey next to Holyrood Palace, the girls suddenly became incensed: "The Scots are great! Why couldn't the English let them be independent? It isn't fair! It isn't right!" Visiting London and then Edinburgh had taught them a lot about British history in a short time, and they identified with the Scots, so much like their Southern Appalachian neighbors back home in East Tennessee.

You know what they say about pearls coming from the mouths of babes. My daughters' comments forced me to think about parallels and connections between Scotland and Appalachia less obvious and more consequential than comparing ballads, fiddle tunes and Jack tales. When I re-examined Rodger Cunningham's *Apples on the Flood*, I finally began to fathom what he was saying about the roots of Appalachian self-estrangement in the Scottish experience of subordination and the consequent impetus to heal the divided self.

When I revisited Scotland in the summer of 1991, I began collecting interviews with leaders of the Scottish folk revival with the intention of comparing it with similar developments in Appalachia. As it happened, four years passed before I returned to Edinburgh. Nonetheless, I remained interested in pursuing this study. Chapter Three was written when I was reconsidering my theoretical assumptions concerning cultural revitalization and seeking to expand beyond my primary concern with revivals of folk and traditional music, which I had investigated in my 1975 doctoral dissertation on the rise of the Old Time Fiddlers Association Movement in the United States. In 1994, I visited and interviewed my old friend Flora MacDonald Gammon of Waynesville, North Carolina, whose family played a key role in initiating the Grandfather Mountain Highland Games, now one of the largest Scottish heritage gatherings in North America. Chapter Four presents her life-long involvement with Scottish heritage activities and Appalachian folk revivalism. About the same time, I had read Edinburgh University sociologist David McCrone's illuminating book *Understanding Scotland: The Sociology of a Stateless Nation* (1992) and began to correspond with him via e-mail in 1994. Chapter Five discusses McCrone's book and its implications for understanding identity politics in Appalachia, including a comparison of David McCrone's critique of American sociologist Michael Hechter's application of Immanuel Wallerstein's world systems theory in his book *The Celtic Fringe* (1975) with Appalachian/Scottish-American sociologist Roberta McKenzie's penetrating analysis of the intellectual history of the concepts of world systems theory and internal colonialism in the discourse of Appalachian Studies since the early 1970s.

When I visited face-to-face with David McCrone and his colleague social anthropologist Anthony P. Cohen in Edinburgh for the first time in 1995, I had to acknowledge that the Scottish folk revival, though tremendously interesting to me, was only one component of a wider cultural and political movement paralleling the rise of the Appalachian Studies movement in the United States. In 1996, I had the opportunity to talk at length with some of Scotland's leading scholars, artists and activists concerning cultural revivals and identity politics.

Chapter Six compares Jim Wayne Miller's "Brier Sermon" with Hugh MacDiarmid's "A Drunk Man Looks at the Thistle." Chapter Seven presents Hamish Henderson's reflections upon the folk revival and its interconnections with poetry and other facets of contemporary Scottish cultural nationalism. Chapter Eight begins with a critique of Ian McKay's deconstruction of the twentieth century folk revival in Nova Scotia in his book *The Quest of the Folk*, strongly influenced by Appalachian cultural critic David Whisnant's *All Things Native and Fine* (1983) and ends by identifying key points of convergence in the careers of cultural leaders in Scotland and Appalachia. Chapter Nine documents that many leading figures in Appalachian Studies, like their counterparts in Scottish cultural nationalist circles, have sought to reclaim vernacular speech ways suppressed by colonialistic school teachers intent upon imposing elite linguistic standards. Chapter Ten is an edited transcription of a conversation with Joy Hendry, editor and publisher of a major Scottish literary magazine. Her lucid observations concerning poetry as a paradigm for all genres of creative self-expression highlight the central concern of this book: how peripheral people like Scots and Appalachians seek to recover their native voices as they struggle to define themselves in their own terms. This book concludes with reflections on the re-establishment of the Scottish Parliament on the first of July 1999 and a call for expanding trans–Atlantic dialogue concerning connections and parallels between Scotland and Appalachia.

So now this book begins as it will conclude, with the assertion that connections and parallels between Appalachia and Caledonia are real and well worth exploring. Hopefully *The Thistle and the Brier* will stimulate further trans–Atlantic dialogue concerning points of convergence between Scotland and Appalachia.

1

Tracing Scottish Allusions in American Discourse on Appalachia

*W*hen should we begin our exploration of points of convergence between Scotland and Appalachia?

About two hundred and fifty million years ago, according to current theories concerning the formation of the continents and mountain systems. Before North America and Europe drifted apart to form separate continents, geologists nowadays tell us that the Appalachian mountains of eastern North America and the Caledonian mountains of Scotland were connected, forming a primordial Appalachian-Caledonian mountain system.[1]

During the Permian period of the Paleozoic era, the shifting of the earth's tectonic plates caused the ancient island of Appalachia to fold itself against the continental shield and sink westward into the ocean, forming the first Appalachian Mountains roughly 250 million years ago. Over eons of time, the accumulation and decomposition of immense quantities of ancient plant life would produce the fossil fuel deposits that made possible the industrial revolutions in Scotland, Appalachia and the rest of the modern world.

The massive ranges of the Appalachian continental mountain system we know today stretch roughly 1,950 kilometers (1,212 miles) northeast to southwest from the craggy coasts of Newfoundland and Labrador to the rolling sandhills of North Alabama and Mississippi. The Appalachian Highland continental mountain system includes five geological provinces: the New England-Acadian Province, the Piedmont, the Blue Ridge, the Valley and Ridge System, and the Appalachian Plateau. Concentrated in the Appalachian Plateau, the anthracite coal deposits of northeastern Pennsylvania and the bituminous coal fields of West Virginia, Virginia, Kentucky, Tennessee and

Alabama fueled the industrialization of the United States following the American Civil War.

The Appalachian South has been a subservient hinterland throughout its history, whose inhabitants have never controlled its immense natural wealth. Instead, outside business and government interests have largely overseen the exploitation of the region's vast reserves of coal, timber, minerals, and water, along with its cheap labor. What factors have kept Appalachia impoverished and underdeveloped?

The shape of the land itself is a major factor, but not the sole source of Appalachia's poverty and dependency. Transportation has been problematic until recent times. There are relatively few navigable streams and rivers in the southern Appalachian highlands of the United States of America. Though much of Appalachia has been landlocked since prehistoric times, the region has never been totally cut off from the outside world. Animal and human migration patterns naturally followed the valleys and gaps.

Human beings have lived in this part of the world for about twelve thousand years according to the archaeological record; European explorers first wandered through this region in the sixteenth century. In the latter decades of the eighteenth century, increasingly great numbers of settlers moved into the mountainous Southern Back Country, mostly English, German and Scottish in origin. Prominent among them were the so-called "Scotch-Irish" (Scots-Irish or Ulster Scots in current British usage), whose ancestors emigrated from the Lowlands of Scotland to colonize the Ulster Plantations in Northern Ireland in the early seventeenth century. Many of these pioneer settlers in the Southern Back Country were uncertain, unaware, or openly defiant of frontier lines demarcated in pre-revolutionary treaties between the British colonial government and the indigenous inhabitants of the region.

In *Apples on the Flood* (1987) Rodger Cunningham says that the Appalachian personality suffers from "uncertain ego-boundaries." We must understand that neither the native inhabitants of the region nor the settlers who displaced and intermarried with them ultimately defined their own boundaries. Powerful outsiders did that for them. The seats of political, economic, social and cultural power and authority lay elsewhere, far removed from the peripheral Appalachian back country. The descendants of the early inhabitants of Appalachia were condemned to marginality and dependency, stereotyped as uncouth barbarians beyond the pale of civilization, defined, of course, by elite metropolitan standards. This may explain why so many people in the Appalachians are resistant to external labels of any kind, including the term Appalachia itself.

When and where does the term Appalachia originate? What language does it come from? What is its literal meaning? How to pronounce it?

Appalachian sociologist David S. Walls meticulously traces Appalachia's etymological history to the very beginnings of European exploration of North America in his definitive 1977 essay "On the Naming of Appalachia." Early dictionaries attribute the first reference to Appalachia to Spanish explorer Hernando De Soto, who could have learned it from the Muskogee tribe or various other Muskogean-speaking Southeastern tribes including the Choctaw, Creek, Yamassee or Hitchiti, possibly even the long-extinct Apalatchi tribe themselves. The Apalatchi, whose name means "Great Water People" or "People Who Live on the Other Side of the Water" lived at the mouth of the Apalatchi River on Apalatchi Bay in northern Florida until a British force destroyed their village and dispersed them in 1703. It is not known whether these hapless early victims of colonialism called themselves Apalatchi or if other Muskogean-speaking neighbors applied that appellation to them.

(A brief digression concerning the pronunciation of the name of the region is in order: most Americans tend to pronounce "appellation" and "Appalachian" similarly but as far as most natives of Southern Appalachia are concerned, "Appalachia" rhymes with "apple at 'cha." What we have here is a textbook illustration of a shibboleth, a linguistic boundary marker that distinguishes locals from non-locals.

(Edna Nowlin, born and raised in the southwestern Virginia coalfield town of Appalachia, was secretary of the sociology and anthropology department when I arrived at East Tennessee State University as a new assistant professor in the fall of 1970. One day she asked me if I knew how Appalachia got its name. Her answer? "Adam and Eve were picking fruit for supper in the Garden of Eden. Adam started getting fresh with Eve, who said, "quit messin' with me or I'll throw this apple at 'cha!").

Although Hernando De Soto has traditionally received credit for the first reference to Appalatchi or Apalachen, David Walls notes that these words do not appear in the records of his expedition. Curiously, they do show up in the journals of the lesser-known conquistador Panfilo de Narváez in 1528. "Apalachen" first appears on a Spanish map drawn by Diego Gutierrez, published in 1562. French cartographer Jacques le Moyne de Morgues, member of a Huguenot expedition in Florida in 1564, was the first European to specifically apply "Apalachen" to a mountain range rather than a village, native tribe, or region of southeastern North America. His map also plainly identifies the village of Apalatchi, which the British destroyed in 1703. Walls attributes the first English language reference to "Apalatchi" to English adventurer and explorer Richard Hakluyt in 1586.

The aboriginal inhabitants of the southern Appalachian mountains known today as the Cherokee did not originally call themselves by that name. Like Appalachia, the term Cherokee is also Muskogean in origin. Cherokee is English for *Tsalagi*, a disdainful Muskogean epithet for the Iroquoian-speaking people who lived in the highlands of the Southern Appalachians comparable to hillbilly, ridgerunner or brierhopper. (Or *teuchter*, a derisive Lowland Scots label for Gaelic speaking rustics up north in the Scottish Highlands derived from *teuch*, the Scots cognate of *tough*. Basically a synonym for "peasant," etymologically *teuch-ter* is analogous to the English "ruffian" — "rough-'un.")

According to the great early American ethnologist James Mooney in *Sacred Myths and Formulas of the Cherokee* (1900), *Tsalagi* comes from the Choctaw "chalk," meaning "cave people." The Cherokee term for cave people is "kituah gi" and curiously, Kituah ("Cave") is what they called their ancient capital in the heart of the Great Smoky Mountains.

Rodger Cunningham, however, has recently proposed an intriguing alternative etymology, contending that: "*Tsalagi* is a Cherokee borrowing of a Muskogean word meaning 'chatterers, barbarians' (the Berbers of North Africa borrowed the Latin word in the same way)." Whatever its ultimate meaning or source, we must understand that "Cherokee" was not originally a Cherokee term. Like the self-designations of so many other Native American peoples, their oldest native appellation for themselves "Ani Yun Wiya," literally means "The (First or Real) People."[2]

The names Scot and Cherokee might have emerged in the same way. Geoffrey of Monmouth and earlier medieval chroniclers of British national myths and legends identified Scota, daughter of Pharoah, as the primordial mother of the Scots. Nonetheless, the ultimate meaning and derivation of the term Scot remains uncertain. One possible source is the Latin "scotti," meaning "raiders." Like Cherokee, Berber, or Jim Wayne Miller's pen name, The Brier, "Scot" could have originated as a badge of shame and been transmuted into an emblem of pride. (Arguably, that process of transmutation is still underway.)

It is uncertain how long The First People occupied the heartland of Southern Appalachia before De Soto's arrival. When De Soto's expedition first encountered the people who became known to the world at large as the Cherokee in 1540, these Iroquoian-speaking farmers and hunters occupied a territory covering more than 40,000 square miles. Straddling both sides of the Southern Appalachian range, the Cherokee lands included extensive sections of the present-day Carolinas, Virginia, Kentucky, Tennessee, Georgia, and Alabama. Though the Choctaw labeled them "cave people," in fact they mostly lived in independent agricultural towns situated on the headwaters of the region's major rivers (King 1979: ix). Many rivers and streams in Southern Appalachia still bear Cherokee names, such as Watauga, Nolichuckey, Citico, and, of course, Tennessee.

Linguistically and culturally related to the Iroquoian tribes of the northeastern United States and Canada, the ancestors of the modern Cherokee presumably migrated south at some undetermined point in prehistoric time before European contact. In *The Cherokee Indian Nation: A Troubled History* (1979), Duane H. King notes that archaeological estimates of Cherokee occupation of the Southern Appalachian region vary from only two or three centuries before the arrival of the Spanish explorers to perhaps a thousand years ago (King 1979: x). In *Snowbird Cherokees: People of Persistence* (1991), Sharlotte Neely contends that the Cherokee have inhabited the Southern Appalachians for approximately four thousand years. This earlier date agrees with current estimates of divergence between the northern and southern branches of the Iroquoian language family.

According to their own origin myths, The Great Spirit created the Ani Yun Wiya in the Great Smoky Mountains at the beginning of time. Based on existing archaeological evidence, human beings have been living, hunting and travelling through this region roughly twelve thousand years. Small bands of migratory hunting and gathering people, so-called Paleoindians, killed huge prehistoric mammals including the mastodon with large, concave stone pointed spears and foraged for wild edible plants. (9500–8000 B.C.E.) The end of the last Ice Age saw the emergence of familiar modern North American animals and plant species. During this Archaic period (8000–1200 B.C.E.), hunting and gathering were still primary means of subsistence, though there is some evidence of early attempts to raise domesticated plants. The subsequent Woodland period (1200 B.C.E.–C.E. 1000) produced significant cultural developments including pottery, bow and arrow, and cultivation of maize, or Indian corn. Increasingly efficient food production supported permanent settlements whose leaders erected massive earthen mounds serving as burial and ritual sites. (See Boyd 1989: 15–27.)

Subsistence and settlement patterns in the Late Prehistoric period (1000–1540) were even more varied. The building of mounds in palisade-enclosed fortifications, along with elaborate ritual items and trade goods, indicate that some of these people were long-settled agriculturists involved in an extended market economy when Spanish explorers first happened upon them in the mid-sixteenth century. (According to Scottish historian Jim Hewitson, De Soto's expedition included a soldier named Tam Blake, the very first Scot known to set foot in Appalachia. See Hewitson 1993.)

The influx of European explorers and traders during the Protohistoric period (1540–1750) brought about drastic changes. Europeans spread infectious diseases that ravaged many tribes, while the introduction of firearms and other trade goods including alcohol caused many Native Americans to become dependent upon the Europeans. The British radically altered the political life of the Cherokee, designating a senior chief king of the Cherokee nation and dealing with the several towns through him, establishing a colonial mercantile economy based on importing muskets, lead, and gunpowder and exporting great numbers of deer hides, eventually shipping tens of thousands annually back to Britain. In *The First American Frontier: Transition to Capitalism in Southern Appalachia, 1700–1860* (1996), Appalachian historian Wilma A. Dunaway contends that at no point since the beginning of European colonization have Appalachia's inhabitants, including its aboriginal population, ever been totally self-sufficient or completely isolated from an externally imposed international market economy. As Dunaway explains, "To finance their importation of European commodities, the Cherokee increased their deerskin production, thereby increasing their debt peonage. Relentlessly the Cherokee were locked into an 'unequal exchange' that drained away Appalachian surpluses to benefit the expanding core" (1996: 49).

The Historic Period (1750–present) saw further Cherokee assimilation of European culture and continued displacement from their remaining lands. By the mid-eighteenth century immigrants from the British Isles and other parts of northwestern Europe began moving into the mountainous back country of British America, often in violation of royal treaties with the native inhabitants. Before the end of the eighteenth century, the Cherokee had ceded much of their original territory including most of the Southern Appalachian region to the British colonialists and then to the new American government.

Most of the Cherokee supported the British during the Revolutionary War, hoping to stop the invasion of their territories. They would sadly discover that the treaties and leases they negotiated with British and later with American governments gave them no protection from unscrupulous, land-hungry settlers. The sale of tribal lands by the older peace-seeking chieftains infuriated young warriors who led rebellious raids against the American settlers, who retaliated by burning Cherokee towns.

Military defeat and overwhelming numbers of incoming settlers prompted many Cherokee to adopt the ways of the white people. There were many marriages between Cherokees and whites. Since the traditional Cherokee kinship system was matrilineal, children of Cherokee mothers and European fathers were considered full members of the seven matrilineal clans of the tribe.

Perhaps the most famous of these so-called White Indians was John Ross, whose Cherokee names were Cooweescoowe ("large water bird with unwebbed feet resembling a snipe, probably the large grey heron") and Tsan-Usdi ("Little John"). Ross served as Chief of the Cherokee Nation from 1839 until his death in 1866.

He was born in 1790 in the southeastern corner of what became the state of Tennessee when it entered the Union in 1796. Ross's Scottish father hired a tutor to educate the future Cherokee chief at home and later sent him off to boarding school. Apparently this was partially at the insistence of Ross' maternal grandfather John McDonald. Born in Inverness, Scotland, circa 1747, McDonald established a frontier trading post at Ross's Landing on the Tennessee River, nucleus of present-day Chattanooga, and married the daughter of a Scottish father and a Cherokee mother. As Scottish historian Jim Hewitson notes in *Tam Blake & Co.: The Story of the Scots in America*: "'Old McDonald,' as he was known, insisted that his descendants should be reared as Scots and not Indians, and as a child wee John would often beg his grandfather to allow him to wear Indian clothes rather than the Highland dress" (Hewitson 1993: 165).

Presiding over the Cherokee National Council from 1817 to 1826, Ross often visited Washington, D.C. as a delegate in treaty negotiations between the Cherokee nation and the U.S. government. Ross opposed ceding tribal lands and voluntary westward migration, but to no avail. In 1838 Ross reluctantly led the forced removal of a major part of the Cherokee nation from their homeland in the Southern Appalachian Highlands to Indian Territory, which entered the Union as the state of Oklahoma in 1907.

This infamous episode in American history, remembered as "The Trail of Tears," is comparable to the Highland Clearances in Scotland. Ironically, those descendants of Scots and other European settlers who dispossessed the Cherokee of nearly all of their ancestral lands in the heartland of Southern Appalachia would be vilified in turn as marginal semi-savages; ignorant hillbillies, ridgerunners and brierhoppers obstructing the progress of Western civilization. Viewed in a more paternalistic and romantic light, these same southern mountain people, like the Scottish highlanders with whom they would frequently be compared, were transformed into a species of "noble savage." Potentially capable of improvement, these worthy but uncultivated folk required the tutelage of energetic agents of civilization. Like Chief John Ross's maternal grandfather Old McDonald, many teachers operated upon the colonialistic assumption that their students' indigenous cultural traditions and languages needed to be uprooted like weeds to prepare a proper seedbed in which seeds of a higher cosmopolitan culture could take root and flourish, transforming a tangled thicket of thistles and briers into a formal garden lined with pruned pear-trees and potted primroses (see Best 1999).

The personal dilemma of John Ross highlights the generic crisis of identity of the peripheral individual Rodger Cunningham terms "the divided self, " borrowing the phrase and concept from the title of Scottish psychiatrist R.D. Laing's popular book (1959). Though Laing may have invented the term, the concept of the divided self has a long, prickly history in Scottish intellectual discourse concerning personal and national identity.

In his provocative exploration of Appalachian psychohistory, *Apples on the Flood* (1987), Cunningham proposes that the insecurity and fragmentation of the Appalachian personality stems from the subordination of the diverse inhabitants of Scotland over the course of centuries, arguably millennia, of successive invasions and displacements. Deconstructionist cultural critics including Tom Nairn in Scotland and Allan Batteau and David Whisnant in Appalachia claim that romantic movements like regionalism and nationalism historically associated with folk revivalism perpetuate the dominance of an established order. Nonetheless it can be argued that contemporary cultural revival movements help bring about what Cunningham calls "healing of the divided self." In Scotland, Appalachia, and elsewhere, subordinated groups striving for autonomy rediscover (and fabricate) expressive symbols such as costume, traditional foods, arts, handicrafts, music, dance and perhaps most significant in their mass appeal, songs, poems and other genres of literature incorporating vernacular dialects and languages, reviving communal identity. As Alan Riach notes in his essay, "Reading Hugh Mac-Diarmid": "The suppression of native languages is followed by the transplantation of inappropriate modes of cultural expression, the recognition of political and psychic disruption and the transformation of that condition into one of regenerative possibility" (Riach and Grieve 1992: xiv).

The recovery of muted native voices and the creative exploration of their regenerative possibilities as poetic language are uniting themes of cultural movements in twentieth century Scotland and Appalachia. In both places the poet has played a key role as an expressive leader: "…holding up a mirror so that those within can gain a transcendental look at the ethos of the culture … serving as midwife for the rebirth of individuals, he serves his culture similarly" (Best 1999: 118). Much more remains to be said regarding identity politics and contemporary revivals of vernacular language and folk culture in Scotland and Appalachia.

Returning to early points of convergence between Scotland and Appalachia, it is purely coincidental yet nonetheless notable that the term "Appalachia" first appeared in print the same year John Ross became the first elected chief of the Cherokee nation. In an essay published in 1839, the celebrated author of "The Legend of Sleepy Hollow," Washington Irving (1783–1859), born in New York City to Scottish immigrant parents from Shapinsay, Orkney, proposed "Appalachia" and "Alleghenia" as alternatives to the European-derived "America" honoring Italian explorer and navigator Amerigo Vespucci (Walls 1977).

Washington Irving never meant his tongue-in-cheek proposal to re-name America to be taken seriously. Just the same, imagine an alternative United States of Appalachia with a national capital (like Brasilia) deliberately relocated from the East Coast in or near the mountains. (An early group of frontier populists actually proposed moving the new republic's seat of government from Washington, D.C., to Washington County, Tennessee, the oldest administrative unit west of the Appalachian range honoring the first American president.) Then try to imagine an Appalachia whose people see themselves and are seen by their nation as central instead of marginal to the national enterprise, who control their own political institutions and economic assets rather than being dominated and exploited by outside interests, whose regional speech patterns define national language standards instead of labeling their speakers as backward and inferior.

When exactly does Appalachia emerge as a distinctive region in American national consciousness? Though most commentators on the region have asserted that mainstream America only became aware of Appalachia following the American Civil War, historian Henry D. Shapiro contends in *Appalachia on Our Mind* (1978) that American consciousness of Appalachia's otherness actually begins with the establishment of Berea College in Kentucky in 1855. William Goodell Frost (1854–1938), third president of Berea College from 1892 to 1920, was the first American academic to define Appalachia as a cultural and geographic region.

Frost's essay "Our Contemporary Ancestors in the Southern Mountains" (1899) is a cornerstone of American discourse concerning Appalachia. First published in *Atlantic Monthly* magazine in 1899, Frost's frequently quoted and reprinted essay presents vivid images of Appalachian backwardness, poverty, illiteracy and feuding, along with detailed descriptions of old-fashioned subsistence patterns, distinctive log architecture, archaic folkways and speech patterns stemming from geographic isolation, tempered by "creditable" (largely English and Scots) ancestry, patriotism, and inherent native intelligence only wanting cultivation to blossom forth.

Seemingly never at a loss for memorable phrases, Frost influenced other major commentators including John Fox, Jr., Emma Bell Miles, Horace Kephart and John C. Campbell, who in turn shaped popular impressions of the region and its people in the first half of the twentieth century. When we examine Frost's landmark essay, we immediately discover numerous Scottish allusions: concrete evidence to support the thesis that from its inception American discourse concerning Appalachia has been grounded in Scottish references and metaphors.

A geographic determinist who attributed Appalachian backwardness to physical isolation, Frost contrasts the region with Switzerland and Scotland: "This is one of God's grand divisions, and in default of any other name we shall call it Appalachian America. It has no coast-line like Scotland or navigable rivers and lakes like Switzerland ... as a place for human habitation, the entire region has one characteristic — the lack of natural means of transportation."

Frost makes no further references to Switzerland, but the rest of his essay teems with Scottish allusions. No other nation except England figures so prominently in Frost's presentation of Appalachia's ethnic history. If Frost highlights the British element in the population of Appalachia, he totally ignores its early German settlers. Though an equally substantial number of Germans also settled in the Southern Back Country, one of the curious gaps in Appalachian Studies has been the relative lack of attention to the Germanic element in the early population. Historian Thomas Jefferson Wertenbaker in *The Old South* (1961) describes a "strange triangular battle of civilizations" that thwarted the conflicting cultural aspirations of the English, Scots-Irish, and Germans on the colonial southern frontier, contributing to the disunity and inner conflict of their descendants, the present-day inhabitants of Appalachia.

Sensational journalistic accounts of feuding had already tarnished the reputation of Appalachia's mountaineers before the end of the nineteenth century. Frost takes pains to accentuate the honorable (predominantly British) origins of southern mountain people:

> The impression has been made that some of the early settlers in the Southern colonies were "convicts," but it must be remembered that many of them were only convicted of having belonged to Cromwell's army or of persisting in attending religious meetings conducted by "dissenters." But whatever their origins, the "leading families" of the mountains are clearly sharers in the gracious influences which formed the English and Scotch people, and when a mountain lad registers by the name of Campbell or Harrison we have learned to expect that he will not be unworthy of his clan [in Best 1997: 11].

Praising the old-fashioned modesty and propriety of mountain women, Frost advocates the revival of spinning and loom weaving as wholesome feminine pursuits. Then Frost offers his own interpretation of Appalachian feuding: "As an institution it has its roots deep in Old World traditions. Yet it seems to have been decadent when the confusions of the civil war gave it new life" (Best 1997: 12).

Decrying the narrow sectarianism and literalism of Appalachian religion, Frost recounts a humorous anecdote about exceedingly literal Berea College students from the mountains who found John Fox, Jr.'s short stories set in the Cumberlands morally offensive. He concludes with an allusion to "the 'unco gude' of a generation ago." Here Frost displays his familiarity with Robert Burns' poem, "Address to the Unco Guid" (1787) lambasting Scotland's "rigidly righteous" Calvinist moralists, who regarded fiction and all manner of worldly frivolity as works of the devil. Horace Kephart retells this same anecdote verbatim in *Our Southern Highlanders* (1913).

Frost's final statement concerning the need to uplift Appalachian America through education alludes to a fictional Scottish village: "Mountain boys will walk a hundred miles, over an unknown road, in quest of an education they can but dimly comprehend. Why may we not expect to see our people as worthy and intelligent as those of Drumtochty?" (in McNeil 1995: 106)

Frost does not bother to identify the source of this allusion; he apparently assumes that his readers will know that Drumtochty is the locale of "Domsie," a short story included in *Beside the Bonnie Brier Bush*, published in 1894 under the name of Ian MacLaren. "Ian MacLaren" was the pen name of the Rev. John Watson (1850–1907), founder and leading proponent of the school of late Victorian Scottish local color fiction known as Kailyard (Scots for "cabbage patch"). The title of MacLaren's collection of short stories set in Drumtochty, *Beside the Bonnie Brier Bush* (and the appellation of the bucolic literary genre it inspired), allude to Burns' rendering of an old Jacobite song, the first line of which is "There grows a bonie brier-bush in our kail-yard."

"Domsie" is the nickname of an old school master or "dominie" who convinces a wealthy farmer, Drumsheuch, to provide scholarships to poor but promising youths, "lads o' pairts," from Drumtochty so that they can go to university and better themselves. Since it was Frost's mission as Berea College's president to raise funds to educate and uplift the poor but promising youths of Appalachian America, it is easy to understand why he would identify so strongly with "Domsie":

> Suppose that Drumtochty had only a bridle path to connect with the world, so that its farmers and shepherds could reach the market town only once or twice a year instead of twice a week; suppose there had been no university on the far horizon to beckon to aspiring lads; and suppose that Drumsheuch and the "meenster" had been illiterate men, jealous of all "high-heeled notions" from the outside world. Who would have ever known if there was ever a scholar born in Drumtochty or not? [Frost in McNeil 1989: 106].

In his book *Understanding Scotland: The Sociology of a Stateless Nation* (1992: 95–96), University of Edinburgh sociologist David McCrone observes that much of the published work of MacLaren and the Kailyard School was specifically directed towards a readership of nostalgic overseas Scots. In 1895 *Beside the Bonnie Brier Bush* was the best-selling fictional book in the United States. (The Reverend John Watson alias Ian MacLaren actually died in Mount Pleasant, Iowa, in 1907 during his third literary tour of the United States.) Were Frost's allusions to Burns and MacLaren conceivably meant to inspire philanthropic Scottish-American readers of *The Atlantic Monthly* to support the good works of Berea College?

Whatever his motivations might have been, Frost clearly felt confident that the readers of the *Atlantic Monthly* would grasp his allusion to the work of one of the most widely read Scottish authors of that period, whose popularity compared with that of Appalachian local color writer John Fox, Jr. (1862–1919), best known for his novels *The Little Shepherd of Kingdom Come* (1903) and *The Trail of the Lonesome Pine* (1908).

Two years after Frost's essay appeared in the *Atlantic Monthly* John Fox, Jr. published "The Southern Mountaineers " in the April–May 1901 edition of *Scribner's Magazine*, reprinted in W.K. McNeil's *Appalachian Images in Folk and Popular Culture* (1995) [1989]. W.K. McNeil notes Fox's fascination with the contrast between mountain culture and the modern world rapidly impinging upon it at the turn of the twentieth century. In most of his fiction, this dichotomy is personified by "a lowlander who is representative of civilization and thus stands in marked contrast to the ancestral culture of the mountaineers" (McNeil 1995: 122), a theme also found in Sir Walter Scott's 1814 novel *Waverley*.

In Scott's *Waverley*, as in Fox's *Trail of the Lonesome Pine*, entering the highlands instantly transports us back to the dark side of the never-never land of Brigadoon, a perpetual past without a future, a timeless black hole foreshadowing the bestial hillbilly fantasies of James Dickey's *Deliverance* (1969). In all of these novels, lowlanders penetrate peripheral highlands where they proceed to go native, taking on the atavistic characteristics of the barbaric highlanders who know nothing of progress or history but are bound up in endless cycles of mindless violence (see Craig 1996: 46). Scottish literary historian and cultural critic Cairns Craig proposes in *Out of History* that Scott's lowlanders seek to enter history even as his highlanders yearn to recover the mythic: "To enter history successfully is to leave Scotland behind" (1996: 62). A native of the central lowland Bluegrass region who moved to the peripheral highlands of Eastern Kentucky, Fox felt the same way about Appalachia.

Fox expands upon Frost's contention that the mountains are physically responsible for the isolation and poverty of mountain people. The cultural conservatism and distinctiveness of mountain folk is a global phenomenon, not restricted to the Appalachians (see McNeil 1995: 123). Like Frost, Fox contends that mountaineers are living like their pioneer ancestors due to geographic isolation. Likewise, Fox repeats Frost's assertion that the loyalty of the southern mountain folk to the Union cause first brought them to national consciousness (McNeil 1995: 123–24).

Fox discusses survivals of British folk culture in Appalachia including the "rough-and-tumble fight of the Scotch and the English square stand-up and knock-down boxing match," and also makes note of various superstitions and witchcraft (McNeil 1995: 126). American historian David Hackett Fischer would repeat Fox's comments nearly verbatim in his widely cited *Albion's Seed: Four British Folkways in America* (1989).

In *Albion's Seed*, Fischer seeks to demonstrate that American culture as

we know it today stems from the interplay of four colonial American subcultures with clearly defined roots in four equally distinctive British regional
traditions. The Puritan culture of New England derives from East Anglia.
The Cavalier culture of Tidewater Virginia can be traced back to southern
and western England. Quaker culture was transplanted from the Northern
Midlands of England to the Delaware Valley of Pennsylvania. Southern Back
Country culture is rooted in the Lowlands and Borders of Scotland as well
as Northern England and the Northern Irish province of Ulster, which contributed heavily to the early population of Appalachia.

In the United States these Protestant emigrants from Ulster are com-
monly known as the "Scotch-Irish," which grates upon the ears of present-
day Scots accustomed to "Scots-Irish" or "Ulster Scots," who nowadays only
apply the adjective "Scotch" to items like salmon and whisk(e)y, not human
beings. Appalachian historian H. Tylor Blethen explains the origins of this
term in his introduction to *Ulster and North America: Trans-Atlantic Perspectives on the Scotch-Irish:*

> The term "Scotch-Irish" is an American usage. It was seldom used in the
> eighteenth century when "Irish" was far more common. After the massive
> migration to America driven by the Irish Potato Famine of the 1840s, many
> Americans of Irish Protestant ancestry seized upon the name to distinguish
> themselves from the culturally different Catholic Irish immigrants, whom
> the Scotch Irish perceived as inferior [Blethen and Wood 1997: 1].

The impact of these Northern Irish Protestant settlers upon the culture
of the southern frontier has inspired what might be called a "border thesis"
in Appalachian Studies. Cratis Williams, who proudly claimed Ulster Scots
ancestry, staunchly maintained that the "Scotch-Irish" had profoundly
influenced the cultural and social life of the region. Throughout the literature dealing with the connections between Scotland, Northern Ireland, and
Appalachia there runs a recurrent theme of *cultural preadaptation,* propos-
ing that the core beliefs, values, habits, and customs of the Southern Back
Country are extensions of the cultural legacy of the borderlands of Northern Britain. Descendants of ancestors who had endured centuries of priva-
tion and lawlessness in the disputed borders of Northern England and the
south of Scotland, their colonial experience in Northern Ireland had *preadapted*
the Ulster Scots for the American frontier. Their cultural baggage included
a warrior ethic, belligerence towards an indigenous population ("wild Indians" taking the place of "wild Irish" Gaels), alienation from a metropolitan
government, a dissenting, nonconformist religion (indeed, antipathy towards
centralized regulation of any sort), and strong traditions of clannish famil-
ialism.

McDonald Family String Band from Mosheim, Greene County, Tennessee. Fiddler James McDonald (front center), born 1842, was the father of A.H. McDonald, born 1884 and A.C. McDonald, born 1879, both standing behind him holding banjos, and T.K. McDonald, born 1882, seated with fiddle. (Courtesy of Archives of Appalachia, East Tennessee State University.)

Even more so than Frost, Fox stresses the essentially Scotch-Irish character of the Southern mountain folk: "the strongest and largest current of blood in their veins comes from none other than the mighty stream of Scotch-Irish" (McNeil 1995: 140–41). To support this claim, Fox asserts, "From 1720 to 1780, the settlers in southwest Virginia, middle North Carolina and western South Carolina were chiefly Scotch and Scotch-Irish ... Scotch-Irish family names in abundance speak for themselves, as do folk-words and folk-songs and the characteristics, mental, moral, and physical of the people" (McNeil 1995: 141). Dialectologist Michael B. Montgomery has meticulously documented the Ulster Scots contribution to Appalachian folk speech in his authoritative 1997 essay, "The Scotch-Irish Element in Appalachian English: How Broad? How Deep?" in H. Tylor Blethen and Curtis W. Wood, Jr., eds. *Ulster and North America: Trans-Atlantic Perspectives on the Scotch-Irish.*

Like Frost, Fox was keenly aware that modernity was rapidly changing life in the Appalachian mountains. Regarding the twin burdens of Appalachian poverty and isolation, Fox concludes: "To my mind, there is but one strain of American blood that could have stood that ordeal quite so well, and that comes from the sturdy Scotch-Irish, who are slowly wresting from Puritan and Cavalier an equal share of the glory that belongs to the three for the part played on the world's stage by this land in the heroic role of Liberty" (McNeil 1995: 144).

Growing American consciousness of Appalachia converged with a revival of Scotch-Irish identity in the United States. In his authoritative article "How Distinctive Are the Scotch-Irish?" (1991), historian Kenneth W. Keller notes that the Scotch-Irish in post–Revolutionary America appeared to be rapidly losing any coherent sense of identity. However, the arrival of Catholic immigrants from the South of Ireland in the 1820s and thereafter set off waves of nativistic revivalism during the course of the nineteenth century. Between 1831 and 1870, Twelfth of July marches celebrating the victory of William of Orange at the Battle of the Boyne in 1690 sparked riots in major cities including New York and Philadelphia. Ulster-American nativism also took more benign forms, including the establishment of the Presbyterian Historical Society (1852) and the Scotch-Irish Society of America (1889). Keller observes that the Scotch-Irish revival "proved useful to reformers seeking to spread an understanding of Appalachian life to the nation at large." Frost, Fox and the major regional commentators they inspired "began to speculate about the connection between the Scotch-Irish and these people whom they began to call the "Southern Highlanders" (Keller 1991: 85).

John Fox, Jr. in particular played a key role in shaping American ideas about Appalachia and its connections to Britain as a whole and Scotland in particular. The United States was just emerging as a world power at the beginning of the twentieth century, and its intellectual and political leaders were striving to articulate a coherent national identity. Like Fox, President Theodore Roosevelt extolled the patriotism of the Scotch-Irish Presbyterians who settled the Southern Back Country in his popular history *The Winning of the West*, published in 1905.

That same year, pioneering Appalachian cultural activist/artist/writer/ school teacher Emma Bell Miles (1879–1919) published what is still one of the most readable and evocative books about Appalachia. From cover to cover, Miles' *The Spirit of the Mountains*, originally published in 1905 and reprinted by the University of Tennessee in 1975, is suffused with Scottish imagery and allusions, typified by this romantic depiction of a mountain woman weaving in her cabin home: "The mother is crooning over her work, some old ballad of an eerie sadness and the indefinable charm of unlooked-for minor endings, something she learned as a child from a grandmother whose grandmother again brought it from Ireland or Scotland" (1975: 30).

Miles' vision of the links between Scotland and Appalachia is utterly, unabashedly romantic: "My people, like the Hindoos and the Scotch High-landers, have the faculty of dealing with the occult, of seeing and hearing that which is withheld from more highly educated minds. Always there is some souvenir of the spirit-world in a nook of the mountaineer's brain" (1975: 118).

An avid self-taught folklorist, Miles' description of social games is particularly rich in Scottish references: "Young men and women enjoy the 'kissing games,' ...half dance, half romping child-play":

> Hit's over the river to feed my sheep,
> Hit's over the river, Charley;
> Hit's over the river to feed my sheep,
> and see my lonesome darling [1975: 160].

Clearly, this verse comes from the well-known "Weevily Wheat," which Miles describes as "very old and very popular. It is more like a dance than a game":

> O law, mother, my toes are sore,
>   Tra la la la la la la;
> Dancing on your sandy floor,
>   Tra la la la la la la;
> Your weevily wheat isn't fit to eat,
>   And neither is your barley;
> I won't have none of your weevily wheat
>   To make a cake for Charley.
> Charley he is a handsome lad,,
>   Charley he is a dandy;
> Charley he is the very one
>   That sold his hat for brandy.
> Your weevily wheat isn't fit to eat ,
>   and neither is your barley;
> We'll have some flour in half an hour
>   To bake a cake for Charley.

Miles comments, "It is not improbable that the "Charley" of these songs is the Prince Charlie of Jacobite ballads. "Over the River, Charley," may or may not be an echo of "Over the Waters to Charlie," for a large proportion of the mountain people are descended from Scotch Highlanders who left their homes on account of the persecutions which harassed them during Prince Charlie's time and began life anew in the wilderness of the Alleghenies.

Be that as it may, the mountain people do sing many ballads of old England and Scotland. Their taste in music has no doubt been guided by these, which have come down from their ancestors (1975: 159–63).

A few descendants of Scottish highlanders did indeed settle in the Southern Appalachian region. However, later commentators on the ethnic composition of Appalachia's early population, most notably John C. Campbell, would go to great lengths to demonstrate that the vast majority of Appalachian settlers of Scottish background originated in the Lowlands, not the Highlands. The Scottish (and Irish) contribution to Appalachian folk music (and North American traditional music in general) is nonetheless substantial and indisputable. Perhaps 40% of the Child ballads are distinctly Scottish in origin; most ballads found in Appalachia are still current in Ireland and Scotland. Some of the best known Appalachian fiddle tunes were originally Scottish, such as "Hop High Ladies" ("Miss McLeod's Reel"), "Leather Britches" ("Lord MacDonald's Reel"), and "Too Young to Marry," the tune of Robert Burns' song, "My Love She's but a Lassie Yet" (Blaustein 1996: 652).

Miles envisioned a regional literature drawing upon Appalachian folklore and vernacular speech: "Let no one who would welcome an expression truly national despise the quaint lore of the Southern mountaineers. We have had no Robert Burns as yet; but I expect him" (1975: 189).

Like Frost, Miles was not only also a devotee of Burns but also an advocate of handicrafts as an alternative to factory work for mountain people. Shifting from subsistence farming to wage labor degrades the mountaineers, corrupts their pre-industrial values and traditions. To realize their potential, mountain people must first become conscious of their distinctive identity.

Depicting southern mountaineers as "a people asleep, a race without knowledge of its own existence" (1975: 200–201), Miles concludes The *Spirit of the Mountains* with one final Scottish allusion: "Looking upon the fresh, sweet young faces of the children of the Log Church school, I often wonder which of them is destined to carry forth the word to his people for a Gathering of the Clans, not to war but to work — work that shall uplift instead of degrading; work that shall make the influence of the mountaineers a peculiar and beneficent force in their beloved country and in the world of men" (1975: 201).

Miles clearly hoped to spark a consciousness-raising movement in the Southern Appalachian mountains: "I make the statement more as a hope than a prophecy, but I feel sure of my ground in saying that these North American Highlanders will yet become a grand race" (1975: 199–200).

Miles' reference to "North American highlanders" inspired much more than just the title of Horace Kephart's *Our Southern Highlanders: A Narrative of Adventure in the Southern Appalachians and a Study of Life Among the Mountaineers,* first published in 1913, revised and republished in 1922, and reprinted by the University of Tennessee Press in 1976. Along with Frost and Fox, Kephart cites Miles throughout his still widely quoted book about life in the Southern mountains in the early decades of the twentieth century. Emulating his major influences, Kephart's discussion of Appalachia in *Our Southern Highlanders* is shot through with allusions to Scotland reflecting his extensive reading of Scottish history and literature.

Kephart compares the rugged terrain of the Great Smokies to "what Burns called Argyleshire: 'A country where savage streams tumble over savage mountains, thinly overspread with savage flocks, which starvingly support its savage inhabitants...'" (Kephart 1976: 29).

Explaining the prevalence of illicit distilling for which the Southern Appalachian region had become notorious by the early twentieth century, Kephart reminds his readers that "The people of Great Britain, irrespective of race, have always been ardent haters of excise laws.... And we still recall Burns' fiery invective" (from his poem "Scotch Drink" [1786]):

> The curst horse-leeches o' the Excise
> who make the whisky stills their prize!
> Haud up thy han', Deil! ance, twice, thrice!
> There, seize the blinkers! [wretches]
> An bake them up in brunstane pies
> For poor d-n'd drinkers [1976: 148].

Like earlier commentators on Appalachia, Kephart stresses the predominantly Scottish and Scots-Irish origins of the people he calls "our southern highlanders":

> They were a fighting race. Accustomed to plenty of hard knocks at home, they took to the rough fare and Indian wars of our border as naturally as ducks take to water. They brought with them, too, an undying hatred of excise laws, and a spirit of unhesitating resistance to any authority that sought to enforce such laws [1976: 150–51].

Kephart proceeds to discuss the post–Revolutionary Whiskey Rebellion in the Appalachian back country during Washington's administration (1976: 152–60) and subsequent changes in liquor laws and taxes in nineteenth century America that brought about the flourishing moonshining and bootlegging industries of his day.

Like Frost and Fox, Kephart comments upon the aversion of Appalachian Mountain people to external appellations:

> Strange to say, it provokes them to be called mountaineers, that being a "furrin word" which they take as a term of reproach. They call themselves mountain people, or citizens; sometimes humourously "mountain boomers," the word boomer being their name for the common red squirrel

which is found here only in the upper zone of the mountains.... It is next to impossible for anyone to write much about these people without offending them or else falling into singsong repetition of the same old terms.

Kephart actively studied Appalachian folk speech and was particularly interested in Scottish linguistic survivals:

> It has been my habit to jot down, on the spot, every dialectical word or variant or idiom that I hear, along with the phrase or sentence in which it occurred; for I never trust memory in such matters. And although I tell frankly what I am about, and why, yet all the folks can or will is that —
>
> a chiel's amang ye, takin' notes
> and, faith, he'll prent 'em.

Here again Kephart exhibits his familiarity with the works of Robert Burns (1759–96), best known as a poet but also actively interested in diverse aspects of Scottish traditional culture including fiddle tunes, legends, myths, beliefs and customs, as well as championing the Scots tongue as a literary language. The source of Kephart's unidentified allusion is Burns' humorous poem, "On the Late Captain Grose's Pereginations Thro' Scotland — Collecting the Antiquities of That Kingdom."[3]

The analogy here is particularly apt. Captain Francis Grose, like Horace Kephart in Appalachia, was an outsider, the English-born and educated son of a Swiss jeweler who had settled in Middlesex, who became interested in collecting and studying what became known as "folklore" only after W. J. Thoms coined the term in 1846. Burns and his late eighteenth century contemporaries knew it as "popular antiquities." Burns met Captain Grose in 1789 during his travels through Scotland collecting lore from the locals he interviewed. Kephart excerpted Burn's first stanza of this poem, included in the additions of the Edinburgh Edition of 1793. The full stanza reads:

> Hear, Land o' Cakes, and brither Scots
> Frae Maidenkirk to Johnie Groat's
> If there's a hole in a' your coats,
> I rede you tent it.
> A child's amang you takin' notes,
> 　　And faith, he'll prent it.
> [*Complete Poetical Works of Burns*, Cambridge Edition, 1966: 94[3]]

A particularly notable allusion to Burns emerges when Kephart retells William Goodell Frost's anecdote about the excessively literal Berea students from the mountains who found John Fox, Jr.'s stories morally offensive:

President Frost relates that when John Fox gave a reading from his Cumberland tales at Berea College "the mountain boys were ready to mob him. They had no comprehension of the nature of fiction. Mr. Fox' stories were either true or false. If they were true, then he was 'no gentleman' for telling all the family affairs of people who had entertained him with their best. If they were not true, then, of course, they were libellous upon the mountain people. Such an attitude may remind us of the general condemnation of fiction by the 'unco gude' of a generation ago [Kephart 1976: 282].

Kephart urges missionaries and educators working in Appalachia in his day to respect the pride and dignity of the people he dubbed "Southern Highlanders":

> The highlanders are Scotch-Irish in their high-spiritedness and proud independence. Those who would help them must do so in a perfectly frank and kindly way, showing always genuine interest in them but never a trace of patronizing condescension [1976: 282–83].

At this point Kephart expands upon Frost's allusion to Burns: "Allow me to add that this is no place for the 'unco gude' to exercise their talents, but rather for those whose studies and travels have taught them both tolerance and hopefulness" (1976: 283). (Kephart's spelling of "gude" follows Frost's rendering of Burns's "guid.")

Kephart continues, "Some well-meaning missionaries are shocked and scandalized at what seems to them incurable perversity and race degeneration. It is nothing of the sort. There are reasons, good reasons, for the worst that we find in any Hell-fer-Sartin or Loafer's Glory. All that is the result of isolation and lack of opportunity. It is no more hopeless than the same features of life were in the Scotch highlands two centuries ago" (1976: 284).

Kephart proclaims that the southern highlander is essentially and unalterably British: "…he is simply his ancient Scotch or English ancestor born over again. Such was the code of Jacobite Scotland and Tudor England. And *back there* is where our mountaineer belongs in the scale of human evolution" (1976: 421–22).

Kephart's ensuing discussion of Appalachian poverty and backwardness summons forth stereotypes of Celtic irrationality and disorganization dating back to the Roman historian Tacitus, stereotypes which still shape interpretations of Southern Back Country life by modern American historians including Grady McWhiney, Forrest MacDonald and David Hackett Fischer: "Is the case of our mountaineers so much worse than that of the Scotch highlanders of two centuries ago? We know that those Scotchmen did not 'vanish — the quicker the better.' What were they before civilization reached them?"

To support his argument, Kephart quotes the eminent nineteenth century British historian Thomas Babington Macaulay (1800–1859) regarding English antipathy to Celtic culture: "In the south of our island scarcely anything was known about the Celtic part of Scotland; and what was known excited no feeling but contempt and loathing.... The English were then abundantly inquisitive about the manners of rude nations separated from our island by great continents and oceans.... The only barbarian about whom there was no wish to have any information was the Highlander" (1976: 461). Macaulay elaborates upon the barbarism, the laziness, the illiteracy, and the paganism of the Scottish highlanders, most of whom lived in primitive conditions rife with filth and disease. Kephart concludes that the Southern Highlanders of Appalachian America exhibit the same virtues and flaws as the Gaels of the Scottish Highlands and their Celtic ancestors: "Let us remember, Sir and Madam, that we ourselves are descended from white barbarians" (1976: 466).

Writing in 1913, a year before the outbreak of the First World War, Kephart obviously assumed that his readers were well-educated middle class white people like himself. After all, racial segregation was the law of the land in the United States and most people thought in racist terms. Concepts like eugenics and racial degeneration were still the stuff of seminars and after-dinner conversations; the gas chambers and ovens of the Nazi death camps were three decades and two world wars away in an unimaginably horrible future.

Engaging and picturesque reading, *Our Southern Highlanders* quickly became accepted as an authoritative source of information concerning Appalachia. Though Kephart repeatedly expresses his appreciation and respect for his southern mountain neighbors, in the end he stereotypes them as barbarians, and this is what remains with his readers.

An inherent problem with great works like Kephart's *Our Southern Highlanders* is that once they become authoritative sources, any biases and misinformation they contain are embedded (like fossil insects in amber) in the canonic body of knowledge along with the brilliant insights and images which caused them to be considered great in the first place. Kephart strongly influenced English historian Arnold Toynbee, who described the people of southern Appalachia as semi-barbarians who once possessed civilization but slid back into illiteracy and superstition. As we have already noted, in his widely cited *Albion's Seed: Four British Folkways in America* (1989), the American historian David Hackett Fischer cites *Our Southern Highlanders* as a primary reference regarding the cruelty and brutality of the North British borderers who settled the Southern back country.

Kephart ends his book with an honorific volley of quotes from his primary influences, John Fox, Jr. and William Goodell Frost. Like Emma Bell

Miles, he calls for vocational education and model farms to enable Southern Appalachian youth to have a sustainable future in the region. From preface to conclusion, Kephart's *Our Southern Highlanders* is a major contribution to America's emerging discourse concerning parallels and connections between Scotland and Appalachia.

It is noteworthy but perhaps not entirely coincidental that one of the most insightful contributors to American discourse concerning points of convergence between Appalachia and Scotland was the American-born son of a Scottish highlander who migrated to the United States before the American Civil War.

Born September 15, 1868, in La Porte, Indiana, John Charles Campbell became director of the Southern Highland Division of the philanthropic Russell Sage Foundation in 1912, was a founder in 1913 of the Council of Mountain Workers, the same year Kephart's *Our Southern Highlanders* first appeared in print. This regional association of teachers and service workers evolved into the single most influential organization concerned with Appalachia from the 1920s through the 1960s, the Council of the Southern Mountains, publisher of the widely read and highly influential magazine *Mountain Life and Work*.

Campbell died at the age of fifty-one in 1919. (Emma Bell Miles and John Fox, Jr. also died that same year.) Founded in 1926, the John C. Campbell Folk School in Brasstown, North Carolina, perpetuates its namesake's concern with folk culture and vocational education, inspired by the Danish folk school movement.

Campbell is perhaps best remembered as the author of *The Southern Highlander and His Homeland* (foreword by Rupert Vance, Lexington: University Press of Kentucky, 1969 [1921], introduction by Henry D. Shapiro), which was published posthumously. It was the devoted and energetic Olive Dame Campbell (1882–1954), herself a leading advocate of folk arts and vocational education, who saw to it that her husband's book, unfinished at the time of his death, was published under his name.

A high school principal at the time they met, Campbell became acquainted with Miss Olive Dame, the vivacious academically and artistically inclined bluestocking daughter of a Medford, Massachusetts, college professor, on holiday in Scotland in 1906. A chance shipboard meeting brought the couple together, and a romantic tour of the Scottish countryside led to their marriage. As Olive Dame Campbell recalled:

> It was natural that travellers so congenial on shipboard should plan to
> continue on together after landing at Glasgow, through the Trossachs to
> Stirling, and by "fair Melrose" which my mother, June, Ruth, John and I
> saw from the top of a surrounding fence by the poet's "pale moonlight," and

so on to Edinburgh where we delighted in the castle, the plaids and the bag-pipes, and the romance of Holyrood with its memories of Mary, Queen of Scots. Later on in the summer we joined again for a coaching trip through Cornwall and Devonshire, and a boat trip down the Thames to London" ["The Life and Work of John Charles Campbell," Olive Dame Campbell 1968: 104–105].[5]

In his introduction to *The Southern Highlander and His Homeland*, Campbell expressed his deep sense of affinity between Appalachia and Scotland:

> I first went to the Highlands of the South nearly a quarter of a century ago. To be honest, it was not that I felt a great mission to uplift anybody. The pioneer call was irresistible as it came in striking contrast to the call of the conventional. Perhaps, too, there was what I then felt to be the call of the blood, for my people in earlier times were Highlanders in those other Highlands; but beneath all was gratitude to the South for having taken within its hospitable doors, during a great epidemic in antebellum days, a lad just from Scotland who had come to seek his fortune in this land of promise — a lad whose memory is very dear to me. If there was any thought of uplift it was not recognized as such, but regarded merely as a debt of gratitude to be repaid by his son [1969: xix–xx].

Following the lead of earlier regional commentators including Frost, Fox and Kephart, Campbell humorously grapples with the thorny question of what to call people allergic to externally applied appellations:

> To circumscribe territory and give it a name is one thing; to call people by a name not of their choosing is quite another. Obviously, if the term Southern Highlands be allowed for the land, native-born residents of the region are Southern Highlanders. Yet within the Highland area are many native-born inhabitants of urban or valley residence who do not regard themselves as mountain people. The writer has two friends, one living in the Greater Appalachian Valley and one in a prosperous mountain city, and both devoted to the interests of their own people, who refer in conversation to "those mountain folks," although at other time jocosely alluding to themselves as "mountain whites." This opprobrious term, coined as a term of distinction by well-meaning advocates of the mountaineer, is resented by all who dwell in the Highlands, by whatever name they may be designated [Campbell 1969: 18].

Apparently the compilers of the revised fourth edition of ethnologist George Peter Murdock's *Outline of World Cultures* (1972) never read Campbell's book or they ignored it if they had, because they saw fit to designate Southern Appalachian mountaineers as "NN5 — Mountain Whites" (1972: 112).

A cautious, exhaustive scholar, Campbell draws upon the works of the leading American historians of his day, Henry Jones Ford, *The Scotch-Irish in America* (1915) and Charles A. Hanna, *The Scotch-Irish* (1902), in recounting the history of European settlement of the Southern Appalachian region in the eighteenth century. Campbell writes:

> For an explanation of the first large movement into the mountain country, we must turn from the South to Pennsylvania. Hither, between 1720 and 1770 approximately, came many thousand Germans from the Palatine, Ulster-Scotch or Scotch-Irish from the north of Ireland, and immigrants from other countries ... they were on the whole a sturdy, virile people, fitted by nature and experience to meet the hardships of pioneer life [1969: 23].

Campbell identifies John Finley or Findlay, as a "Scotch-Irish trader" who may have preceded Boone and Walker in exploring the territory west of Cumberland Gap (1969: 28). Though proud of his Scottish ancestry, Campbell refrained from indulging in romantic speculations concerning the origins of the Appalachian region's diverse settlers:

> Conjectures have been many as to the ancestry of Southern Highlanders. Some would make their progenitors Scottish chieftains, transplanted to the Highlands of the South, unchanged, save that here they preferred the rifle to the broadsword, the hunting-knife to the dirk, the buckskin and homespun to the brighter hued tartan. Others find in them the offspring of English redemptioners and indentured servants, swept beyond the mountain ridges by the swollen tides of immigration flowing through the valleys and left to subside in the hollows and grow stagnant. In just resentment to this claim, other theories more sane have been put forth, but often with such extravagance as to make those not of "illustrious Scotch-Irish descent" or "purest Anglo-Saxon lineage" shrivel before the effulgence emanating from such stock.
>
> Inquiries of the Highlanders themselves as to family history and racial stock rarely bring a more definite answer than that grandparents or great-grandparents came from North Carolina or Virginia, occasionally from Pennsylvania, and that they "reckon" their folks were "English," "Scotch," or "Irish"— any of which designations may mean Scotch-Irish — or "Dutch," which may and usually does mean German [Campbell 1969: 51].

(Cratis Williams quotes Campbell nearly verbatim in "Who Are the Southern Mountaineers?")

Campbell concludes that the Scotch-Irish and Germans each comprised roughly a third of the population of Pennsylvania in colonial days (1969: 54–56). Campbell says, "The Scotch-Irish strain is strongest in some mountain sections; the English in others; and in some sections may be surmised an influence of German ancestry. All of these people "were blended into a homogeneous people — the type which has come to be called 'American'" (1969: 71).

Campbell's discussion of the backgrounds of the settlers of what Turner called the Southern Back Country is even-handed. Nonetheless, in the end he does emphasize the Scots and Scots-Irish elements in the population of the colonial Southern frontier: "the up-country people were, before the Revolution, predominantly Presbyterian, while the Tidewater aristocracy in whose hands lay most of the legislative power were largely of the Established Church" (1969: 95). Conflict between Dissenters and the Established Church continued during colonial times which Campbell interprets as a rejection of the temporal as well as the spiritual authority of the Anglican tidewater planters.

Campbell stresses the pro-revolutionary stance of the Presbyterians in the colonial South: "At the outbreak of the war they stood prominently for the cause of independence, seeing in the defeat of the Mother Country not only their political enfranchisement but the overthrow of the 'persecuting ecclesiastical arm of the English Government'" (1969: 161). Though David Hackett Fischer has recently contended in *Albion's Seed* that economics, not religious persecution, was primarily responsible for the Presbyterian exodus from Ulster to the Southern Back Country, Campbell maintains otherwise: "...religious grievances as well as political had their part in bringing about the Battle of Alamance" (1969: 162). The colonial government of North Carolina suppressed the anti-establishment Regulators, mostly Presbyterian, prompting many of these settlers to migrate to the west where they established the Watauga Association in present-day Northeast Tennessee and declared their independence from British colonial authority.

The Watauga settlers (also known as the Overmountain Men) led by Arthur Campbell, Landon Carter and John Sevier (who later became governor of the short-lived State of Franklin and then first governor of Tennessee) defeated loyalist colonists under the command of a Scottish officer, Colonel Patrick Ferguson, at the Battle of Kings Mountain on the border of the Carolinas on October 7, 1780. On the twenty-sixth of September, Presbyterian minister Dr. Samuel Doak had blessed the Overmountain Men at Sycamore Shoals on the banks of the Watauga River in the name of the "Sword of The Lord and Gideon," which became their battle cry at Kings Mountain.

Campbell quotes Theodore Roosevelt's comments in his popular history *Winning of the West* (1905) concerning the fervent support of Scotch-Irish Presbyterians for the revolutionary cause in the uplands of the Southern colonies. The insistence of Presbyterians on an educated ministry became increasingly difficult to sustain in frontier conditions, creating opportunities for Baptist and Methodist evangelism, which became the dominant denominations of the Southern Appalachian Highlands (1969: 164–65).

Campbell's painstaking scholarly influence pervades Paul E. Doran's essay, "The Backgrounds of the Mountain People," *Mountain Life and Work*, January 1936, reprinted in Bill Best's anthology *One Hundred Years of Appalachian Visions* (1997). Doran, a Presbyterian minister from East Tennessee, provides an overview of Appalachia's ethnic and religious history with a strongly Scots-Irish Presbyterian emphasis. Published the same year Jim Wayne Miller was born and two years before the death of William Goodell Frost, Doran's concise 1936 essay enables us to quickly review some major points of Appalachian history addressed in this first chapter.

Concerning the geographical location of southern Appalachia, Doran comments, "The Mountain district, as we know it, has almost the same boundary line as the old Cherokee nation…. This area is almost exactly what we now call the Southern Highlands" (Best 1997: 29–30). When Doran remarks that southern mountain people bitterly resent the appellation "mountain whites," he evokes a recurring motif in Appalachian discourse, which surfaces again in Cratis Williams' wry observation at the conclusion of his article, "Who Are the Southern Mountaineers?" *(Appalachian Journal*, vol. 1, no. 1, 1972) that mountain people resent anything written about them (1972: 30).

Reflecting Campbell's influence, Doran cautiously delineates the origins of the inhabitants of Southern Appalachia: "The mountain people have been referred to as the purest strain of Anglo-Saxon stock in the world. Now this is a fine rhetorical phrase but it is not the truth. The first settlers came from Ireland [presumably the North?] and Scotland and swept along with them a few Welsh, who are also Gaelic [more precisely, Celtic] and some English. There came also a few French, German and Danish." Doran's description of the ethnic origins of the early Appalachian settlers closely agrees with Frederick Jackson Turner's and also John C. Campbell's concept of a "composite nationality," not as predominantly British as Frost or Fox would have it.

Doran brilliantly encapsulates the historical experience of southern mountain people: "In the beginning we were persecuted, then later we were forgotten; when we were rediscovered, we were looked down upon as inferior" (Best 1997: 32). Anglican persecution of Scotch-Irish Presbyterians generated support for the revolutionary cause in the Southern Back Country.

By 1730 Scots-Irish Presbyterians were moving into the Southern colonial frontier. As elsewhere in British America, oppressive taxation alienated these Southern settlers, giving rise to the Regulators who took up arms against British authorities by 1771 at Alamance Courthouse in North Carolina. Hundreds of Regulators who supported the Mecklenburg Declaration renounced allegiance to the Crown years before the outbreak of the American Revolution "It is no wonder that in England it was called the Presbyterian Rebellion in America" (Best 1997: 34).

These pious rebels were descendants of Covenanters and Cameronian hillmen or hillfolk, Seceders and Dissenters who opposed the restoration of the Stuarts, the progeny of Billy Boys who supported the Protestant Prince William of Orange, "King Billy." Like Campbell, Doran stresses the significance of Kings Mountain, a decisive victory for the American revolutionary cause. Following the Revolution, the new American government rewarded patriot soldiers with grants of lands confiscated from the Cherokee, who had supported the British in hopes of regaining their territory. In the following century Appalachian emigrants of Scottish ancestry like Andrew Jackson and David Crockett would play major roles in the westward expansion of the United States.

Development of railroads and industry was well underway in the southern mountains by 1850 but came to an abrupt halt when the American Civil War erupted. Doran graphically describes the torching of mountain schools and libraries, which set back education and fostered widespread illiteracy in the region well into the twentieth century.

Cratis Williams, a prime architect of Appalachian Studies, would often repeat Doran's reference to illiterate descendants of early settlers unable to read the great books their ancestors had carried with them into the Southern Highlands. Cratis transformed it into a rallying cry of the emerging Appalachian identity movement in the sixties and seventies; a challenge to educated mountain people to write authentic Appalachian literature and history from the inside out, voicing indigenous viewpoints and insights.

Paralleling the rise of contemporary Scottish cultural nationalism during this same

Cratis Williams attending an early meeting of the Appalachian Consortium. (Courtesy of Archives of Appalachia, East Tennessee State University.)

period, the Appalachian Studies movement arises from the same fundamental human desires that motivate all peripheral people to get back in touch with their roots, to define and express themselves in their own terms.

NOTES

1. Rodger Cunningham, personal communication, August 13, 1998.
2. Rodger Cunningham, personal communication, August 13, 1998.
3. Quote provided courtesy of Ewan MacVicar, School of Scottish Studies, Edinburgh University.
4. Quote provided courtesy of Philis Alvic, Lexington, Kentucky.

2

Appalachian Studies Comes of Age

*F*or the most part, Appalachian people have not defined and expressed themselves in their own terms. Historically they have been presented to the world at large as comic numskull hillbillies, degenerate barbaric relics of isolation, romantic mountain folk preserving the quaint folkways of a frozen frontier, as well as pathetic, fatalistic victims of deprivation and exploitation requiring uplift. Only rarely have they been portrayed sympathetically, realistically, or heroically. Persistent stereotypes of marginality and backwardness shape internal and external perceptions of Appalachia to this day.

Appalachia presently has a population of roughly 22 million, slightly less than a tenth of the national population. Large families, small farms and an historically high percentage of landless people created a superabundant cash-poor labor force under the political and economic domination of local elites cooperating with outside investors and developers to exploit the region's coal, timber and other natural resources.

Driven by a boom and bust industrial economy, roughly 3.3 million people left Appalachia between 1940 and 1970, looking for work elsewhere. A hillbilly accent was not an asset in the industrial northern and midwestern United States. Some migrants from the Appalachian South attempted to change or cover up their distinctive speech patterns, blend into standard mainstream American blandness. The term "Appalachia" itself still evokes prickly feelings of shame and defensiveness in many natives of the region.

The term "Appalachia" first appeared in a U.S. Federal Government publication in 1935, a year before Jim Wayne Miller was born. However, "Appalachia" did not gain widespread currency as a popular designation for the region until the early 1960s. In 1957 Berea College president W. D. Weath-

47

erford received a Ford Foundation grant to underwrite an exhaustive regional study, *The Southern Appalachian Region: A Survey,* published in 1962, which marks the dawning of the present-day Appalachian Studies movement.

Michael Harrington's *The Other America,* also published in 1962, fixed the attention of John F. Kennedy's administration on entrenched poverty in Appalachia. Other influential books like Harry Caudill's *Night Comes to the Cumberlands* (1962) and Jack Weller's *Yesterday's People* (1965) raised national consciousness of Appalachia during the early sixties. Lyndon Johnson's establishment of the Appalachian Regional Commission in 1965 further heightened awareness of the problems besetting the region.

The Johnson administration's War on Poverty and the creation of the Appalachian Regional Commission led to federal funding for experimental programs through the Office of Economic Opportunity. Appalshop, now an internationally renowned nonprofit media production center in Whitesburg, Kentucky, began as a learning project for disadvantaged youths in the coalfields of southeastern Kentucky. Social service programs like VISTA and Appalachian Volunteers brought a new generation of idealistic young teachers and public service workers into the region. Conflicts between old-line liberals and new-left radicals created an irreparable rift within the Council of the Southern Mountains that eventually led to its demise. Tensions between confrontation-oriented activists and reform-minded gradualists continued to flare up in the 1990s at the annual meetings of the Appalachian Studies Association, which grew out of an initial Appalachian Studies Conference held at Berea College in 1977.

Efforts to set up Appalachian Studies programs in regional colleges and universities were underway by the late sixties. Scholar-activist Helen Mathews Lewis, a native of rural Georgia with a doctorate in sociology from the University of Kentucky, organized a groundbreaking interdisciplinary program in Appalachian Studies at Clinch Valley College in Wise, Virginia, in 1970. The Appalachian studies program Lewis established at Clinch Valley College in the coal country of southwest Virginia proposed to bring about fundamental changes in consciousness, empowering students from the region "to control their own lives, make important decisions, and not be controlled" (Lewis 1982: 163).

Though now technically retired, Helen Lewis, recently elected president of the Appalachian Studies Association for 2001-02, still advocates a revolutionary if non-violent agenda for radically transforming regional education. In the community consciousness–raising tradition of the Highlander Center in New Market, Tennessee, of which she became senior scholar-activist in residence following the death of Myles Horton in 1991, Lewis calls for participatory research to break down hierarchical divisions between students, scholars, and community groups. (Founded in 1932 in Grundy County, Tennessee, as a center for educating union organizers in the Southern coalfields and textile mills, the Highlander School played a key role in the Civil Rights Movement during the fifties and sixties and is still very actively concerned with social justice issues including health, environment and migrant labor).

Drawing inspiration from Brazilian educator-activist Paulo Freire as well as the homegrown empowerment pedagogy of Myles Horton and the Highlander School, Lewis proposes that personally and socially liberating knowledge emerges from articulating the collective experience of the subservient group. Colonialistic teachers typically stifle expression of that collective experience, imposing instead a prescribed regimen of canonic knowledge, indoctrinating rather than empowering students in the process of their education. Counter colonialistic movements like Appalachian Studies must challenge and cast off the hegemony of entrenched elite establishments, enabling subordinated peripheral people to regain control of their lives through learning how to define and express themselves in their own terms.

The Appalachian Studies movement blossomed during the seventies. In 1970, representatives of regional colleges, universities, government agencies and other regionally concerned organizations founded the Appalachian Consortium with its headquarters located at Appalachian State University in Boone, North Carolina. Appalachian State University took on a leading role in Appalachian Studies, commencing publication of the *Appalachian Journal* in 1972. In 1976, Appalachian State University sponsored the Cratis Williams Symposium to honor one of the most influential proponents of the Appalachian Studies movement.

This pivotal event inspired the first Appalachian Studies Conference in 1977, which in turn led to the establishment of the Appalachian Studies Association.

The late Cratis Dearl Williams (1911–1985) was a native of the Big Sandy Valley section of Eastern Kentucky who began his career in education as a teacher in a one-room mountain schoolhouse. After receiving the Ph.D. in American literature from New York University in 1961, Cratis (pronounced "*Cray*-tus"; it is impossible for anyone who actually knew the man personally to think of him in more formal terms) went on to become the dean of graduate studies and for one year acting chancellor of Appalachian State University in Boone, North Carolina. Scholarly yet down to earth, Cratis Williams always presented the history and culture of southern mountain people affectionately and respectfully. Appalachian Studies wasn't merely a career to Cratis; it was a true profession, akin to a religious mission or spiritual calling.

Loyal Jones, another prime mover in Appalachian Studies who directed the Council of The Southern Mountains during the tumultuous 1960s and then went on to direct the Appalachian Center at Berea College, notes that

Three founders of Appalachian Studies. Left–right: Loyal Jones, Cratis Williams, W.D. Weatherford. (Courtesy of William Leonard Eury Appalachian Collection, Appalachian State University.)

Cratis Williams was only seventeen years old when he published the first item listed in his curriculum vitae, a letter titled "Why a Mountain Boy Should Be Proud," printed in the December 12, 1927, edition of his high school newspaper, *The Louisian.*

In their introduction to the second volume of his posthumously published memoirs, *The Cratis Williams Chronicles: I Come to Boone* (1999), Cratis' son David Cratis Williams and cultural anthropologist Patricia Beaver, director of the Appalachian Studies program at Appalachian State University, note that Cratis had already learned to feel ashamed of being an Appalachian mountain boy three years earlier. Shortly after entering Louisa High School at the precocious age of fourteen, young Cratis was cruelly humiliated by his freshman English teacher before his classmates during an oral presentation for unwittingly using the archaic Middle English "hit" still common in vernacular Appalachian speech instead of the standard modern English "it" (see Best 1999: 13).

At the time, fourteen year old Cratis Williams felt intense shame and resolved to reinvent himself and his speech patterns. He felt divided, split

Presenting Outstanding Local Talent at Appalachian State University. Left–right: Cratis Williams, Rogers Whitener, Doc Watson and Merle Watson. (Courtesy of William Leonard Eury Appalachian Collection, Appalachian State University.)

between two worlds. Fortunately, sympathetic teachers who did recognize his potential encouraged him to be proud of himself and his Appalachian folk heritage, setting him upon the path that would make him one of the prime movers of the Appalachian Studies movement. Studying traditional ballads helped to spark the sensitive young East Kentucky mountain boy's budding interest in the historical roots of southern Appalachian speech (Williams and Beaver 1999: v–vii).

(Incidentally, Chaucer used "hit" for "it" in his *Canterbury Tales*. As it happens, "hit" also occurs in vernacular Lowland Scots, a shade of a vowel shy of the Dutch "het." Scottish children at play count out "one-two-three, you are *het*.")

It took Cratis Williams thirty-seven years to finally overcome that distressing experience. That thorny wound to his self-esteem only completely healed when Cratis completed his monumental, encyclopedic doctoral dissertation, no less than 1,650 pages long in three volumes. An eclectic interdisciplinary opus integrating history, ethnography, linguistics, literary criticism, folklore and other scholarly fields, *The Southern Mountaineer in Fact and Fiction* (1961) is one of the primary intellectual wellsprings of Appalachian

Studies as we know it today. The first issue of the *Appalachian Journal* (1972), published at Appalachian State University under the editorship of J.W. (Jerry Wayne) Williamson included an excerpt from Cratis's dissertation titled "Who Are the Southern Mountaineers?" outlining the complex history of European settlement in the Southern Appalachian region. Ambrose Manning and Robert J. (Jack) Higgs, professors of English at East Tennessee State University, reprinted this essay in their trailblazing Appalachian anthology, *Voices from The Hills* (1975).

A close reading of this essay shows that Cratis Williams, like Paul Doran, drew heavily upon John C. Campbell's account of the settling of the Southern Highlands. The settlement of Southern Appalachia is part of the greater Westward Expansion of the American Frontier. Like that noted historian of the American frontier, Frederick Jackson Turner, Cratis observed that North Britons (lowland Scots and the so-called Scotch-Irish; Ulster Scots or Scots Irish in preferred British usage) played a predominant role in the settling of the Southern Back Country. The Scotch-Irish, along with English settlers and other Northwestern European Protestants, particularly Western Germans and a few French Huguenots like John Sevier's forebears, were to become part of what Turner had called "a composite nationality." One of the most significant links between these diverse people was "the essential non-conformist quality of their religious views." Though many of these people were antagonistic to the authority of the British establishment, vested in the Hanoverian monarchy and the Anglican Church, we should not automatically assume that all backcountry settlers, particularly the Scotch-Irish, supported the Revolutionary cause.

How did Appalachia become an impoverished hinterland? According to Cratis, isolation from the main currents of American society, combined with overpopulation and reliance upon subsistence agriculture, contributed to the intellectual as well as material impoverishment of the mountain people, intensified by the impact of the Civil War and the return of ex–Confederates to political dominance in the Southern states following the collapse of Reconstruction. Overpopulation, undercapitalization, and lack of formal education left the mountain people vulnerable to external exploitation and domination. Evoking a recurring motif of American discourse on Appalachia, Cratis humorously concludes that the people of the region have generally not labeled themselves as mountaineers (or Appalachians), and their defensiveness towards outsiders, though frequently justified, causes them to resent anything written about them. Students of Scottish cultural history will quickly identify this prickly mixture of pride and defensiveness as a trans–Atlantic cousin of the "Scottish Cringe," a subspecies of the generic colonial inferiority complex Frantz Fanon termed "inferiorism," stemming from a common history of marginality and subordination.

Why do other Americans think of Appalachians as a people apart? Where and when do negative and impaired images of Appalachia originate? How have stereotypes shaped internal and external perceptions of the region and its inhabitants? The 1976 Cratis Williams Symposium held at Appalachian State University in Boone, North Carolina, brought together Appalachia's leading scholars and writers to grapple with these thorny, intertwining questions of personal, regional and national identity.

Regional historian and novelist Wilma Dykeman, native of western North Carolina and longtime resident of East Tennessee, contributed a penetrating essay to the Cratis Williams Symposium titled "Appalachia in Context" (1977). Dykeman proposes that we examine Appalachia in three contexts: 1) Appalachia as an alternative to the Old South, 2) Appalachia as an alternative to mainstream America from the end of the Civil War until the great Depression, and 3) Appalachia as an internal Third World country challenging American complacency.

Dykeman challenges the longstanding notion dating back to William Goodell Frost that Appalachia's distinctiveness is solely the product of geographic isolation. From colonial times, the mountainous back country of southern Appalachia was socially, culturally and economically alienated from the slave-holding Old South. The loyalty of Unionists in the southern uplands would lead to political retribution when vengeful former Confederates regained control of their state governments following the collapse of Reconstruction. Confederates who supported the Lost Cause were portrayed as aristocratic latter-day Cavaliers; Southerners who remained loyal to the Union were scornfully labeled poor white trash and scalawags: "The Civil War not only divided America. It divided Appalachia from the South"(1977: 34).

Dykeman challenges the romantic myth of self-sufficient contemporary ancestors dwelling in a frozen frontier, which obscures the historic vulnerability of a region rich in labor and natural assets but lacking economic and political autonomy. Apologists for the unregulated spread of industry in the American South lauded its progressive effects on the benighted people of the highlands while decrying their alleged backwardness and barbarism, a classic example of "blaming the victim."

Colonialists throughout history have applied the same belittling, dehumanizing terms to the people they have subjugated and exploited. Though her rhetoric is less overtly revolutionary, in the end Wilma Dykeman, like Helen Lewis, sees little if any difference between Appalachian people and other victims of colonialism around the globe. If the people of Appalachia are poor in material things, they are rich in the realm of the spirit. Like Lewis, Dykeman believes that Appalachia can teach mainstream America and the rest of the so-called advanced world some badly needed lessons about human values such as respect and appreciation, caring and sharing.

Like Wilma Dykeman and Cratis Williams, historian Henry D. Shapiro reminds his readers that since the 1870s progressive America has perceived Appalachia as a land apart from the mainstream. Shapiro's Cratis Williams symposium essay, "Appalachia and the Idea of America: The Problem of the Persisting Frontier," touches upon many of the same themes explored at length in his controversial book *Appalachia on Our Mind* (1978). America's fascination with Appalachia reflects national ambivalence concerning the ascendancy of Hamiltonian notions of urban-industrial progress and the demise of an idealized, self-sufficient Jeffersonian agrarian society, which Allen Batteau in *The Invention of Appalachia* (1990) describes as "sacrifice of nature in the service of civilization."

Even as mainstream metropolitan America looks down upon the primitivism of backwoods Appalachia, there is also a sense of remorseful nostalgia, a nagging suspicion that irreplaceable spiritual values are being traded for material rewards of dubious worth. A great outpouring of romantic local color literature (paralleling the emergence of the Kailyard School in Scotland) takes place between the 1870s and 1890s, just as industry comes to the old colonial frontier of Appalachia and the western frontier is finally closed. Paradoxically, as Wilma Dykeman has observed, it is during the industrial boom that Appalachia is portrayed as a land frozen in time, whose inhabitants, though viewed as benighted and unprogressive, still presumably retain the primitive virtues of their ancestors.

Shapiro sees elements of White Anglo-Saxon Protestant racism and xenophobia in the fabrication of this nostalgic, nativistic literature at a time when swelling immigration from southeast Europe and East Asia, mushrooming urban industrial centers, the rise of labor unionism, socialism, syndicalism and anarchism, and the continuing decline of American farming were rapidly transforming the fundamental character and complexion of American society (1977: 27–28). The nostalgic, romantic side of the local color literature of the late nineteenth century was countered by recurrent barbaric motifs of moonshining and feuding, representing southern mountaineers as lawless savages, comparable to the hostile Western plains tribes only recently subjugated at the beginning of the new century. Americans concerned with social progress and uplift saw the frontier legacy of the southern mountaineers "as a sign of their pressing need for assistance so that they might cast off a discredited or at least a useless past, and join the rest of the nation in the present" (1977: 30).

Is there no future in the Appalachian past? Is the Appalachian past totally useless, a dead end, a beguiling romantic mirage akin to the Celtic Twilight that spread its crepuscular pall over the Scottish cultural landscape during Victoria and Albert's idylls at Balmoral? In his essay on "Appalachian Literature," one of the highlights of a special issue of the *Appalachian Journal* titled

Jim Wayne Miller (1936–1996) in his study. (Courtesy of Mary Ellen Miller.)

"A Guide to Appalachian Studies" (vol. 5, no. 1, autumn 1977), the late poet/
scholar/cultural leader Jim Wayne Miller (1936–1996) describes a vital regional
literary movement dating back to the 1880s as a continuing search for a
"usable past."

Literary imagery has shaped the world's perceptions of Appalachia; the
creation of an indigenous regionalist literature has been a principal element
in the emergence of Appalachian Studies and the regional identity movement
associated with it. Miller notes that in *The Southern Mountaineer in Fact and
Fiction* (1961), Cratis Williams divided Appalachian literature into three major
epochs. During the first period, including fictional and non-fictional writings dealing with the Southern mountains from the journals of colonial trav-
elers through the frontier romances and comedies of the antebellum era until
1880, the Southern mountaineer is not distinguished from the pioneer or
backswoodman. Only after the American Civil War does the Southern mountaineer emerge in national consciousness as a distinct regional type.

The second era of Appalachian writing, in which the mountaineer is distinguished from other Southern rural or backwoods whites, commences in
the 1880s with the novels of Mary Noailles Murfree. Murfree's novels inspired
the development of a romantic genre of Appalachian local color fiction

epitomized by the hugely popular works of John Fox, Jr. which were continued until the early 1930s by derivative writers, many of whom Williams
identifies as outsiders. Native-born Appalachian writers like James Still, Jesse
Stuart, Thomas Wolfe, and Harriette Arnow dominate Williams' third era
of Appalachian writing, extending from the thirties to the mid-fifties.

The current era, from the mid-1950s to the present, is arguably the rich-
est and most varied period in the history of Appalachian literature. The artistic and scholarly works of the founding figures of the modern Appalachian
Studies movement like Cratis Williams, Wilma Dykeman, and Jim Wayne
Miller have inspired an outpouring of regional fiction, poetry, and criticism
that has continued unabated from the early 1960s to this very day. This latest
wave of creative, insightful homegrown Appalachian literature has played a
key role in converting teachers in the region's schools, colleges and universities into proponents of Appalachian Studies.

In "The Politics of Nostalgia: Uses of the Past in Recent Appalachian
Poetry" (*AppalJ*, vol. 8, no. 1, autumn 1980), Frank Einstein repeats Miller's
contention that modern Appalachians (like their contemporaries in Scotland,
and modern people in general) are searching for a usable past to reintegrate
their divided identities. Jim Wayne Miller's most frequently quoted poem,
"The Brier Sermon: You Must Be Born Again" (1980) offers personal testi-
mony of identity reformulation following the classic sequence of separation,
marginality and return common to rites of passage, heroic quests, healing
ceremonies, and cultural revitalization movements. Miller's poetic alter ego,
The Brier, experiences *separation* from his original home and community,
the locus of his primary sense of selfhood and belonging. Separation leads
to feelings of ambivalence and self-alienation typical of *marginality*, which
the Brier resolves through a symbolic homecoming or *return*, reconstruct-
ing a coherent identity that combines the best of now and then: "going back
to what you were before/ without losing what you've since become." (Gurney Norman's brilliant, humorous novel of Appalachian rediscovery, *Divine
Right's Trip*, follows the very same archetypal pattern).

The Brier proposes a happy medium, a creative alternative to parochial
narrowness and rootless cosmopolitanism:

> You don't have to live the way your foreparents lived.
> But if you don't know about them
> If you don't respect them
> you're not going anywhere.
> You don't have to think ridge to ridge
> the way they did.
> You can think ocean to ocean [Miller 1980: 55].

By the turn of the eighties, Appalachian scholars and activists were heed-ing the Brier's call to think ocean to ocean, exploring a diversity of comparative perspectives in order to understand their regional situation better. Ten years after Cratis Williams' "Who Are the Southern Mountaineers?" appeared in the first issue of the *Appalachian Journal,* Thomas McGowan and Jerry Williamson of Appalachian State University co-edited a special edition of *AppalJ* titled "Assessing Appalachian Studies" (winter-spring 1982). In his essay "Image and Identity in Appalachia," Ohio-based Appalachianist Bob Snyder applies sociologist Immanuel Wallerstein's ideas concerning a global capitalist world-system divided into dominant metropolitan cores and subordinate peripheries (and semi-peripheries) to the case of Appalachia. Like Helen Lewis, David Walls, John Gaventa and David Whisnant, Snyder identifies Appalachia as an internal colony of the United States, peripheral to the national metropolitan core.

Using economist Kenneth Boulding's theory of "eiconics" as his point of departure, Snyder asserts that rather than being passively shaped by social and cultural forces, individual human beings actively reformulate their personal identities and reinvent entire social and cultural systems. Appalachian (and Scottish) intellectuals naturally seek to resolve the dilemma of dependency and flawed identity in local terms, but they are arguably coming to grips with localized expressions of worldwide political and cultural struggles in the current post-imperial, post-colonial era.

In light of the subsequent collapse of Soviet hegemony in Eastern Europe in the late eighties, it is notable that as early as 1982 Snyder stresses the obstinate persistence of ethnic and nationalist identity movements: "socialism is not as automatic a solution to the failures of capitalism as it once was" (1982: 78); he also argues that attributing the low status of Appalachians in American society solely to social class ignores cultural differences that are not purely economically determined, though they have very real economic consequences.

Like Bob Snyder, David Whisnant came to the conclusion that the basic assumptions of orthodox Marxist analysis could not account for the slippery, exception-ridden complexities of the Appalachian situation. As Whisnant maintains in "Developments in the Appalachian Identity Movement: All Is Process" (*Appalachian Journal,* vol. 8, no. 1, 1980): "the region's history has both radical *and* conservative (even reactionary) dimensions; Appalachia has been exploited by insiders *and* outsiders; its culture is the product of both indigenous creativity *and* a sometimes unfortunate eclecticism; a few Appalachian values are in tension with mainstream values, but many are not" (1980: 40).

Author of two highly regarded scholarly books on Appalachia, *Modernizing the Mountaineer* (1980) and *All Things Native and Fine: The Politics of Culture in an American Region* (1983), Whisnant grew up in a western North

Carolina factory town where his father worked in a textile plant. Whisnant briefly considered a career as a chemical engineer, then switched to English literature. Whisnant had to leave Appalachia before he could identify with the region and learn to appreciate the stigmatized local culture his upwardly mobile family were doing their best to reject, which romantic outsiders were expropriating and gentrifying beyond recognition in the name of preservation. In graduate school, Whisnant first came in contact with some of the early leaders of the emerging Appalachian identity movement in the late 1960s.

Whisnant outlines the history of the subordination of Appalachia in his first book *Modernizing the Mountaineer: People, Power and Planning in Appalachia* (1980), republished by the University of Tennessee Press in 1994. He argues that nearly all public and private efforts to develop Appalachia have tended to romanticize the region's pre-industrial past while ignoring corporate and bureaucratic abuse and degradation of its human population and natural resources.

Most of *Modernizing the Mountaineer* focuses upon the Appalachian situation. In his conclusion, however, Whisnant draws an "historical analogue" between the destructive impact of federal development schemes upon the people of Appalachia and the Highland Clearances in Scotland. Reading Scottish historian John Prebble's *The Highland Clearances* (1963) inspired Whisnant to construct this analogy between Scotland and Appalachia.

Whisnant tells us that he routinely dismissed statements concerning Appalachia's Celtic Connections as romantic myth making: "Nearly every romantic statement ever concocted to explain Appalachian people — from John Fox, Jr., to CBS' "Sixty Minutes" — has told wistfully of their proud Scotch-Irish forebears" (Whisnant 1994: 268). Whisnant's reading of Prebble's account of the Highland Clearances suggested striking parallels to the displacement of Appalachian people in the twentieth century in the name of progress. (Whisnant's interpretation of the Highland Clearances is evidently based solely upon Prebble's popular history, since he refers to no other source of historical information on the subject.)

Whisnant proceeds to describe the Agricultural Improvement Movement and its effects upon Scottish Highlanders. Throughout the Highlands, huge flocks of sheep replaced thousands of tenants driven from their homes by their lairds and chieftains in the name of "improvement." It is noteworthy (and highly ironic) that Whisnant extols the decency of Sir John Sinclair, who demonstrated concern for the welfare of his Highland tenants. This same Sir John Sinclair was a founding member and early historian of the Society of True Highlanders. Emulating Allen Batteau in his deconstructive 1981 *AppalJ* review of Malcolm Chapman's *The Gaelic Vision* (1978), Whisnant denounces this aristocratic group for appropriating and falsifying the cultural legacy of displaced Scottish Gaels. (See Hugh Trevor-Roper, "The Myth of the Highlands" in Hobsbawm and Ranger, eds., *The Invention of Tradition*, 1983.)

Whisnant states the Scottish lairds deliberately stripped themselves of Gaelic language and culture in their eagerness to assimilate metropolitan English values and norms, voluntarily committing ethnocide and linguicide. Curiously, within a very short period of time, he reports that these very same Scottish aristocrats (including the aforementioned Sir John Sinclair) are actively seeking to preserve and revive selected aspects of Scots Gaelic cultural identity.

In his haste to debunk and deconstruct, Whisnant does not stop to question this seeming paradox which raises the unsettling possibility that the founders of the Highland Society, though privileged aristocrats, were nonetheless leaders and patrons of a bona fide nativistic cultural revitalization movement resisting the total assimilation of a subordinated minority into a dominant metropolitan culture. Like Grady McWhiney and Forrest Mac-Donald in *Cracker Culture* (1988) and David Hackett Fischer in *Albion's Seed* (1989), Whisnant takes the observations of a hostile commentator like Prebble at face value because they support his own ideological position. Whisnant's facile portrayal of the Highland Society as fatuous London dandies amusing themselves by dressing up as Highland Scots does not merely trivialize the historical facts: it misrepresents them to support his political preconceptions.

The Disarming Act of 1746, which followed Bonnie Prince Charlie's defeat at the Battle of Culloden, specifically prohibited displays of Scottish national symbols, including kilts, tartans, plaids, and Highland bagpipes. Loyalist Highland regiments, however, were exempted from the bans on the pipes, along with cattle drovers, "due to the lonely and dangerous nature of their work," which explains the Highland Society's selection of a yearly cattle fair, the Falkirk Tryst, as the site of their first piping contest in 1781, a year before the repeal of the Disarming Act (Alburger 1986: 160).

The Scottish nobles who were the officers of the loyalist Highland regiments refined modern Scottish martial music and costume, inventing regimental tartans, which in turn inspired the clan tartans we know today. In 1778, a group of these same Scottish gentlemen founded the Highland Society in London, so that they could periodically gather together "...in that garb so celebrated as having been the dress of their Celtic ancestors, and on such occasions at least to speak the emphatic language, to listen to the delightful music, to recite the ancient poetry, and to observe the peculiar customs of their country" (Sir John Sinclair, 1807, quoted by Hugh Trevor-Roper, "The Invention of Tradition: The Highland Tradition of Scotland" in Hobsbawm and Ranger 1983: 26). This group successfully petitioned the House of Commons to repeal the ban on Highland dress and other strictures of the

Disarming Act in 1782. In return for their continued loyalty to the Hanoverian monarchy during the critical years of the American Revolution, these Scottish nobles gained cultural concessions that gave rise to modern Scottish romantic sub-nationalism within the emerging British Empire. Understanding this historical context helps to explain why so many twentieth century Scottish artists and intellectuals including prominent cultural commentators like John Prebble and Tom Nairn have railed against tartan, kilts and bagpipes as emblems of false consciousness fostering mindless, tasteless, syrupy romanticism, obscuring Scottish complicity in British colonialism and imperialism.

Whisnant does not investigate the cultural politics of a relatively sympathetic character like Sir John Sinclair (who nonetheless dispossessed many of his own tenants). Instead, he rehashes Prebble's account of the Clearances, focusing upon the wanton cruelty of the Duke of Sutherland, who forcibly evicted thousands of hapless tenants in the process of enclosing and "improving" his lands (1994: 270).

The writings of the Improvers, particularly James Loch, rationalized the removal of the Highlanders in the name of the advancement of civilization. Whisnant sees an analogy between the rationalization of the Highland Clearances and the liberal progressive philosophy that imposed the Tennessee Valley Authority and the Appalachian Regional Commission upon the common folk of Appalachia for their own good but without their consent. Says Whisnant, "Much of the 1964 planning document of the President's Appalachian Regional Commission could have been written by James Loch two hundred years earlier" (1994: 271).

Expropriation and falsification of folk culture has been a recurring theme in Whisnant's writings on Appalachia. He focuses upon this topic in a section of his conclusion to *Modernizing the Mountaineer* aptly titled "The Uses of Cultural Nostalgia": "I return to my analogue. While the Duke of Sutherland was eager to have done with the burdensome Highlanders themselves, he and his peers took unto themselves the more picturesque trappings of a romanticized version of Highland culture. They found their model in Sir Walter Scott, who, as Prebble notes, took the highlander out of his environment, disinfected him, [and] dressed him in romance" (1994: 277).

Whisnant quotes Prebble regarding Scottish nobleman Alistair Ranaldson MacDonnell, heir to the MacDonnell estate in Glengarry: "Even while continuing to evict tenants, he helped to organize the Society of True Highlanders" (In support of the Dress, Language, Music and Characteristics of Our Ancient and Illustrious Race" [1994: 278]). But the laird of Glengarry was dispossessed in his own turn. As Whisnant records, "Ironically, an English baronet William Ward purchased the Glengarry estate where he draped himself in tartan and organized highland games for his friends" (1994: 278).

Though Whisnant is evidently unaware of this connection, an earlier chieftain of this same clan, Ian MacDonnell of Glengarry, was in fact partly responsible along with English Quaker foundryman Thomas Rawlinson for the invention of the modern pleated Scottish kilt, which had already become a Scottish nationalist symbol before the battle of Culloden.

It is hard to say exactly when the Highland costume, including the kilt and tartan, emerged as a symbol of Scottish national identity. In a lecture on the subject of "Tartans" at the School of Scottish Studies in the summer of 1989, the late Alan Bruford challenged the contention of English cultural historian Hugh Trevor-Roper, Lord Dacre, that the familiar and distinctive Scottish national costume, particularly the kilt, was a recent and totally spurious invention.

Alan Bruford was neither the first nor the last Scottish scholar to accuse Lord Dacre of Scotophobia. Bruford maintained that the modern kilt is based on the plaid cloak, the Celtic equivalent of the Roman toga, which aristocrats wore draped over their long tunics in peacetime and which their followers wrapped loosely around their waists in battle. Trevor-Roper admits that this latter garment, the *breachan* or belted plaid, was probably made of tartan material by the sixteenth century, providing the foundation of the modern kilt (also see Dunbar 1989). The term "kilt" is first used to describe a Scottish garment in 1727, and then as a designation for the *breachan* and not the separate pleated item of dress which was specifically banned by the Disarming Act of 1746.

Even before 1745, Highland dress was already controversial. To quote Trevor-Roper, "After the Jacobite rebellion of 1715 the British parliament had considering banning it by law, as the Irish dress had been banned under Henry VIII. Such a ban, it was thought, would help to break up the distinct Highland way of life and integrate the Highlanders into modern society" (1983: 21).

Historically speaking, the modern kilt is a product of the early Industrial Revolution in the highlands of Scotland. Trevor-Roper notes that its inventor was an English Quaker, Thomas Rawlinson, who entered into partnership with Ian McDonnell of Glengarry to operate an iron foundry near Inverness around 1727, the same year the term "kilt" first appears in print. Observing the inconvenience of the traditional belted plaid and long tunic still worn by his Highland laborers, Rawlinson had a tailor in Inverness produce the prototype of the modern kilt, "...which was achieved by separating the skirt from the plaid and converting it into a distinct garment, with pleats already sewn" (1983: 22). According to Trevor-Roper, once the McDonnells adopted the new garment, it quickly spread throughout the Highlands and several of the Northern Lowland counties before the last Jacobite Rising in 1745.

Even by Trevor-Roper's admission, the modern Scottish kilt is not a totally spurious fabrication. On the contrary, the selective adaptation of an older traditional garment transformed it into an enduring emblem of Scottish identity. Even if an Englishman did actually invent the first modern kilt, that did not stop Scots from very quickly making it their own distinctive identity symbol. That last telling point is somehow lost on debunkers like Trevor-Roper, Prebble, and Whisnant, who sees such a compelling allegory of the expropriation of Appalachia's cultural and natural assets in Prebble's highly colored account of the Highland Clearances.

Whisnant concludes *Modernizing the Mountaineer* with one last quote from Prebble: "In the beginning the men who had imposed the change were of the same blood, tongue and family as the people. They used the advantages given to them by the new society to profit from the new, but in the end they were gone with their clans. The Lowlander has inherited the hills, and the tartan is a shroud" (1994: 284).

Whisnant completes his analogy and his book by asserting, "But if we continue systematically to destroy the social and cultural fabric of the United States in the service of economic development — or whatever other high-minded rhetoric — we will get our shrouds nevertheless" (1994: 284).

David Whisnant has undeniably made a substantial intellectual contribution to Appalachian Studies in general, and particularly to discourse concerning connections and parallels between Scotland and Appalachia. Nonetheless, in the end Whisnant's elegantly framed historical analogue is warped by the same dismissive, deconstructive scorn that major twentieth century Scottish cultural commentators from Hugh MacDiarmid to Tom Nairn have heaped upon popular romantic icons such as tartan, bagpipes and the bucolic fantasies of the Kailyard school.

Even if such symbols are artificial constructs, that does not seem to stop most ordinary human beings from investing meaning and value in them, regardless of shifting academic fashions like deconstructionism and post-structuralism. Rather than trying to debunk and explode them, we need to better understand why so many people need to identify themselves with these so-called artificial constructs. Whatever we do, we cannot afford to ignore or dismiss them.

Are patchwork quilts, mountain dulcimers and John Fox, Jr.'s southern highland romances the Appalachian counterparts of Scottish tartans, bagpipes and the idylls of the Kailyard? Cultural anthropologist Allen Batteau would have us believe so. Like David Whisnant, Batteau argues that the people of Southern Appalachia have only played a negligible role in fabricating the popular imagery of their region. For the most part, outsiders (like Batteau himself) have interpreted and marketed Appalachia to the world at large.

At the 1983 Appalachian Studies Conference, cultural anthropologist Melinda Bollar Wagner of Radford University in Virginia chaired a forum on Appalachian imagery including Batteau and labor historian-folklorist Archie Green (see Wagner, Batteau and Green 1983).

Batteau's response to Wagner's questions concerning the genesis of Appalachian stereotypes sketches out ideas he discusses at length in his book *The Invention of Appalachia* (University of Arizona Press, 1990).

Above all, Batteau is concerned with the evolving poetics of Appalachia: "At bottom, *all consciousness is poetic.* All forms of seeing the world, experiencing the world, placing faith in the world, are derived from, refracted from, or prefigured by mythopoetic forms" (1990: 8).

Batteau asserts that "Appalachia is a creature of the urban imagination" (1990: 1). The mythopoetic forms outsiders have imposed upon the people of the Southern Appalachians are artificial constructs, counterfeit depictions of an idyllic past that never existed except in the overheated imaginations of their romantic fabricators.

Sharing David Whisnant's ideological bias towards economic reductionism, Batteau decries tendencies in capitalist America that systematically reduce all cultural values to commodities. Says Batteau, "To a greater extent than one finds satisfactory, Appalachia today is packaged and sold as a commodity…. The Appalachian region, its stock of natural resources now sadly depleted, is finding its rituals and symbols rapidly mined for export…. Whose Appalachia is this?" (1990: 12).

Acknowledging Appalachia's historical status as an internal colony, Batteau concedes many natives of the region have been willing accomplices in the expropriation of their cultural heritage, along with their coal and timber. Formerly utilitarian artifacts are transmuted into mass-produced nostalgia symbols to satisfy the desires of rootless mainstream Americans for rootedness. These objects of nostalgia are tangible links to an idealized folk community set in an idyllic Golden Age: "a new set of commodities is enlisted to satisfy a public that demands an escape from the commodity system" (1990: 12).

Batteau is particularly contemptuous of promoters and purveyors of folklore: "Without educated interpreters, folk culture would not exist per se…. Folk culture is the symbolic production of a relatively powerless group, selected for its distinctiveness and specificity, and presented to the audience through the intermediation of a properly credentialed authority, so that its audience will know that it is 'authentic'" (1990: 82).

Like Whisnant, Batteau seems unwilling or unable to acknowledge that participants in the Appalachian folk revival movement could possibly be fulfilling personal needs and desires transcending economic profit, such as communion with significant others who identify themselves with distinctive forms of cultural expression that give meaning to their lives. Batteau's failure to appreciate the validity of these fundamental human needs and desires results in a distorted interpretation of an important aspect of the Appalachian identity movement. What also gets lost in these attacks upon folk revivalism is the historical fact that revivals of traditional arts have served (and continue to serve) progressive political purposes, helping subordinate people to cast off feelings of inferiority and dependency, promoting "counter-hegemonic opposition" that dispels the subservient colonial mentality.

Like Whisnant's trashing of Scottish romantic nationalism in *Modernizing the Mountaineer*, Batteau's deconstruction of Appalachian folk revivalism is ultimately more facile than valid. As Scottish novelist Neil M. Gunn's Philosopher says of the Antichrist in *The Serpent* (1943): "The awful thing is that he has nothing to put in the place of that which he destroys" (quoted by Ronald Turnbull and Craig Beveridge, "Recent Scottish Thought," in Craig 1987: 61).

To give the devil his due, Batteau does provide some valuable insights into the problematic character of Appalachian identity. Like Henry Shapiro, Batteau argues that Appalachia is mainstream America's alter ego, manifesting the nation's ambivalence concerning its notions of progress, which he describes in *The Invention of Appalachia* as "the sacrifice of nature in the service of civilization" (1990: 96). Individuals who identify themselves and are identified by others as peripheral people experience what Batteau calls "double otherness," manifested in prickly, conflicting feelings of shame and pride that sociologists might describe less poetically as status anxiety.

The internal conflict of core and periphery Batteau calls "double otherness" is not unique to Appalachia, nor is it anything new in human experience. Folklorist/labor historian Archie Green sagely observes that conflicts between Israelites and Philistines, Athenians and Spartans, Anglo-Saxons and Celts were part of the cultural baggage European explorers and settlers brought with them to the American colonial frontier. Green proposes that the settlers who came to the Southern Back Country developed an ambivalent relationship with metropolitan power centers. These frontier folk blurred the boundaries between savagery and civilization, between Native American and European cultures, between nature and culture, animal and human. Clothed in the skins of wild animals, southern backwoods people like Davy Crockett (1786–1836), born in Appalachian East Tennessee to parents of Scottish ancestry, declared themselves to be "half horse and half alligator." (The expression "half horse, half alligator" brings to mind the Chinese idiom "*ma ma hu hu*"—literally "*horse horse tiger tiger*"—signifying confusion, incongruity, disorder, contradiction, disjunction, internal division).

One of the Appalachian Studies movement's most intellectually adventurous scholars has concluded along with Archie Green that internal divisions in the Appalachian psyche are the legacy of ancient conflicts between metropolitan and peripheral peoples. In *Apples on the Flood* (1987) Rodger Cunningham proposes that southern mountaineers have inherited the "uncertain ego-boundaries" of their ancestors on the Atlantic rim of Europe, overrun and displaced by waves of invaders from the continent, possibly even predating the Celtic settlement of the British Isles.

A native West Virginian of Scottish ancestry with a doctorate in comparative literature from Indiana University, during his youth Cunningham received mixed messages from his Scottish-Appalachian family that left him feeling internally divided, torn between competing cultures of unequal status and authority. Cunningham's descriptions of his family history and youthful experiences in a West Virginia town whose gentry considered themselves to be mainstream Americans and their city part of the Midwest reveal a conscious desire to maintain Scottish ties, expressed in the Lowland Scots terms and sayings his mother carefully taught to Rodger (an emphatically Scottish spelling, distinctive from the English Roger). They also reveal a high degree of status anxiety on his mother's part regarding her family's Eastern Kentucky mountain origins: "A Cunningham uncle once told me that the other kids used to make fun of the young Chapmans as 'countrified.' This must have come as a shock to a girl whose family was 'quality' up Big Sandy.... I felt, long before I could understand, her deep ambivalence about her heritage" ("Meeting the First Time Again," in Best 1997: 136).

In graduate school studying comparative literature on the Bloomington campus of Indiana University, Cunningham discovered that his Appalachian background set him apart from other Americans, who affected not to understand what he was saying, even though he believed his locutions to be standard mainstream American English. He also experienced cultural conflicts with two graduate school roommates. One roommate had a New York Jewish background. Cunningham describes his other roommate as "a young man of smoothly processed whitebread opinions." This young man's father, a wealthy plastic surgeon residing in a posh suburb of Detroit, had evidently undergone the cultural equivalent of cosmetic surgery to efface the Appalachian identity Cunningham would go on to explore in *Apples on the Flood*.

In *Apples on the Flood*, Cunningham focuses upon the psychological consequences of colonization, positing a connection between geopolitical marginality and what he terms "insecure ego-boundaries." Reading David Whisnant's *Modernizing the Mountaineer* and Helen Lewis *et al. Colonialism in Modern America* inspired Cunningham. David Walls' article in *Colonialism in Modern America* introduced Cunningham to Immanuel Wallerstein's world systems theory: metropolitan cores deliberately subjugate and impoverish peripheral regions; "underdeveloped" regions are subjected to intentional "underdevelopment" (Cunningham 1987: xix).

Cunningham's reading of Malcolm Chapman's *The Gaelic Vision in Scottish Culture* (1968) led him to draw parallels between the historical experiences of the peoples of Scotland and Appalachia. The dominant English culture has appropriated elements of the subordinate Scottish Gaelic culture "...to create a stereotype that implicitly denies Gaelic and all "Celtic" cultures the attributes of adult competency to wield power" (1987: xix). Such "symbolic appropriation" (to use Chapman's phrase) prevents the subordinated culture from defining itself in its own terms, but only in alien terms dictated by dominant others.

Cunningham envisions Appalachia and Scotland as intermediate zones between civilized cores and savage peripheries: "My basic themes, then, are two: identity, both individual and collective; and peripheralization — what it means to be looked on constantly as someone on the fringe of things" (1987: xxii).

Cunningham proposes that the people of the Atlantic fringe of Europe have been retreating before the advancing continental mainstream for millennia. Anglicized Lowland Scots sought to subdue the wild Gaelic speaking highlanders, then the wild Irish Gaels of Ulster, and then treated the wild Indians of the Southern Back Country the same way.

Cunningham rejects the simplistic, racist notion that the genetic irrationality and emotionality of "Celtic culture" is the root cause of Appalachian (or Southern) subordination by "Teutonic" or "Nordic" Yankees, as historians Grady McWhiney and Forrest McDonald have argued:

> Sentimental Celtophiles are fond of saying that the Celts, in their battles against the Germanic tribes, were hampered by "Celtic traits" such as "individualism" and "lack of organizing spirit." This is usually said as if to lament their passing in a sentimental sense, while at the same time, distancing oneself from it by making it seem inevitable, a law of nature. The student of Appalachia will see the dismal parallel [1987: 14].

According to Cunningham, a dichotomy between "civilized" Lowland Scots and "wild" Highlanders emerges in Scotland by the fourteenth century. The Highlander becomes the unruly child, the ignoble savage, the Lowlander must suppress to become more like the superior civilized rationalistic paternalistic Englishman. The assimilation of English language and culture by Lowland Scots was self-imposed. All of this is prologue to the settlement of Lowland Scots in the Ulster Plantations in 1610. The Union of the Thrones marked the loss of Scottish autonomy, capped by the Union of the Parliaments in 1707

Simply put, Cunningham's primary thesis in *Apples on the Flood* is that imposition of feudal Anglo-Norman culture in Lowland Scotland and suppression of Celtic traditions created internal divisions that still vex the

Appalachian psyche. Cunningham adopted the concept of the divided self from R.D. Laing (1927–1989). The controversial Glasgow-born psychotherapist's popular books *The Divided Self* (1959) and *The Politics of Experience* (1967) drew an analogy between rites of passage and psychosis as processes of identity reformulation. Cunningham's sophisticated application of Laing's concept of the divided self in tracing the Scottish roots of Appalachian self-estrangement represents a great intellectual leap forward in American discourse concerning the Appalachian-Caledonian connection.

In the process, Cunningham seems to have independently invented (or rediscovered) Caledonian anti-syzygy, an extraordinarily cumbersome term first published in C. Gregory Smith's *Scottish Literature* (1919), adopted by Scottish nationalist poet Christopher Murray Grieve alias Hugh MacDiarmid and other leaders of the Scottish Renascence of the 1920s.

Equally difficult to spell or pronounce, "Caledonian anti-syzygy" basically means "Scottish disjunction." (Derived from the Greek *zygon*, "yoke," syzygy is a synonym for conjunction or alignment). Scottish historian Edward J. Cowan provides support for Cunningham's ideas when he suggests that the Ulster Scots settlers of early Appalachia carried this anomalous state of mind with them into the Southern Back Country:

> Is it possible that the Scotch-Irish shared the Scottish characteristic described by Gregory Smith as "a strange union of opposites," the notion of "The Caledonian Antisyzygy," which so inspired Hugh MacDiarmid, Scotland's greatest twentieth-century poet? The idea discussed by both Smith and MacDiarmid is that inherent contradictions exist within every individual as well as within societies, ethnicities or nations [Blethen and Wood 1997: 22–23].

According to Scottish literary historian Alan Bold, R. D. Laing drew upon this concept of internal disjunction to explain schizophrenia as an understandable response to "a disturbing environment." Bold declares, "What Laing (who studied medicine in Glasgow) calls the Divided Self corresponds to what Gregory Smith called the Caledonian anti-syzygy and Byron called the antithetical mind."

I experienced an uncanny sensation of *déjà vu* when I first read Bold's 1983 *Scotsman* article, "Healing Scotland's Divided Self," during the summer of 1996 in Edinburgh. I had encountered those very same ideas before — in *Apples on the Flood*. Shortly after I returned to the United States, I photocopied Bold's article and sent a copy to Cunningham, asking for his reaction. He wrote back to say that he saw great similarities between Bold's ideas and those in his own book, still in manuscript form when Bold's 1983 article appeared in *The Scotsman*. In fact, he even commented that reading Bold's ideas at that point in time would have definitely influenced the shape and direction of *Apples on the Flood*.

Entirely unaware of twentieth century Scottish discourse concerning Caledonian anti-syzygy, Cunningham's ideas converge at nearly every point with Bold's reflections on the fragmented Scottish personality published in *The Weekly Scotsman* [Edinburgh] on Saturday May 7, 1983.

Scotland is a complex and deeply divided nation, writes Bold: "Division is more than a physical presence, it is a mental condition. Maybe there really is something to the notion that the trauma of subordination, being labeled as inferior and dependent, has split the Scottish personality."

Nostalgia for a Gaelic Golden Age stems from the trauma of defeat and displacement. Scottish language is divided; therefore Scottish thoughts and feelings are divided. In the eighteenth century, the Scottish Enlightenment denied the value of Gaelic and Scots, striving for "universality" through the linguistic medium of Received English, though as we well know, early romantic nationalists like MacPherson and Burns were championing Gaelic and Scots through their poetry. Because so much writing about the Scottish Enlightenment is grounded in unexamined elitist values, it is assumed that the sacrifice of the vernacular for the sake of universality is inherently progressive and positive. As University of Edinburgh historian Owen Dudley Edwards puts it, "An act of extraordinary violence took place which permitted Scotland to grow intellectually, but at the cost of losing its native voices" (personal communication, May 28 1996).

In Scotland as in Appalachia, generations of colonialistic school teachers deliberately attempted to silence their students' native voices through verbal and physical abuse in the name of progress and enlightenment. Sadly, this was not at all a unique situation. Cherokees and other Native American children were routinely beaten, sometimes even had their mouths washed out with lye soap for speaking their aboriginal languages in government boarding schools administered by the Bureau of Indian Affairs to facilitate their assimilation into the American mainstream (see Best 1999: 13).

The 1872 Education (Scotland) Act legally suppressed Gaelic and the Scots tongue in Scottish schools. Official repression of Gaelic and Scots continued until relatively recent times. In *Revolving Culture: Notes from the Scottish Republic* (1994) essayist Angus Calder describes these colonialistic schools as "miniature Bastilles which beat Scots and Gaelic out of bairns" (page 9).

Bold says, "Gaelic civilization is still seen as the innocent childhood that was denied the Scottish nation." Nostalgia for the Celtic Twilight permeates J. M. Barrie's "Peter Pan" and even Lerner and Loewe's "Brigadoon," calling to mind ancient Gaelic legends of Tir na nOg, that mysterious land beyond the western edge of the known world: "That spiritual nostalgia is the soft centre of Scottish culture."

Twentieth century Scottish writers have struggled to overcome the cloying Victorian sentimentalism of the Celtic Twilight and the Kailyard School, even as modern Appalachian writers have rejected the romanticism of turn of the century regional local color novelists like John Fox, Jr. and his imitators. Bold concludes, "The best modern Scottish writers are individuals seeking to express the undivided self in an image of artistic wholeness".

The Scots have trans–Atlantic counterparts in Appalachia, who have also suffered prickly psychic wounds because of their marginality and have likewise struggled to heal their divided selves through creating scholarly works, art, music, fiction and poetry to reconnect them with their roots and restore unity to their psyches.

When sociologist John Shelton Reed stated that "Appalachia has always been the South's South" (1986: 42), he deftly pinpointed the source of Appalachia's double otherness: its marginality. Regional and sectional prejudices are still very much alive in the United States. Regardless of all the ethnic and racial pride movements that have taken place since the early sixties and the advent of the era of political correctness, marginal low-status Southern types like hillbillies, crackers and rednecks are still the butts of crude jokes and slurs. As Reed puts it, "Just as rednecks seem to be the last identifiably ethnic villains, so hillbillies appear to be the last acceptable ethnic fools" (Reed 1986: 43).

Popular historical studies published in the 1980s positing survivals of British regional subcultures in the United States have resurrected hoary stereotypes of congenital Celtic barbarism dating back to Tacitus and Herodotus. In their widely quoted book *Cracker Culture* (1988), historians Grady McWhiney and Forrest McDonald assert that no less than seventy five percent of the settlers of the hinterlands of the Southern colonies were transplanted Celts, whose cultural baggage included traditions of shiftless pastoralism, laziness, intemperance, sensuality, violence and anarchic individualism.

In the winter 1990 edition of the *Appalachian Journal* (vol. 17, no. 2) in an essay titled, "Cracker, Your Breed Ain't Hermeneutical," Rodger Cunningham accuses McWhiney and MacDonald of uncritically accepting degrading characterizations of their Celtic forebears at face value, an insidious manifestation of ethnic self-hatred, Frantz Fanon's "inferiorism" in action. However, Cunningham finds weighty evidence in David Hackett Fischer's *Albion's Seed* (1989) to support his own thesis that descendants of the North British settlers of Appalachia suffer from an impaired sense of autonomous identity and self-worth, the psychological residue of centuries of insecurity and violence troubling the unstable borderlands of Scotland and Northern Ireland.

Blurred boundaries generate mixed messages and double binds, signaling unresolved inner conflict between the dominant core and the subordinate periphery. Evoking Sigmund Freud's concept of projection, John Shelton Reed contrasts the peripheral "id culture" with the "superego culture" of the core: "The idea is that members of the group doing the stereotyping project their unacceptable impulses onto the group being stereotyped, and thus deny that they have those impulses" (1986: 45).

Whether we are talking about Appalachians, Scots, vanishing noble savages, or any other dominated, peripheral group, it is interesting that the qualities which distinguish "superego" and "id" cultures remain constant, for ultimately they are expressions of unequal power relationships:

(+)	(-)
Dominant	Subordinate
Core	Periphery
Superego	Id
Left Brain	Right Brain
Rational	Irrational
Advanced	Backward
Hardworking	Lazy
Refined	Uncouth
Cleanly	Slovenly
Organized	Fragmented
Apollonian restraint	Dionysian excess
bureaucracy	folk society
United States	Southern states
Southern states	Appalachia
United Kingdom	Scotland
Lowlands	Highlands
Teutonic	Celtic

In *The Gaelic Vision* (1968), Malcolm Chapman neatly assesses the paradoxical image of the Highlanders in Scottish culture: "The Highlands have long been derided as the barbarous antithesis of southern culture and sophistication, yet they have at the same time become the location of all of the virtues that civilisation has felt itself to lack" (1968: 13). Like the Scottish Gael, the Appalachian highlander comes to embody the inner conflicts of the metropolitan core, "at once a fit object for the location of primitive traits, and a fit object for taming, schooling and 'improving'" (1968: 20).

This is true of The Folk in general. As folklorist Alan Dundes comments, "The folk is a backward, illiterate segment of the population of which elitist intellectuals are ashamed. On the other hand, the folk represents the glorified, romanticized remnants of a national patrimony which is something for zealous intellectuals to celebrate ... the same situation applies in most countries. Intellectuals were both embarrassed by and proud of their folk and folklore" (1989: 44).

The assumption that advancing core cultures must inevitably displace peripheral cultures has historically provided the impetus to study and celebrate vanishing folk traditions and, indeed, has led to the initiation of romantic cultural revivals in general. However, before such revivals can occur, their leaders must resolve their feelings of divided identity. Dundes proposes that selective reconstruction or wholesale invention of folk traditions provides a means of shedding demeaning stereotypes and asserting a self-defined social and cultural identity. Embracing the periphery and rejecting the hegemony (the inherent cultural authority) of the core resolves the identity crises of internally conflicted peripheral individuals who become founders and leaders of regionalist and nationalist cultural revitalization movements. As the English sociologist Anthony D. Smith remarks, "The enemy within is loss of identity, self-oblivion, the end of authenticity, which erodes and corrupts the community, dividing and weakening the members and tempting them into cultural imitation and political dependence" (1979: 118). In conquering the inner enemy, which is in fact the internal conflict between core and periphery, marginal intellectuals are transmuted into partisans (or patrons) of the revitalized folk community. To quote Smith, "They go out among the peasants and farmers, commune with nature, record the rhythms of the countryside, and bring them back to the anonymous city, so that rising urban strata may be 'reborn' and possess a clear and unmistakable identity" (1979: 106).

At the very end of *Apples on the Flood*, Rodger Cunningham depicts a sleeping Merlin awaiting rebirth in a fairy mound, a mystical womb-cavern-crucible hidden in the northern borderlands of Albion conjuring up an allegorical process of psychic alchemy separating the dross of the false self from the gold of the authentic self, enabling the self-actualized individual to return home to a reawakened community that has come to know and respect itself again.

Along with folk revivalism, the creation of local, regional, and national literatures voiced in indigenous languages, dialects, and accents expresses that same desire for symbolic rebirth and homecoming. Apparent similarities between the cultural identity movements flourishing in present day Scotland and Appalachia are not coincidental or illusory. They reflect very real points of convergence in the lives of members of marginal groups striving to heal their divided selves. Rather than deconstructing or discounting them, we need to consider how these cultural revival movements in Scotland and Appalachia satisfy universal human desires for meaning and belonging in local and personal terms.

3

Scottish Cultural Revivals:
A Sketch and a Theory

*W*hen most social historians, cultural anthropologists or folklorists use the term "revival," they are generally referring to social movements seeking to restore or revitalize idealized or even imagined communities and their distinctive cultural features.

What are these distinctive cultural features? Language or dialect, costume, music, dance, foods, sports, games, rituals, ceremonies, or anything else that expresses communal identity.

The classic American anthropological definitions of cultural revitalization are found in the writings of Ralph Linton, who defined nativistic revival movements as "any conscious, organized attempt on the part of a society's members to revive and perpetuate selected aspects of its culture (1943: 230), and Anthony F.C. Wallace, who asserted that revitalization movements were "deliberate, conscious, organized efforts by members of a society to create a more satisfactory culture" (1956: 279).

In these movements, we often find that stigmatizing cultural features are transformed from sources of shame to emblems of pride. People deemed to be lacking in history and culture rediscover (or fabricate) counter-mythologies depicting a Golden Age in which their subordinated group was happy, strong, cultivated, and independent while their subjugators were mired in savagery and superstition. Cultural revival movements make it possible for subordinates to recover at least a vestige of that lost primordial autonomy, if only periodically and symbolically.

Scottish cultural revivals have historically been reactions to the loss of sovereignty and the displacement Scotland has experienced since the Union of the Parliaments in 1707 and possibly even as early as the Union of the Thrones in 1603. Some contemporary Scottish scholars, notably David

McCrone and Lindsay Patterson, argue that Scotland retained a high degree of political and cultural autonomy even after the Union of the Parliaments. Rather than merely symbolically compensating for loss of political sovereignty, preserving and promoting various genres of Scottish culture expresses continuing active resistance to English hegemony. Displacements and emigrations were radically transforming Scottish society during the eighteenth century. A new global Scottish culture was coming into being, and nostalgic immigrants were playing a key role in its creation.

Scottish colonists began settling in the American colonies in 1622. By 1657, a Scots Charitable Society was established in Boston, "surely the first of many such societies which Scots were to found in all parts of the world" (Donaldson 1966: 44). Increased Scottish settlement in the eighteenth century saw the establishment of St. Andrew's Societies in Charleston (1729), Philadelphia (1749), New York (1756) and Savannah (after 1750). Then as now, the St. Andrew's Societies not only served charitable purposes but also provided Scottish immigrants with welcome opportunities for renewing cultural and social links with their compatriots. The first fiddling contest known to be held in the American colonies was part of a St. Andrew's Day celebration in Hanover County, Virginia, in 1736. These voluntary associations reorganized traditional social institutions, giving them a modern legal-rational corporate structure, enabling displaced immigrants to assimilate a new way of life while preserving selected aspects of their original cultures.

Though deconstructionist cultural critics may challenge the historical authenticity of "tartanry," there is substantial evidence that Scots in America were already engaged in the romantic reconstruction of their cultural heritage before the American Revolution or the repeal of the Disarming Act. To quote Scottish American historian Gordon Donaldson, "It is, however, curious that so early as 1765 George Bartram, a native of Scotland who had become a cloth merchant in Philadelphia, was advertising 'best Scotch Plaids for gentlemen's gowns and boy's Highland dress; this might suggest that the cult of the tartan flourished on the far side of the Atlantic earlier than it did in Great Britain" (Donaldson 1966: 128).

Scottish cultural revivalism was flourishing on both sides of the Atlantic. The publication between 1760 and 1765 of *Ossian* and other allegedly ancient Scots Gaelic poems by a young Highlander, James MacPherson (1736–96), resulted in vicious accusations of fraud but also generated widespread interest in the poetry of the common people that laid the groundwork for the emergence of folklore as an academic discipline. James Boswell described MacPherson to Dr. Samuel Johnson as "an impudent fellow from Scotland, who affected to be a savage, and railed against all established systems." Today folklorists and cultural historians tend to perceive MacPherson more sympathetically as an archetypal romantic rebel who sought to restore the damaged self-esteem of his subjugated people through the "rediscovery" of a counter myth. *Ossian* asserted the primordial superiority of a humiliated subject nation. Macpherson revealed a Golden Age in which the ancestors of the Highlanders were producing exquisite, cultivated poetry while the Irish and English were "sunk in primitive barbarism" (See Dundes 1989: 49).

The 1760s was a period of increasing Scottish cultural pride; many collections of Scottish music and dance were being published, including the first detailed analysis of the Scottish elite piping tradition, *ceol mor* or *piobreachd, A Compleat Theory of the Scots Highland Bagpipe,* which was written circa 1761 by a nostalgic immigrant scholar-performer, Joseph McDonald, on a sea voyage to India where he died shortly after taking up a post with the East India Company. McDonald's career prefigured that of later immigrant amateur scholars whose pursuit of their musical roots provided respite from their workaday lives as bureaucrats and functionaries, like Captain Simon Fraser, a military officer and collector of Scottish fiddle tunes or Chief Francis O'Neill, Irish-American police superintendent and perhaps the most productive collector of Irish melodies in modern times.

The continued expansion of British industry and empire during the eighteenth and nineteenth centuries led to the establishment of more Scottish immigrant organizations and romantic nationalistic institutions. Burns' Birthday was celebrated in New York as early as 1820; by 1836, the Highland Club of New York held its first annual Highland Games. Within a very short time, Caledonian Games were being held in major Scottish settlements in the United States, Canada and New Zealand, including most of the sports and performing arts competitions which are still part of the contemporary Highland Games (see Redmond 1971). Though initially organized to celebrate Scottish culture, the Caledonian Games were soon open to the general public, regardless of national origin. During their peak years, the Caledonian games attracted tens of thousands of spectators and participants. Scottish-Americans were leaders in the development of modern collegiate athletics in the United States, which actually led to the decline of the Caledonian games at the end of the nineteenth century and the emergence of the modern Highland games, which are more exclusively Scottish in content and focus. The same period also saw the formation of modern clan societies that reinvented the traditional Scottish system of hereditary chiefs and retainers within the framework of a novel institutional structure, the voluntary non-profit organization. The modern system of clan tartans was also elaborated during the course of the nineteenth century, an extension of Scotland's martial subculture. Thus by the turn of this century, most of the features we now associate with modern Scottish romantic nationalism were already in existence.

The varying forms of cultural revitalization we find in present-day Scotland and Scottish immigrant communities represent divergent visions of

Scottishness. Contemporary Scottish nationalists may see the kilt and Highland pipes as symbols of subservience to British imperialism and colonialism while immigrant Scots may see these same cultural artifacts as links to a cherished communal history. Calling James Macpherson a forger does not negate the enormous influence *Ossian* had upon the development of romantic nationalism; unraveling the cult of the kilt does not stop it from functioning as a valid symbol of cultural identity—for those who find positive meaning in it. As Alan Dundes says, folklorists cannot prevent people from believing that fakelore is folklore. Traditions emerge and evolve, reflecting the desire of living people for meaningful patterns of affiliation in a constantly changing world.

Flora MacDonald Gammon of Waynesville, North Carolina, has seen traditions emerge and change in her own lifetime. A self-proclaimed missionary for cultural heritage, Flora has been actively involved in Scottish heritage activities and the Appalachian folk music revival in the Southeastern United States since childhood. She poetically describes the Scottish traditions that have been handed down to her not as threads but as thick ropes that securely tie her and her family to a people and an ancestral homeland with which she identifies herself. Her perceptive reflections on her personal experiences shed light upon the meaning and value of traditional culture to contemporary people in general.

4

Conversation with a Cultural Missionary: Flora MacDonald Gammon, Waynesville, North Carolina, 17 January 1994

One of Flora MacDonald Gammon's favorite ballads is "The Palace Grand," which she learned from David Morris of Ivydale, Clay County, West Virginia. Morris, born in Appalachia and Scottish by ancestry, had learned this ballad from a Clay County woman who in turn had acquired it from a woman of Scottish background who had moved up to West Virginia from Georgia. Flora not only values this ballad for its mournful melody and tragic story, but also because it reminds her of points of convergence between Scotland and Appalachia in her own life.

Born May 17, 1946, in Fayetteville, North Carolina, in an area of the eastern section of the state heavily settled by Scottish Highlanders, Flora grew up in a family that delighted in celebrating its Scottish heritage. Her mother was raised in Carolina Community, a town in Dillon County, South Carolina, settled entirely by natives of the Isle of Skye. As a child, Flora took her given names and family names for granted, but as she matured, she became increasingly aware of her ancestral ties to Scotland. She feels sorry for children whose newly made-up names have no history or meaning behind them, nothing to provide a sense of communion with their forebears. In the cultural enrichment programs Flora presents to Western North Carolina school children, one of her main objectives is to help them understand that names are not just arbitrary assemblages of sounds; they are symbolic links between living individuals and their ancestors, fulfilling basic human desires for meaning and belonging.

Flora has been married since 1987 to John Dall, a native Scot whose father's family hailed from Fife. They live in the Iron Duff community near Waynesville, North Carolina. Like many Scots, John's family had to leave Scotland to make a living. As Flora comments:

> His father was not interested in his Scottish heritage or culture and knew that the only way he could make a decent living was to anglicize himself. And he did. So his father never wore the kilt, never had anything to do with being Scottish. Got rid of his accent as soon as possible and everything. His mother's parents were native Scots. His father was a farm overseer in Ireland, and so his mother was actually born in County Cork and she grew up in Ireland but she was of Scottish parentage. When she was growing up and when she was an adult, people would ask where she was born and she would say "County Cork." "Oh, you're Irish!" She would look at them with absolute disdain and that typical arrogance of the Scots and would inform them in her nice lilting accent that Christ was born in a stable but you didn't call the lad a horse.

John Dall was underage when he enlisted in the British marine commandos in World War Two. He migrated to Canada, then to the States where he became a naturalized citizen. Now retired, John is active in Scottish heritage activities, including making authentic replicas of medieval weapons for Scottish historical re-enactment groups and regalia for fraternal organizations like the Knights Templar.

Flora doesn't have any children, nor does her cousin Jamie or her Uncle Donald MacDonald, a cofounder of the Grandfather Mountain Highland Games and a great advocate of Scottish traditions. Flora didn't self-consciously think about the role of tradition in her life until she became involved in folk revival in the sixties. Up until that time, she took her family heritage for granted along with the names that had been handed down to her.

Flora's mother, her uncle Donald's sister, was also deeply devoted to Scottish history and traditions, reflected in the historical names she bestowed upon her oldest daughter. Flora isn't a direct descendant of the Flora MacDonald who carried Bonnie Prince Charlie over to Skye after Culloden, but she is nonetheless closely related to her:

> I am a direct descendent of her mother and stepfather, not Flora MacDonald herself. Her father died when she was a small child. Her mother Miriam MacDonald was a MacDonald from South Uist who married a MacDonald, and her second husband was also a MacDonald, but a MacDonald from Skye, from Armadale. And she married Hugh MacDonald of Arma-

dale, and together they had another family, two daughters and at least one or two more sons, one of those daughters being named Flora. And I'm a descendent of that second Flora.

All of Flora's genealogical lines have been thoroughly traced: "My mother's ancestry is very simple: all Highland Scots from the Isle of Skye." She's very proud of the fact that she is "pure Scot" as she says (laughs), and I say what's that, because that's a mixture already. She's very proud of the fact that all of her ancestors came from the Isle of Skye:

> Then, my father's side is a combination, as I say, a "Duke's Mixture," They are some Highland Scot, Lowland Scot which became Ulster Scot, English, Dutch, French Huguenot, that's it. A real mixture of things. Even though he was brought up in Brazil with most of the family still living in southwestern Virginia and Northeast Tennessee, when they came back up here, they would always go visit. The family was still very much aware of its roots basically as Scottish and English in origin. Our family has never had one immigrant ancestor. We trace all the female lines, too, and then the male–female lines from those female lines. So therefore we've got all those different immigrant ancestors; they came in lots of different times, mid-1700s, late 1750s and early 1760s into early 1800s.

Flora's father was a Presbyterian minister, and her mother's family had a long history of involvement with the Presbyterian ministry:

> My mother's family, the MacQueen side of the family, for seven genera-tions over in Scotland had been ministers. And then the line broke over there sometime during the Covenanting—sometime after Culloden. But then, it picked up again over here, and for five full generations over here, there was a minister in every single generation of our MacQueen line in this country.
>
> My father's father was a teaching missionary in Brazil. And his mother was also a teaching missionary. But my father and one of his brothers went into the ministry and two sisters went in as teaching missionaries and stayed in Brazil as teaching missionaries. There were five children in my father's family, and out of all five, four of them went into the Church. Only the fifth brother, the middle one, went into business and did not go into any line in the church at all.
>
> It was kind of funny, though, when I was growing up and my father was moving to different churches, I often had the little old ladies of the church who would have known of the Gammon ministries in Brazil asking me, "Are you going to be a missionary like your grandparents when you grow up?"
>
> And I would sit there and my mind would be saying, "Hell, no! You couldn't pay me to be a missionary! But at the same time, I've come to real-

Flora MacDonald Gammon and kilted boy singing at Grandfather Mountain Highland Games ceilidh. (Courtesy of Jim Thompson.)

ize that I am a missionary, but not with the church. I'm a missionary of culture.

Flora considers herself very lucky to have grown up in two families that were very conscious of their Scottish family histories and traditions. Flora and her cousins were encouraged to perform for older family members when they got together for family visits. Without using the term as such, they were unselfconsciously carrying on the old Scottish tradition of the *ceilidh*, which simply means "visit" in Gaelic.

Flora describes putting on shows with her cousins at the old MacDonald homestead, a large log house that had been gentrified by adding white clapboards and square columns to approximate the appearance of a classical plantation house. From the time she was a toddler, Flora took part in these family frolics; her uncle Donald taught her how to do the Highland fling and sing Harry Lauder songs:

> Whenever our family gathered, we always organized entertainment. It was always the little ones that did the entertainment, but Uncle Donald was the one who organized us. And he would teach us songs; he would teach us

Flora's uncle Donald MacDonald. (Courtesy of Hugh Morton.)

dances. We would make up plays; just anything and everything. And we would put on a performance for all the adults sometime during the visit.

He taught us Highland dancing; he taught us Scottish country dancing, and it was nothing unusual to us. It was simplified, yes, and it wasn't done according to the rules and regulations for competition and all that, but we were doing it just for fun. Then we put on these performances, these *ceilidhs*, for the members of the family. I was the one who loved it the most. Cousin Jamie [MacDonald] loved it, too, but he was a whole lot younger, so he didn't get in on it quite as much as I did, because I was the oldest grandchild. Jamie's the one who was at the School of Scottish Studies and got his Ph.D. in Gaelic. He is the first American to be teaching Gaelic in Scotland. I'm so proud of him; it just tickles me to death to be able to say that.

The oldest of twelve cousins, Flora and her cousin Jamie have become strong advocates of Scottish heritage like their Uncle Donald:

I guess the main interest in it came through my uncle Donald MacDonald, my mother's brother, because he's the one with the real active interest in our heritage and things Scottish, period. He was fascinated by the Harry Lauder songs and the Harry Lauder period, the music hall, yeah, so that sparked some of his interest. But he was also interested in the older culture, too. He didn't know anything about it, because there was no way to really study it over here. His interest had always been there, because our family never lost sight of who they were. They always talked about the family coming from the Isle of Skye, and that we had so-and-so granddaddy's fiddle that was made in Skye and he brought over here when he was a small boy, various things like that, so that the heritage of the family was always there.

After returning from Scotland after his first extended visit, Donald, then a journalist, began writing on Scottish subjects in the now-defunct *Charlotte News*. Agnes McCrae Morton, wife of an heir to the Morton Salt fortune, read one of Donald's articles about the Braemar Highland Games in Scotland and contacted him to ask his help in setting up a family reunion at her property in Western North Carolina, McCrae Meadows on Grandfather Mountain.

She had been reading in *The Charlotte News* some of the articles he had written about games in Scotland and Scottish things, and she was interested in organizing a big McCrae reunion and wanted to know from him how to go about this and to help these McCraes understand more of their Scottish heritage. And between the two of them — she had the monetary means and a place, because they owned Grandfather Mountain, and he had the idea of starting the games.

He really wanted to start them somewhere around Montgomery County, North Carolina, in the Uwherrie Mountains, because that's where those first Highland Scots settled, and the MacDonalds did, and Flora MacDonald and her step-father Hugh MacDonald, our ancestor. So he really wanted to start the Highland Games down there, which would have been the logical place because it was where the Highland Scots settled.

But she had the place up here in the mountains, and so they were started at Grandfather Mountain. She gave up the idea of just having a family reunion and made it a Scottish reunion. So that's why it started, and that's why we say today that Scottish Games in this country are more like a family reunion. But not just of one family, but of that whole extended Scottish family. But that's why the atmosphere is of a family reunion, cause it was set up like that in the very first place.

But then his interest got bigger and bigger. He had gone back to Scotland and met a woman who was a native of Lewis, and she was a folk singer, a Gaelic singer from Lewis, and they got married over here at Grandfather Mountain during the Games in 1960. That was the first time that our family all came together for something Scottish. My mother had assisted him with the worship service at the Games ever since they started in 1956, but the rest of the family had not really come and become involved in it until 1960 when the family came up for the wedding. And half the family was in the wedding (laughs).

That was the first time I had ever been. And, I guess the major impression I had was that there weren't any people my age there. I was thirteen years old, and there were either little kids or there were college age students and people older than that. Or people in their fifties and sixties. But there was no one my age — no teenagers at all. So as a result, I was always with the adults.

So I went to all the parties and all the gatherings and the *ceilidhs* that occurred, At the *ceilidh* that night, my uncle called me up and had me sing "The Wig-Wig-Waggle of the Kilt" with him. That was one of the first songs he ever taught me.

At first the Grandfather Mountain event was a small, informal gathering, not much more than an overgrown family reunion attached to very traditional

Agnes McCrae Morton and N.J. MacDonald (not one of Flora's immediate relations) at McCrae Meadows with the peak of Grandfather Mountain behind them. (Courtesy of Hugh Morton.)

Highland Games restricted to athletic competitions like foot-races and tossing the caber:

> Well, at that time, the Games were a lot smaller than they are now and so therefore, they were just held on Sunday at that time, cause that's how they were over in Scotland. On Saturday night, there would be a "Tartan Ball/*Ceilidh*," all one thing thrown together. In other words, it was a dress-up occasion, a formal occasion. There was a dance band there for dancing, but there was also entertainment.
>
> And everybody sat around and sang songs together and shared the entertainment together as is done in Scotland. In other words, it would start out with maybe one person, basically my uncle Donald singing some songs, but then as everybody got a little more liquor into themselves, they started singing along, too. Of course, at that time in the 1950s, more people were aware of Harry Lauder's songs, because that was the age group that also remembered Harry Lauder.
>
> So they were used to singing "Roamin' in the Gloamin'" and things like that, so they'd all join in singing. People were used to singing more in those days than they are now. They would gather in the Esceola Lodge pool pavilion; there was a building right beside the pool at the lodge in Linville, and they would gather in there for that evening's entertainment. And then the next day the games would start with a worship service that was set up as interdenominational based on Presbyterian lines but at the same time interdenominational; just merely a Christian service really, after which the games would start. There were no guests from Scotland; there was no Parade of Tartans. There was nothing but the competition in the athletic events and the Highland dancing and drumming events. There was AAU track and field, because that is traditionally Highland. All of your running events, those were Highland type athletic events, besides the tossing of the caber, the tossing of the sheaf, the Highland wrestling and all that.

However, the Grandfather Mountain gathering quickly became much more than just an athletic event. It became a major Scottish-American powwow, attracting tens of thousands of participants with widely diverging and occasionally conflicting concepts of Scottishness. While the older generation who founded the event had been reared on the tartan music hall songs of Sir Harry Lauder, Flora's generation became devotees of Appalachian and Scottish traditional music during the great folk boom of the sixties. Folk music had been part of her family's gatherings from the beginning, and while she was in college, Flora acquired an Appalachian dulcimer made by Ed Presnell of Beech Mountain in Watauga County, North Carolina, which she still plays today:

> I was already involved in the Scottish games and music when the hippie movement moved in with me, with college age stuff. Remember, I said when

Kilted competitors lifting caber at Grandfather Mountain Highland Games. (Courtesy of Hugh Morton).

I first started going to the Highland Games, there was nobody there my age. There was never anybody there my age until the late 60s, early 70s. And that's when all of a sudden the hippies discovered (I'm just using the term … my generation discovered) the Highland Games. And it became the in thing to do to go camp out at the Highland Games and become part of this culture for the weekend. All of a sudden I had my own age group there, which I'd never had before. It was bringing the folk side of it to what had already become the cocktail party circuit and the tartan bandwagon, as I call it, to the games. Because the games moved away from being a real folk thing. And of course the games continued to move on in this direction, of cocktail parties.

Flora sees great irony in the way Scottish Americans kowtow to the Scottish clan chiefs and nobles who were the honored guests at these posh country club soirees:

My uncle started the tradition of bringing a chief over from Scotland for the Games to be the honored guest. And he rues the day he ever started that. Here are all of these Americans falling all over themselves to party and show off for this Scottish chief who was born in England, grew up in English schools, has no more interest in his Scottish heritage than the Pope does, and yet is usually a direct descendent of the people who actually threw all of us out. And yet we're over here kowtowing to them and telling them how wonderful they are. And having all these parties for them and showing them off, making them out to be the biggest thing in history.

Why in the world are we doing it? I think it's that old American love of pomp and circumstance, for one thing, and love of kingship and all that kind of stuff. But enough time has evolved so you romanticize it.

The old feelings aren't there that used to be there, so now it's something just sort of clouded in time and history, so it becomes pretty. The dirty part, all the bad part, the real part gets knocked away because you don't need that; it's not part of it anymore. Because we're not close enough to it to have remembered what it was like, to have survived those times. We don't have any memory of what it was like to eat seaweed to survive, before we could finally get in the hold of some filthy ship and get over here and hopefully survive to get over here and not die in the middle of the ocean. So we don't have that kind of memory, therefore any of that is just pretty stories now, so it doesn't upset us the way it would have generations ago.

So anyhow, Donald got these Highland chiefs coming over as honored guests. And then he started this Parade of Tartans. Well, actually, he didn't start this parade of tartans; he didn't want that, but it got started. You get to march around behind your chieftain displaying your tartan ... all the peacocks got to show off with what they're wearing.

Meanwhile, around the campfires on Grandfather Mountain, Flora was able to find a refreshing alternative to the pretense and social climbing of the country club scene with friends of her own generation who were exploring connections between Scottish and Appalachian traditional music. These included outstanding West Virginia musicians of Scottish background such as singer-guitarist David Morris, fiddler and bagpiper Franklin George and his wife Jane, a teacher of Scottish country dancing:

> I had to live in both worlds of the games. People who would see me at the *ceilidhs* would then see me later up at the campgrounds and they would say, "Would the real Flora Gammon please stand up?" Because they would see a different person. I would get up to the campgrounds and I could be me; I could relax and just sit around the campfire and sing songs and get up and dance when I felt like it and do step dancing and hoot and holler all I wanted to. Whereas down at the *ceilidhs* and cocktail parties I had to be Miss Priss, as all the adults were doing. So there were these two elements to the games.
>
> During this period of time at the *ceilidhs*, I had gotten to know Frank George and David through campground experience and all. I kept wanting my mother to have Frank at the *ceilidh*: "I'm not going to have any of that fiddle music; that's not Scottish!" But Mother's whole concept of Scottish

The Parade of Tartans at Grandfather Mountain. (Courtesy of Hugh Morton.)

was what she had learned from Donald and what she had learned from books. It was all Harry Lauder; it had nothing to do with the old culture at all. It was what had been given in the history books and what had been put out through this Victorian period, the resurgence with Queen Victoria, King George IV and Queen Victoria and the love of things Scottish. But they weren't the love of things Scottish; they were the love of what they decided was going to be Scottish. Just as the love of what people decided was going to be Appalachian became the thing, right, which had nothing to do with the culture of the people in the first place.

So that's what my mother wanted her Scottish entertainment to be; she wanted people ... she never did have well known people from Scotland ... but people either in the style of Harry Lauder or then Peter Morrison, Arthur Kennedy ... the people from Scotland who are the music hall, the Tartan Bandwagon people, singing the style that came out of the Victorian period; the parlor music that Sir Walter Scott gave to the world. At the same time, I was trying to bring in the "real" element (laughs), the natural element of the fiddle music and all the old instruments and old style of doing things. But to my mother, all she saw was beards, and beards meant hippies. Now, she never noticed that the hair was short. All she saw was the beards, and that meant hippies to her. And therefore that wasn't what she wanted. And it didn't happen until she was sick and I got 'em in!

That was around '70, '71. That's the way things were going. Of course, Frank didn't care in the least either way. But he came in and did some fiddling, it was like he stood there and of course gave everybody this history lesson, and they're all sitting there going "Ahh!" and I'm saying, "Go on, Frank, sock it to 'em! Tell 'em how it is! Tell 'em the real story!" I knew it was real. I had never studied it, but inside I knew it was real. And that was the real thing and the right thing, and what I was getting the rest of the time wasn't right at all. So that kept me in this double life style [laughs] up at the games.

Frank got into it because when he was in the Army he was stationed in Scotland and he got his enjoyment of learning the pipes over there. He was already a fiddler, saw Scottish fiddling over there, but it does fascinate me that our style of fiddling over here is more the Irish style of fiddling. It evolved from Irish fiddling, not from Scottish fiddling, because Scottish fiddling is much more classical in style. As to whether it was really classical in style to begin with, I doubt it. During the days of Niel Gow and all of them, when all of that music was being written, I doubt it was all classical in style. However, once it got written down and published it was the Victorian period and there it went into classical and got fixed and orchestrated. And so you have John Turner playing Scottish fiddle music and giving this whole style to the United States and it is so formal; it is not the music of the people, really. You need to go to the pubs.

So what we think of as fiddling music of the people in this country is actually the Irish style, because that's the only style that stayed real and didn't get fixed into another type. It stayed as an oral tradition, so I think

West Virginia fiddler Franklin George playing with kilted guitarist and drummer at Grandfather Mountain. (Courtesy of Hugh Morton.)

the history of these tunes was passed down in Frank's family. And then he got over there in Scotland and found the same tunes but they were on the bagpipes and that sparked his own historical interest of "oh, what I'm playing was originally a pipe tune, not a fiddle tune! And I'm playing the modern evolution of that old tune."

So Frank got into it more and saw some Highland Games over there, so by the time he came back here and was in his heyday as the musician to know and all that, the publicity for Grandfather Mountain had gotten good enough so that he heard about it. And so he came down. He enjoyed it and went back and by then had met David.

And David, of course, being back from Nam and being absolutely haywire and not knowing what in the world he wanted to do, latched onto it, too. Cause Frank said, "Hey, you've got to come down here and see this! You'll love it!" And so David came, and the year that Frank brought David was the year that I met them. Because at the end of the games on Sunday afternoon, a few people were still kinda hangin' around. Frank was standing there playing fiddle, David was playing guitar, and they were playing old pipe tunes, and I started dancing the highland fling to what they were doing.

And somebody took a picture of us, because Grandfather Mountain was right behind us.

I said something to Frank — here we'd been communing through the music for forty-five minutes to an hour, never said a word to each other; never passed any conversation between us. When we finished, I said something to Frank and asked him his name. And Frank laughed and said, "You'll never remember it anyway. And I said, "Try me." And he said "Franklin George!" And periodically through the year I would flash back this name, Franklin George.

And the next year when I saw him, I walked up to him and said, "Hello, Franklin George. How are you?" He looked at me like "How'd you remember my name?" and I said "You said I'd never remember your name and I knew I would." And that's how he and I got to know each other. And David of course came back with him. So David was always there, and David being a singer, Frank not, so David and I started singing together. It would end up, we'd sit around tents. It would start raining and everyone would fly under the same tent. And we'd sit there and start singing. See, I automatically harmonize.

I sing lead, but at the same time I really like to harmonize. So when David would start singing, I'd just automatically harmonize with him. Well, David and I have the same timbre to our voice; we sing in exactly the same pitch. In fact we have sung with our foreheads touching, and our voices are vibrating at exactly the same pitch, totally in tandem. And it's very unusual to find someone that you can sing with, you know, that jells that well. And so we did a lot of singing together. And that's eventually how I got him up at the *ceilidh* was to sing with me and then do some on his own, you know.

David Morris and Flora MacDonald Gammon singing under Clan Hay tent, Grandfather Mountain Highland Games, July 1974. (Courtesy of Kent Hay Atkins and Flora MacDonald Gammon.)

Once my mother met them — and of course, both of them would fall into their "parlor mode," as I would call it, their "meet the public mode" — they just charmed her to death, and she just loved them and thought they were wonderful! And what they looked like didn't make any difference anymore. As long as they wore the kilt, they were okay. Which they did.

Except for the fact that David always wore his kilt with his brogans and [laughs] his big old thermal socks instead of kilt hose! [laughs] Either that, or he wore it barefooted. [laughs] "Where's ma shoes?" [laughs] Oh me, so that's kinda how that got started.

I knew them during the days of that big resurgence to the music period, and then I got to know Frank's wife Jane before they got married and were first dating, because she started coming down to the games with him some, too. And that was kinda neat, because Jane was into the dancing. And she taught it as folk dancing, but she was actually teaching basic Scottish country dancing. She said she'd be glad to teach if I wanted her to. At the *ceilidh* I announced that if anybody was interested in staying after the *ceilidh* to do some dancing, we'd do it. Practically everybody stayed, and Jane got him or her up and taught 'em some basic dances which were really basic Scottish country dances; just sort of around the room kind of things. That's how Scottish country dancing got started at Grandfather Mountain. It is the big Scottish country dance of the year in the Southeast — the Grandfather Mountain gala on Friday night.

Flora and her late mother Flora MacDonald Gammon the Elder, who was music director of the Grandfather Mountain games from its inception until 2000. (Courtesy: Jim Thompson.)

When Jane was doing it, we had Frank George playing fiddle for us. When the other people from Kentucky started, it was strictly records; taped music from Scotland. And see, the one thing I've had a hard time with — still do to a certain extent — is the accordion in Scottish music. But I can remember the feelings

I had years ago; every time you put on a record of Scottish dance music — you never got the fiddle. The fiddle was in the background.

Flora's mother served as director of music at Grandfather Mountain from 1962 until 2000, when she finally relinquished that position to Flora, who had assisted her mother all of those years. Assisting her mother gave Flora an ideal vantage point to observe the changes that were taking place in the music events at the games. In the meantime, she was also developing a regional reputation as a performer of Scottish and Appalachian music.

Well, I started with the Grandfather Mountain games with my uncle there at the *ceilidhs*. I've performed there every summer since then since 1960. While I was in college, I would periodically be asked to give programs of Scottish music or Scottish dancing or do something Scottish, and so I would go to schools and give programs; one of them was a Scottish folk dancing class in high school one time when I was in college — it was their PE stuff that they were doing, and so I taught them the stuff that Jane had been teaching at the games; I'd go to an elementary school and talk about something Scottish, things like that. Then after I graduated from college, I was doing the games here all the time.

But then the Highland Games in Gatlinburg got started, and as they were getting ready to start those games, those people went to Grandfather to specifically see how things were done and set up what they wanted to do their own way.

The person in charge of music called me, because he'd seen me at the *ceilidhs* and found out that I lived just over the mountain and called me and asked if he and his wife could take me to dinner and talk to me about Scottish music for the games. Then he asked me ... that was the year that David Morris and I were working together on a record album ... and so he asked if David and I would come over and do entertainment for a dinner in late November — '79, I think — when all the people involved in getting the games started were having a formal dinner — a Saint Andrew's dinner — and asked us to provide the entertainment. Then I was hired to come and perform at their first games. I performed at their first two games at their ceilidhs and on the field. And then I've gone back periodically several times since then. That was really the first time since the Grandfather games, but then in between the Gatlinburg games starting and me having done all this at Grandfather.

After I moved back here from Colorado, which was in '76, then some friends you probably know — Liz and Lynn Shaw, traditional musicians — they were in charge of a program by a local arts council here to do a recording of local musicians and we called it "Our Mountain Musical Traditions." We got musicians and dancers and storytellers from all over the county to participate in this record album, so I'm one of twelve or fifteen musicians and people on this album, and each of us had one cut, you know. And so that was my first formal recording experience.

Flora MacDonald Gammon onstage with celebrated scholar/performer of Appalachian traditional music Mike Seeger. (Courtesy of Jim Thompson.)

And then, doing the Gatlinburg games and then I would be asked to do a Kiwanis club or something like that; various and sundry little things would happen. And I would do a little bit more and a little bit more.

And then the Stone Mountain [Georgia] Games got started, and they asked me to come down and actually emcee their *ceilidh* and perform there. And so I performed at Stone Mountain. Then the Flora MacDonald Games got started and they asked me to come perform there, and the Waxhaw Games, and different Highland Games in this area in the Southeast; the Charleston Games and all. So I would be asked to come down and sing for them.

A typical *ceilidh* in this country is based upon what people have seen at Grandfather Mountain, which is the model for it. Which is not a real *ceilidh*; a *ceilidh* is a gathering, a visit. That's all the word means.

I remember as a child — I don't know if you all did it where you grew up — but in the 40s and 50s people did more visiting and did more singing, because there wasn't TV to entertain you all night. So the family got together after dinner and the dishes were done, and there was that little bit of time between then and time to go to bed, and you sat and you visited with each other . And you talked, and sometimes you got into telling stories. And if your family was a musical family, you inevitably started singing or playing music or whatever was the musical side of your family. If you had a piano, everyone got around the piano and you sang. That's what happened in my family. That's a *ceilidh*, and we've been having *ceilidhs* over here in this country for hundreds of years, and nobody knew that's what they were.

But once they got started at Grandfather Mountain, it was the evening entertainment. And it evolved into a planned evening, because it was very difficult to take a group of individuals from all over, gather them together in a room, and say, "Let's have a *ceilidh*. Who wants to do something?" Because, by then, this is late fifties and early sixties, somebody says "Let's have a *ceilidh*; who wants to do something?" and everybody sits there. It took enough liquor in 'em to get 'em loosened up enough to stand up and sing their party piece, as I would call it today—the thing that they were always known for singing or saying or doing or whatever.

So the *ceilidhs* then became a planned thing, whereby it wasn't always professional entertainment or professional performers; it was just that you planned on who you were going to have, instead of just arbitrarily saying "who wants to get up and do something?" It became, "We're going to have so-and-so next; we're going to have so-and-so next" and you introduced your acts, if you want to call it that.

So that it was planned and formalized. But then, other people, as they started Highland Games, didn't like this, because a *ceilidh* is supposed to be spontaneous; that's what it is. Well, knowing that, they wanted to have a real *ceilidh*.

And so Gatlinburg did. They had their formal thing that they billed as a *ceilidh*, and everybody paid money to come see and all; that was planned entertainment. But they also set up a real *ceilidh*. And what they did was they rented a place and they set it aside. And people would come in and sit around. And everybody came in and sat around waiting for something to happen. And nothing ever happened, because they were expecting something to happen. They didn't know they were the happening themselves. Because Americans aren't like that anymore. Unless you go hanging out somewhere and drinking enough beer or whatever you want to drink.

And so they always failed, and they never could understand. And it's because you cannot tell Americans that we're going to get you together to do whatever you want to; they can't handle that. They have to have it planned for them.

So that's what a *ceilidh* is; it's now planned entertainment. Sometimes it is totally and completely professional entertainment. Those people who do this for a living, and they actually pay those people to come do it. Other times, it is just people as I was all those years who have the enjoyment of it, who would come do it for nothing. They just did it, or maybe if there was a budget, you might give them a place to stay and some meals while they were there but they paid their own expenses to be there. Or sometimes it was people who, you know, they put on a kilt four times a year at the most, but they knew some Scottish songs and they had the guts to stand up in front of a bunch of strangers and sing 'em. And so they weren't even non-professional entertainment; they were just people who just plain had an interest in it.

Flora MacDonald Gammon (fourth from left) and husband John Dall (second from left) leading farewell song at Grandfather Mountain ceilidh. (Courtesy of Jim Thompson.)

But whether they had any real talent or not really didn't make any difference. You get the gamut of all those styles. A few times, my mother has had … if she's heard that somebody's going to be in the audience who's good at doing such-and-such, then she'll call them up. And it looks like a spontaneous thing, but she's heard about them prior to the *ceilidh* and she plans to call them up.

[That's] what we try to do with the *ceilidhs* at Grandfather Mountain, even though the performers are known beforehand, and that's planned, and we do have an order of appearance that we set up that afternoon before we go on. We all know when we're going on and we know how many minutes we've got, which is very few, but we know what our time limit is. At the same time, once someone is out there performing, then whatever happens. And that's the spontaneity of it.

Let's see, somebody has described the ceilidh at Grandfather Mountain as "Scottish Grand Ole Opry." You know how the Grand Ole Opry was set up with all the chairs out on the stage, so that the performers could actually come out and hear the other performers and be a part of it. It wasn't this formal introduction, come out and do your thing and then leave, and then the next formal introduction. You just might be sitting out there and you get introduced and you get out there and do your stuff. That is what the

Grandfather Mountain *ceilidh* is like. In other words, the chairs are out there for us, and we don't have to be the big fancy artistes who hang out backstage and only appear when our names are called; we're out there all the time. And so, if somebody is singing a song that is a waltz, some of us might get up and start waltzing around the stage, have fun with it. If somebody's singing a crazy song, somebody might get up and act out that crazy song, that typical Harry Lauder type of "what does a Scotsman wear beneath his kilt?" Some of the women will get down on their hands and knees and crawl along the stage to look up under the guy's kilt, you know. And of course, the guy that's out there singing it doesn't know what's going on behind him until the audience starts laughing. And he can't figure out why the audience is laughing at him when that's not the time in the song to laugh. [laughs] Until all of a sudden, he feels his kilt moving or something. Silly things like that. That's where it's spontaneous; it's whatever we feel like doing. And none of that is planned; it's just you get the idea and you do it.

There was a guy who performed for us for a while who played the electric organ, and the only way he was comfortable onstage was if he had that organ between him and his audience. Like some people can't do without a microphone on a stand; they've got to have a barrier between them and the audience. But anyway, Jack would be singing some song, and here he would be playing the electric organ. [laughs] And a couple of the guys, one of them being John Turner, another being my husband John Dall, would be backstage, and they would see that there were props left over from a play, toy guns and a mops. So they threw them over their shoulders as Jack's playing and come marching out in fine military fashion. They line up across the stage, they turn around, they say, "ready, aim, FIRE!" And they shoot the organ. And all the time Jack's sitting there playing this song, and the audience is dying laughing. And Jack doesn't even know what's going on until he sees it. And then he gets into it, too. As soon as they go Bang! he goes BLAAGH on the organ. And the organ dies. So we get into it as a spontaneous thing. And that's not planned at all; it's whatever happens. So what is a *ceilidh*? All those things.

Flora was strictly an amateur performer until 1987, when she gave up her career as an operating room supervisor to reinvent herself as a fulltime performer and interpreter of Scottish history and culture. With her husband John's support and encouragement, Flora found her present calling as a performer and teacher, teaching schoolchildren and senior citizens about the Scottish heritage that is such a central part of her personal identity:

> I started performing for Elderhostel and various clubs around this area and more Highland Games. I started contacting some Highland Games; I worked hard on a brochure and a business card and started sending that out, but at the same time I never sat down and did a mass mailing or a real promotion of myself. It was more by word of mouth. I always knew that I

could never make a living off of Highland Games, because Scottish people are not interested in paying money for their entertainment at the Games.

All of those games run on absolute shoestring budgets, and the only place they're willing to pay money is to bring a pipe band over from Scotland. Occasionally if someone working for those games is a real entrepreneur of Scottish folk music or Scottish music and really knows or has contacts with people like Peter Morrison and Jean Redpath, then they'll be willing to pay the money to bring those people in. But otherwise, the rest of us they aren't willing to pay. And so you don't make money going to Highland Games just singing.

Now the way people like Alex Beaton and Carl Peterson make it is because they have tapes to sell, and they stand there and they basically are what John calls "buskers." They are what I call streetcorner musicians. They are buskers, they stand there and they sing all day. Instead of just collecting tips, they sell tapes. That's where they make their money, so they can afford to come into a game for nothing. Well I don't produce a lot of tapes, number one; number two, that's not my style. I don't do well standing out in the hot, broiling sun singing my guts out all day long. My voice won't last, and I know it. Plus, my only bit of ego as a performer is that when I sing, I expect people to sit and listen to me. I do not want them passing by. So therefore I do not like festivals and places where I'm standing up there singing and they're just kinda passing by, and if they want to listen for a minute, they can then walk on.

Nowadays festivals are beginning to give seating of some kind around the little performance area, which psychologically tells people you can come and sit and stay. But even at that, only a few come and sit and the rest of them will come and stand in the background and then they'll leave. And even the ones who come and sit, then you hit a song they're not interested in and they'll get up and leave right in the middle of everything. And I just do not deal well with that; I don't like it. So I know I don't do well outdoors; I do much better indoors. I also deal better with smaller audiences.

Now I can do the *ceilidhs* and stuff where you've got seven hundred people or a thousand people sitting out there — that doesn't bother me — but as part of an entire evening. I'm not having to carry that entire crowd the whole time by myself. Because somebody described me once, "I hear you're very intimate with the audience." I want the lights up when I see the people I'm singing to; I do not want to sing to a black void, which is what you get when you're spotlighted and all the house lights are out. Because I look people in the eyes when I sing to them, which also intimidates a lot of people. They don't want to be noticed; they don't want you to sing to them. They just want to hear the music, and it scares them when you look at them. When I find those people, I just quit looking at them; it really puts them off. Whereas other people really love being noticed and being sung to, and so I will sing to those people. You have to interact with an audience.

I've come to realize that my real market and audience is retired people or older adults, be they in their twenties, thirties and forties, but adults out working and older adults and Americans of Scottish descent. And not even of Scottish descent, because I reach a lot who are not of Scottish descent and really have no interest in it. But I'm teaching them about history. When I come at it from the historical angle, then that interests them. And the cultural angle. That pulls it in so they're willing to listen to it because of that. It starts making them think about their own culture. Because as I say to them, the main message I'm trying to get across to them is that whatever your ethnic heritage is, be proud of it, learn something about it, and pass it along.

So if I want to give myself a label, well, as I said before, I'm a missionary for cultural heritage. But I utilize music and history and teaching, all the different methods, but that's what I'm trying to do: enrich cultural heritage. In doing it, I always point out that I'm sharing the Scottish heritage, but every single culture has a rich heritage. And learn something about it. And quite honestly, with Americans being such a conglomerate of different cultures, look how much more fascinating we are. Because we're not just the same culture anymore; we're a mixture. So many of us are. Here I am learning about my Scottish heritage, but I need to learn about my Dutch heritage, my French heritage, too. They're just as much a part of me as the other is. All of those are the sum that will make up the total whole of me, to help me understand myself.

Core and Periphery:
A Critique of the Internal
Colonialism Model
in Scotland and Appalachia

*F*lora MacDonald Gammon resolved a personal identity crisis by redefining herself as a cultural missionary, devoting herself to promoting
appreciation of the Scottish heritage with which she identifies so strongly.
Flora's richly detailed first person account of her experiences sheds light on
thorny theoretical questions concerning the interplay of personal, social, and
cultural identity in Scotland and Appalachia.

Edinburgh University social anthropologist Anthony P. Cohen maintains that the desire for a satisfying sense of personal identity is one of the
driving forces of contemporary Scottish nationalism:

> ...nationalism has appeared more as a lament for the continuing denial of
> the integrity and authority of Scottish nationhood, in the long wake of the
> loss of the Scottish nation-state that followed the 1707 Act of Union. It is
> essentially a *cultural* response to nationalistic and other reactions that follow
> from the popular perception of the denigration of a culture by a powerful
> neighbor or occupying force. In this sense, Scottish nationalism is a state-
> ment of *identity,* the potency of which is separable from — and independent
> of — its more partisan political program" ["Personal Nationalism: A Scottish
> View of Some Rites, Rights and Wrongs," *American Ethnologist*, 23 (4): 803,
> 1996].

Likewise, the rise of Appalachian Studies in the United States is a statement of identity, a bona fide revitalization movement manifesting the desires

of denigrated marginal people to define and express themselves in their own terms.

Though there are many points of convergence between Scotland and Appalachia, there are critical differences as well. Appalachian identity is much more problematic and tenuous than Scottish identity. Appalachia never had a monarch, capital or parliament. If Scotland can be described as a subordinated nation resisting devolution to the status of a mere region, then Appalachia can be described as a subordinated region showing evidence of the awakening of something akin to nationalistic consciousness, at least among its progressive intellectuals. Few people designated as Appalachian, other than regional activists, artists and scholars involved in the Appalachian Studies movement, use that term to identify themselves; most think of themselves as Americans first, not Appalachians or southern mountaineers. Writing in 1992, Scottish sociologist David McCrone showed by his research that seven out of ten modern Scots thought of themselves as Scottish rather than British. Nine years later, according to an article in the December 17, 2001, London *Times*: "A survey published towards the end of 2001 revealed that 37% of Scots now consider themselves to be Scottish not British compared with 19% in 1992. Asked to make a straight choice in 1992, 57% affirmed that they were Scottish *rather than* British — in 2001, 80% decided to be Scottish."

Identifying with Scotland is by no means limited to native-born Scots. Millions and millions of people born and raised in other countries, like Flora MacDonald Gammon, identify themselves as Scottish, though their ancestors may have left Scotland centuries ago. Nearly 2.5 percent of Americans claim some degree of Scottish ancestry, while approximately 3.3% identify themselves as "Scotch-Irish," Ulster Scots and Scots-Irish, as already noted, being the preferred current British appellations for Northern Irish Protestants whose progenitors emigrated from Scotland (Jones 1980: 895).

Though Scotland lost its political sovereignty following the Union of the Parliaments in 1707, it has nonetheless preserved a high degree of civil and religious autonomy and generated a continuous succession of cultural revitalization movements. For nearly three hundred years, Scots at home and abroad have asserted their distinctive communal identity through literature, language and folk culture. As we have already noted, deconstructionist cultural critics in late twentieth century Scotland and Appalachia have tended to dismiss such romantic nostalgia symbols as spurious fabrications fostering false consciousness and bad taste.

In his review essay, "An Agenda for Irrelevance: Malcolm Chapman's *The Gaelic Vision in Scottish Culture*" (*AppalJ*, vol. 8, no. 3, spring 1981), Allen Batteau urges Appalachianists to read Chapman's study of Celtic romantic nationalism in Scotland, even though it doesn't contain a word about Appalachia in particular:

It ought to be read for its warnings against the traps involved in such romantic constructions as the True Highlanders (or the True Appalachians), and
its discussion of the intellectual dishonesty and political irresponsibility
involved in nostalgia for a past that never existed. The parallels between the
social context of the Highlanders and Gaelic culture on the one hand, and
that of rural Appalachians and "Appalachian culture" on the other, are
sufficiently numerous to invite detailed exposition and, one hopes, new
insights into the problems of each [Batteau 1981: 212].

Like Malcolm Chapman's *Gaelic Vision*, David McCrone's *Understanding Scotland: The Sociology of a Stateless Nation* (1992) has a lot to tell us about
the cultural politics of the Appalachian region, even if it says nothing about
Appalachia per se. McCrone's discussion of Scottish cultural nationalism
focuses upon the antipathy of Scottish intellectuals, particularly Tom Nairn,
the acerbic author of *The Break-Up of Britain* (1977), to romantic, nostalgic,
folksy, kitschy manifestations of Scottishness, specifically tartanry and the
Kailyard school of bucolic local color literature (McCrone 1992: 89–92).

The Kailyard ("cabbage patch") school celebrates lower middle class values in an idyllic rural setting. The success of the "lad of pairts," the Scottish
equivalent of Horatio Alger's "rags to riches" heroes is a central motif of this
genre, which particularly appealed to nostalgic overseas Scots. (Its underlying message is that that Scots with get up and go got up and went, leaving
their less energetic kindred at home to vegetate in the Kailyard.)

Tartan, kilts, bonnets and bagpipes are so indelibly associated with
Scottishness in the popular imagination that it may shock some readers to
learn that many present-day Scots have come to despise them, just as many
Appalachian people loathe black wool hats, corn-cob pipes, bare feet and
denim overalls. Scottish cultural critics coined the derisive term "Tartanry"
to describe the constellation of romantic cultural symbols that degenerated
into sentimental stereotypes following the failure of the Jacobite Movement.
Tom Nairn calls tartanry "the tartan monster" (McCrone 1992: 180–81). As
McCrone observes,

> Tartanry was not a literary movement, but a set of garish symbols
> appropriated by Lowland Scotland at a safe distance from 1745, and turned
> into a music hall joke (Harry Lauder represented the fusion of both Tar-
> tanry and Kailyard — the jokes and mores from the latter, the wrapping
> from the former). [...] tartanry has come to stand for tourist knick-knack-
> ery, visits to Wembley, and the Edinburgh Tattoo. Oddly, no serious analy-
> sis of tartanry, the sets of symbols and images, has been carried out by
> Scottish intellectuals though there are a number of studies of the history of
> tartan [1992: 181].

Nairn's dismissive scorn for tartanry is transparent: "Tartanry will not wither away, if only because it possesses the force of its own vulgarity — immunity from doubt and higher culture" (Nairn 1977: 165). Nairn views these manifestations of Scottish romantic nationalism as pathological expressions of false consciousness: "Two disparate cultural formations have combined into a hegemonic system which locks Scots into a sense of their own inferiority in the face of a powerful Anglo-British culture. Tartanry and Kailyard maintain hegemony over Scotland's sense of self" (McCrone 1992: 186). Nairn argues that "Scottish culture is schizophrenic; its low culture a bastard product, partly indigenous and partly maintained by British imperial mechanisms (the Scottish soldier is the obvious example). This sense of separation, of fragmentation runs through much intellectual analysis of Scotland" (McCrone 1992: 184). Nairn's statements reflect the same ideological assumptions underlying Batteau's assertion that "Appalachia represents the convergence of two traditions, each of which contains its own contradiction" (1990: 27). Nairn and Batteau share intense antipathy to folklore scholarship and folk revivalism, which they predictably interpret as latter-day expressions of mind-clotting romanticism promoting hegemony, or false consciousness.

Though much gentler in tone than Nairn or his American counterpart Batteau, McCrone is nonetheless critical of the post–World War Two folk revival in Scotland. As McCrone observes, "Cultural studies of Scotland, its literature, language and folklore especially, formed the basis of another academic industry, one which extended beyond the academic world to that of the enthusiastic practitioner. One problem with this division of the intellectual map was that culture has seemed cut off from political, economic and social developments in contemporary Scotland. The task was too readily defined as one of conservation rather than development, of protecting the legacy of the past rather than planning the future" (1992: 4). Appalachian Studies was similarly divided. (See Jim Wayne Miller, "Appalachian Studies Hard and Soft: The Action Folk and the Creative People," *AppalJ*, vol. 9, nos. 2–3, winter-spring 1982.)

Ultimately, McCrone believes that debunkers like Nairn are missing the point when they challenge the authenticity of tartan and similar icons of national, ethnic and regional identity on historical grounds: "Traditions may be invented; symbols of national identity are manufactured. Perhaps there is a suggestion in the word 'invented' that myths and traditions are fabricated; what seems to happen is that the cultural raw materials are refashioned in a manner that gives coherence and meaning to action. The task is not to debunk these inventions, but to show how and why they are put to such telling use" (1992: 30).

The basic issues of identity politics in Scotland and Appalachia are strikingly similar, if not identical. It is not surprising that intellectuals in both places found such a compelling explanatory model in Immanuel Wallerstein's world-systems theory. In *Understanding Scotland* McCrone comments upon the responses of Scottish intellectuals to Michael Hechter's *Internal Colonialism: The Celtic Fringe in British National Development, 1536–1966*, an attempt to apply Wallerstein's world-systems theory to Britain: "Hechter's analysis generated considerable interest and controversy, not simply on the 'periphery.' Critics pointed out, moreover, that Scotland was a poor fit for his theory" (1992: 59).

Nonetheless McCrone acknowledges the compelling rhetorical power of the internal colonialism model: "Its power is that of the metaphor rather than explanatory concept, and it is these concepts that have shaped academic work on Scotland by both historians and sociologists alike" (1992: 62).

The metaphor of internal colonialism has shaped the thought and works of Appalachian intellectuals as well. In her insightful essay, "Appalachian Culture as Reaction to Uneven Development: A World Systems Approach to Regionalism" (in Kuhre and Ergood, 3rd ed., 1993, originally published in JASA, vol. 1, 1989), sociologist Roberta McKenzie states: "The region called Appalachia in the United States has been defined over the past half century as a culture apart from mainstream America" (McKenzie 1993: 284). To quote McKenzie,

> Two important themes, one pervasive during the 1970s, and a second
> one which has been developing recently, are intellectual responses to the
> explanations of Appalachians as possessing a culture that is out-of-step with
> the rest of society: 1) the application of the internal colonialism model to
> the situation of Appalachia, and 2) the question of an emergent Appalachian
> ethnic identity.... The *internal* colonialism model is used to analyze a
> "peripheral" or underdeveloped area within the national boundaries of a
> "core" or highly industrialized area (Hechter 1976; Lewis 1978; Walls 1976).
> This model was particularly important in Appalachian Studies during the
> 1970s [McKenzie 1993: 286].

McKenzie's reference to Tom Nairn's *The Break-Up of Britain* (1977) regarding present-day Scottish nationalism reveals more points of convergence between contemporary Scottish and Appalachian discussions of culture and identity politics: "The movement for Scottish separatism within the British Isles, Nairn (1977: 126–28) argues was a 'neo-nationalist' response to 'relative deprivation'—a cultural and political movement characteristic of 'late capitalism'" (1993: 286). McKenzie's discussion of Michael Hechter's concept of the Celtic Fringe stresses the insidious hegemonic power of the internalized dominant culture: "Indigenous culture is denigrated and results in the native's will being undermined to resist the colonial regime" (Hechter 1975: 73).

McKenzie's conclusions concerning Appalachia as internal colony are practically interchangeable with McCrone's concerning Scotland. Like McCrone, who is wary of what he terms "excesses of analytical Third World-ism" (1992: 62), McKenzie is also aware of the beguiling rhetorical power of this construct: internal colonialism must be carefully defined to be more than a catchword.

Is internal colonialism just another exhausted artificial construct to be discarded upon the trash heap of outmoded academic catchwords, or does this concept still have some relevance to the lives of real people? Though Scotland and Appalachia may not have been colonies in the very strictest sense of that term, nonetheless Scots and Appalachians must still address and overcome the lingering effects of internalized colonialistic beliefs in the inherent inferiority of the periphery and the assumed superiority of the metropolitan core.

In *Out of History: Narrative Paradigms in Scottish and British Culture*, Cairns Craig comments, "The history of culture is written insistently from the metropolitan centres: this is deeply ironic, since the most significant creative achievements of the past two hundred years have come from the peripheries" (1996: 29). The rise of contemporary Scots and Gaelic literature is a postcolonial phenomenon, driven by the dissolution of the Empire and the decay of English cultural authority (page 202). Postcolonial literatures are multi-voiced, operating in the linguistic space between vernacular and received standard languages. In Scotland as in Appalachia, poetry (along with folk revivalism and other distinctive forms of expressive culture) has been a primary medium for the recovery of native voices: "It is as though poetry, through its regionalism, seeks to assert what the British political state would deny — that hundreds of years of shared political culture cannot obliterate the spirituality of local experience and local culture" (Craig 1996: 205).

6

The Thistle and the Brier: Poetics and Identity Politics in Scotland and Appalachia

O see ye not that narrow road,
So thick beset with thorns and briers?
That is the path of righteousness,
Tho' after it but few enquires.

From the Scottish traditional ballad,
"True Thomas," concerning 13th century poet
and seer Thomas Learmont of Ercildoune, also
known as Thomas the Rhymer, who encountered
the Queen of Elfland and spent seven years
in her enchanted realm where he acquired
magical gifts of poetry and prophecy

The outside world has been slow to appreciate the richness and depth of contemporary Appalachian literature, let alone acknowledge its very existence. Nevertheless creative writing and literary criticism in Appalachia have flourished and matured, continuing to inspire the Appalachian Studies movement as a whole. One of the leading advocates of Appalachian Studies, Jim Wayne Miller (1936–1996), born and raised in Buncombe County in western North Carolina, was not only a scholar and critic of his native region's literature. He was also a gifted poet with a deep conviction of the power of poetry to heal the divided self. In his 1977 essay, "Appalachian Literature," Miller deftly expressed his sense of the connection between poetics and what is nowadays termed identity politics: "For some time now people in Southern Appalachia, like rising groups everywhere, have been searching for a usable past, attempting to understand who they are by knowing who they were. Literature is always central to such efforts" (*Appalachian Journal* 1977, vol. 5, no. 1, page 82).

Miller's "The Brier Sermon-You Must Be Born Again" (1980) is one of the most frequently quoted contemporary Appalachian poems. The poet's alter ego, the Brier (short for brierhopper, a synonym for ridgerunner or hillbilly) has undergone a personal transformation akin to a rite of passage. Separation from his native community has led to marginality and alienation, resolved through a process of self-renewal or identity reformulation; a sorting out of what is of lasting value in the past and the present. Modern Appalachians, like modern people everywhere, have become self-estranged; the Brier urges them to consider what they may have thoughtlessly discarded in striving to advance themselves according to the outside world's definition of progress (see Quillen 1989: 17–21).

Editor Maxwell Perkins titled one of Thomas Wolfe's posthumously published novels *You Can't Go Home Again* (1940). A native of Buncombe County, North Carolina, like Jim Wayne Miller, Thomas Clayton Wolfe (1900–1938) thought and wrote a great deal about Asheville during his meteoric literary career in New York, but he did not go home again to stay until he suddenly succumbed to tuberculosis of the brain at an untimely age. Wolfe's short story "Only the Dead Know Brooklyn" was published in 1936, the year Jim Wayne Miller was born. Wolfe's narrator, a local working-class type with a burlesque Brooklyn accent, encounters a tall, unkempt out-of-towner (modeled on Wolfe himself) who stumbles onto a subway platform during evening rush hour with a map in his hand. Seeking directions to out of the way sections natives of the borough know to avoid, his outlandish, pointless questions convince the nervous little Brooklynite that the stranger is totally out of his mind.

Thomas Wolfe's nameless stranger with a map on the subway personifies irremediable rootlessness and alienation. Jim Wayne Miller's Brier *can go* home again, but he is also free to be a citizen of the world; the Brier holds forth the possibility of "going back to what you were before/ without losing what you've since become." The voice Miller has given the Brier is simultaneously personal and collective, ironically humorous in its parody of the biblical cadences of Appalachian preaching while sincerely exhorting educated mountain people not to commit the sin of forgetfulness but rather to seek creative alternatives to narrow provincialism or rootless cosmopolitanism:

> But you don't have to live in the past:
> You can't, even if you try
> You don't have to dress old-fashioned,
> talk old-fashioned,
> You don't have to live the way your foreparents lived,

> But if you don't know about them,
> If you don't respect them
> You're not going anywhere.
> You don't have to think ridge-to-ridge
> the way they did.
> You can think ocean-to-ocean.
>   [Higgs, Manning, and Miller 1995: 423]

Or galaxy-to-galaxy and eon-to-eon, as the late Scottish nationalist poet Christopher Murray Grieve (1892–1978) demonstrated in "A Drunk Man Looks at the Thistle," which he published in 1926 under the pen name of Hugh MacDiarmid. It is purely coincidental that the thistle and the brier happen to be prickly plants stubbornly clinging to the thin soil of marginal uplands; there are more cogent analogies to be drawn between "A Drunk Man Looks at the Thistle" and "The Brier Sermon." To begin with, it seems noteworthy that Grieve and Miller chose to create poetic alter egos to give voice to dilemmas of divided cultural identity. In the early stages of his career, Grieve/MacDiarmid wrote in revitalized modern literary Scots to show that it was possible to preserve a local accent and vocabulary and yet address universal themes. As Christopher Harvie comments in *Scotland and Nationalism* (1994), "For MacDiarmid, Lallans was a vehicle for national differentiation and political mobilisation" (1994: 107).

Casting off what Raymond Williams would later term "the internal dominative mode" represented by Received English does not inevitably lead to parochialism and intellectual impoverishment. Instead, resurrecting and reinventing Scots as a modern literary language enabled Grieve, speaking through the medium of MacDiarmid, to express feelings and ideas beyond the limited capacities of conventional English. A heady concoction of braid Scots peppered with cosmopolitan allusions and polyglot phrases generates a surrealistic linguistic polyphony comparable to Pentecostal glossolalia, sustaining a visionary, prophetic tone throughout the nearly 2700 stanzas of "A Drunk Man Looks at the Thistle," which has been compared to the major works of Yeats, Pound and Eliot. The poem's unifying leitmotif is the weird light of the moon shining down upon Scotland's ancient botanical emblem, seen through the eyes of a drunken poet wavering between epiphany and incoherence:

> I never saw afore a thistle quite
> Sae intimately, or at sic an 'oor.
> There's something in the fickle licht that gi'es
> A different life to't and an unco' poo'er.
>   [stanza 305]

                                   * * *

> Plant, what are ye then? Your leafs
> Mind me of the pipes' lood drone
> —And a' your purple tops
> Are the pirly wirly notes
> That gang staggerin' owre them as they groan.
> [stanza 415]

* * *

> Guid sakes, I'm in a dreidfu' state
> I'll ha'e nae inklin' sune
> Gin I'm the drinker or the drink,
> The thistle or the mune.
> [stanza 450]

The shape-shifting thistle reflects the poet's ambivalent identification with Scotland, entangled with the rose of England and Christ's crown of thorns—ironically bringing to mind the rose and brier twined in a true lover's knot at the end of the ballad, "Barbara Allan." The poet is uncertain whether the thistle is alive or dead or whether he himself is dreaming or awake, evoking unresolved internal divisions troubling Scots long before Grieve found it necessary to invent MacDiarmid. If Appalachians suffer from what Allan Batteau in *The Invention of Appalachia* (1990) terms "double otherness," then its Scottish counterpart is "Caledonian anti-syzygy," an analogous state of self-alienation expressed in these following stanzas:

> Hauf his soul a Scot maun use
> Indulgin' in illusions,
> And hauf in gettin' rid o' them
> And coming to conclusions
> Wi' the demoralisin' dearth
> O' anything worthwhile on Earth.
> [stanza 2390]

Translated from the Latin, the motto of the thistle on the royal Scottish badge reads "Let None Touch Me with Inpunity." The poet does not escape unscathed from his entanglement with the chimerical plant he cannot separate from himself:

> A Scottish poet maun assume
> The burdens of his people's doom
> An' dee to brak their living tomb.
>
> Mony ha'e tried but a' ha'e failed
> Their sacrifice has nocht availed
> Upon the thistle they're impaled.
> [stanza 2640]

* * *

For aince its toomed my hert and brain
This thistle needs maun fa' again,
— But a' its growth 'll never fill
The hole it's turned my life intill!
[stanza 2670]

At last the vision fades, along with the moonlight and whiskey fumes. Ranting gives away to silence, as life must ultimately give way to death. The drunk man finally returns home to his wife whose name, perhaps only coincidentally, is Jean, the same as Robert Burns's wife; it is she who has the last word — in braid Scots.

What are we to make of all this? There is no clearcut resolution at the end of "A Drunk Man Looks at the Thistle," which only makes sense when we consider that seventy years after its first appearance in print, Scotland's artists and intellectuals were still sorting out much of the same unfinished business. It is purely coincidental that Jim Wayne Miller, whose "Brier Sermon" is the Appalachian counterpart of "A Drunk Man Looks at the Thistle," happened to die in 1996, which not only marked the seventieth anniversary of Grieve/MacDiarmid's celebrated poem, but also the 200th anniversary of the death of Robert Burns, the 250th anniversary of Bonnie Prince Charlie's defeat at Culloden, and the 700th anniversary of the removal to London by Edward I, the Hammer of the Scots, of the famed Stone of Destiny upon which Scotland's kings were enthroned.

The year 1996 also happened to be a year in which nationalistic feelings were running high in Scotland, with widespread popular support for the re-establishment of a Parliament in Edinburgh to be a ballot item in the British general elections in 1997, 290 years after the last independent Scottish parliament was dissolved in 1707. Optimistic predictions of the UK's devolution and eventual autonomy for Scotland within the European Community were countered by pessimistic allusions to Burns's bitter anti–Unionist refrain, "sic a parcel o rogues in a nation," implying that politicians might sell Scotland out once again for English gold as they had in 1707.

If undercurrents of uncertainty were surfacing in Scotland during the summer of 1996, they sprang from a long, painful history of dashed hopes and internal division. Rodger Cunningham has conjectured in *Apples on the Flood* (1987) that the Scottish ancestors of Appalachia's settlers suffered from a flawed sense of autonomous identity long before the Union of the Parliaments, dating back to the anglicization of the Scottish lowlands in medieval times and possibly into the prehistoric past. While literal-minded scholars may challenge the factuality of Cunningham's historical speculations, the divided self he discusses in *Apples on the Flood* is not a figment of his fertile imagination, nor is its healing a certainty in Scotland or Appalachia. If anything is certain, it is the need on both sides of the Atlantic to carry forward to fruition the unfinished work to which the authors of "A Drunk Man Looks at the Thistle" and "The Brier Sermon" made such inspiring and enduring contributions, each in his own way.

Thinking about poetics and the politics of identity in the Brier's terms—ocean-to-ocean rather than ridge-to-ridge — helps us understand how much Christopher Murray Grieve and Jim Wayne Miller shared in common, especially when MacDiarmid's Drunk Man declared:

> And let the lesson be — to be yersel's,
> Ye needna fash gin it's to be ocht else.
> To be yersel's — and to mak that worth bein'
> Nae harder job to mortals has been gi'en.
> [stanza 745]

The Brier would surely have said "amen" to this last outburst of luminous insight from MacDiarmid, who once likened himself to a volcano, producing heat and light, and also a great deal of rubbish:

> The function, as it seems to me,
> O' Poetry is to bring to be
> At lang, lang last that unity.
> [stanza 2585]

Much more remains to be said concerning points of convergence between poetics and identity politics in Scotland and Appalachia. For now, as the drunk man said when he returned home to his Jean, we'll "clack nae mair aboot it."

7

Self Portrait of a Cultural Activist: A Conversation with Hamish Henderson, Edinburgh, 13 June 1996

*H*amish Henderson (1919–2002) knew the author of "A Drunk Man Looks at the Thistle" personally. As a young aspiring poet and fervent Scottish leftist nationalist in the 1930s, Henderson found inspiration in the older man's innovative use of the Scots language. When he returned from military service at the end of World War II, Henderson was still one of Grieve/MacDiarmid's loyal supporters, even providing the reclusive poet and his family with financial assistance during a particularly low point in their personal affairs:

> When I came out of the army, which was in the forties, the dominant theme that one got was one of very disheartening and offputting philistinism. MacDiarmid, Hugh MacDiarmid, of course, the great stormy petrel of Scottish letters, was alive and kicking, but he was very much kicking against the pricks, you might say. The dominant feeling — one could feel almost an atmosphere of everything being a bit disheartened.
>
> So when I met MacDiarmid, one sensed the same thing. See, MacDiarmid was an amazing cratur [Scots cognate of "critter" or "creature"], as you probably know. On the political side, he'd boxed the compass. At one point, when Mussolini came to power in Italy, he was writing a program for a Scottish Fascism. And, within a few years, of course, almost a few months, he had become a leftwing socialist. He joined the Communist Party and was

Captain Hamish Henderson of the 51st Gordon Highlanders in Italy during World War II. (Courtesy of School of Scottish Studies, University of Edinburgh.)

thrown out of it for nationalist deviations. In fact, most of his life, he was, so to speak, from a political point of view, out of step. I worked with him on the cultural side, insofar as I could, but only on the cultural side. He and his family were ... I mean, he was really on his uppers, you know. Grieve/ MacDiarmid's career was moving from one set of uppers to another set of uppers, you know; the same when he was up in the Shetlands in the thirties, he went through a very, very bad period financially. He succeeded, it seemed to me, in some rather peculiar fashion, in getting a *deus ex machina* organized just at the last minute when he was about to go under. The *deus ex machina* when he was in the Shetlands, when he was nearly at the end of his tether, was the arrival of a bloke named Grant Taylor who volunteered to come up and be a kind of amanuensis, a typist for him. This must have been a tremendous relief to him at a time when he was in very sore straits.

I, up to a point, was a *deus ex machina*, if you can dignify me with that title. Similarly because I found that ,owing to the point for various reasons, that I had a bit of money..well, I had a job in Belfast with the Workers Educational Association and I won a lot of money on a horse [laughs] ... I backed Russian Hero, very appropriate name, in the 1949 Grand National. So I was able to give the Grieves [MacDiarmid's own family name, of course, was Grieve]; I was able to give him and Valda practical assistance at that time. I mention all this just to illustrate the fact that it was not a very bright situation in general.

Hamish Henderson with Hugh MacDiarmid and other literary friends, 1949. Left to right: Morris Blythman, Hamish Henderson, Marion Blythman, Calum Campbell, Hugh MacDiarmid and Archie Meikle. (Courtesy of School of Scottish Studies, University of Edinburgh.)

Born in Blairgowrie in Perthshire on the eleventh of November, 1919, Hamish Henderson spent his childhood in a rich Scottish cultural environment. He learned Scottish step-dancing and country-dancing from an old fashioned fiddle-playing dance master and began collecting traditional songs and tales from his Blairgowrie neighbors while still in his teens.

The untimely death of Hamish's father prompted his mother to seek employment south of the border in England. Young Hamish began the first phase of the rite of passage or heroic quest that would eventually transform him into one of Scotland's best known contemporary cultural activists. Though physically separated from Scotland, Hamish's interest in poetry and Scottish folklore continued to blossom. As an undergraduate at Cambridge, Hamish became part of a group of émigré Scots who gathered together periodically to sing, recite poems and play the bagpipes, asserting their Scottishness in the very heartland of English cosmopolitan culture (MacNaughton 1991: 2).

Adam MacNaughton notes in his tribute to Hamish in *Tocher* no. 43 (published 1991 by the School of Scottish Studies)that young Henderson displayed unusual talent in poetry and foreign languages, and when he went to Italy during World War II, he was able to put his Italian to practical use in communicating with Italian Communist partisans resisting the Fascist regime. While in Italy, Hamish became a member of the Italian Communist Party, which led him to translate the Prison Letters of the Italian Marxist cultural theoretician Antonio Gramsci into English. Even before the outbreak of the war, Hamish was an anti–Fascist, anti–Nazi political activist who had helped to smuggle Jews out of Germany under the auspices of The Society of Friends. Hamish served

Ten year old Hamish Henderson in full Scottish attire.

in North Africa, where he managed to collect folklore from Allied and Axis troops and was inspired to write an award-winning book of poems, "Elegy for the Dead in Cyrenaica." His wartime experiences during the Allied invasion of Italy prompted Hamish to compose a number of topical songs including "D-Day Dodgers" and "Farewell to Sicily" that would become staples of the post-war Scottish folk revival (MacNaughtan 1991: 3).

The years that Hamish spent in England and in the European and North African campaign comprised the marginal phase of his personal rite of passage, a point at which his love of Scottish culture converged with his growing political radicalism. Reading the ideas of Gramsci, a Sardinian folklore enthusiast who became one of the founders and leading ideologues of the Italian Communist Party profoundly shaped Hamish's cultural and political perspectives. Challenging the orthodox Marxist contention that romantic nationalism, like religion, perpetuated subservient attitudes supporting the status quo, Gramsci argued that cultural and linguistic revivals could help suppressed groups recover their own autonomous identities and cast off belief in the innate superiority of their oppressors:

> One of the things that first attracted me to Gramsci was the knowledge that he had been so interested in Sardinian folktales and traditional music. In the letters that are translated, for example, there's a summary of a Sardinian folktale. Gramsci himself went through a particularly rough period at the time of the famous "vuolta" or "twist" or "bend" of the party line in the late 1920s. In fact when he was in prison, he actually at times had to face rather cruel antagonism from some of the other communists or left-wingers in the prison. Still, what you might call the enlightened Communism was one of the reasons why the Communist Party of Italy is so good. It has a cultural thrill to it, which is quite different from the Communist Party here in my experience.

Hamish's return to Scotland at the end of the war marked the beginning of the third and final phase of his personal rite of passage. Though he was now the author of a prize-winning book of poetry and the first radical scholar to translate Gramsci's *Prison Letters* into English, he was still struggling to find his life's work. One of America's best known folk music collectors would play a fateful role in shaping the course of Hamish's future career as a folklorist and cultural activist:

> Well, talk about a *deus ex machina*, as far as I was concerned, Lomax was exactly that for me. It was through Ewan McColl that I learned about him. You see, I'd been in Italy translating *The Letters from Prison* of Antonio Gramsci and was eventually flung out of Italy by the government of that time. As you know, it was like a banana republic, Italy, more or less. De Gasperi's government was under the thumb of, pardon me using the expression, the Yanks. Anyway, they threw me out, and very luckily, because I arrived back just when Alan Lomax arrived from the United States, which you must admit was a fortunate accident or a syncronicity of the first order.
>
> I got a letter from Ewan McColl when I was visiting friends in Cambridge telling me that Lomax was just arriving or had just arrived, in Britain. And Ewan asked me to steer Lomax away from what he called the "dead hens," or something like that [laughs] and to introduce him to the real traditional Scottish singers, which I was delighted to do.
>
> I first met Alan in London where he was with his assistant-*cum*-girl-friend Robin Roberts. He recorded me singing my own songs and some of the songs that I'd learned—collected is too big a word; just picked them up here and there—so these early recordings of me got in the archive here, and in fact, Alan Lomax's tapes, copies of them, from that summer of 1951, these are the first tapes in our own archive. I got a copy, actually, of all his tapes,

and this, up to a point, helped me to get a job here. Though here didn't exist at that time. When I was first hired to do a job for the University, the School of Scottish Studies only existed on paper: it had no building and indeed it had no archive. We were as virginal as you could possibly imagine. It was Alan Lomax, up to a point, who [laughs] got cracking and destroyed its virginity. [laughs]

So, as I say, I'd just translated Gramsci's *Prison Letters*, which didn't get published for quite a long time after that for various reasons that I could explain. Not, I think, because of the quality of the translation but because of the content of the letters, many of which naturally reflected the fact that Gramsci had been the boss of the Communist Party of Italy, the finest Communist Party in the world, I think, better than any I've come across.

Anyhow, Alan Lomax recorded me in London and asked me then if I would take on the job in Scotland of what he was obviously needing to make this Columbia collection; world albums of folk and primitive song. Needless to say, I got on the Scottish album, it being primitive song. [laughs] Anyway, he asked me would I do this to fulfill for Scotland the role, which [was] obviously needed everywhere he went, of resident collector, you might say.

And I naturally agreed to do this and had a very enjoyable summer tour with him when he came to Scotland; that was two or three months after this that he arrived in Scotland. I always noticed the day he arrived, because that was the same day of Burgess and MacLean's disappearance. And reading this with Alan next to me — of all of this about Burgess and Maclean, so I could trace it to the actual day, you know.

Anyway, I went out recording with him to the Northeast and I introduced him to the great Gaelic poet Sorley MacLean with the idea that Mac-Lean's wonderful family would do the same job in the Gaelic world, which they did. So he got a wonderful collection in a comparatively short time, because he was later on just taken around like a puppy on a lead by the MacLeans and up to a point by me.

But it was great for me, because I was able to watch this great collector doing his job, the way that I never dreamt that I would do anything like it. As far my own collections, I was just purely learning things first of all from my own family and then I went around on a push-bike when I was a teenager. I was just naturally interested in meeting one person after another. I was certainly not a conscious collector then. But anyway, I accepted this job from Alan, had a wonderful time, and as I say, the MacLeans, Calum MacLean was the younger brother of Sorley — Sorley was the poet — Sam MacLean, he was a schoolteacher at the time. In his own flat in Queen Street, which had belonged to another Gael called Torqual Nicolson. We were tremendously lucky to have things played into our hands to a large extent. Flora MacNeill, the Gaelic singer, was a telephonist in Edinburgh; Calum Johnston, the brother of Annie Johnston, who had also been a Barra school teacher, was a very fine folklorist, indeed, and I got to know her, as I said, through roving around. Her brother Calum Johnston, who was a fine

HH recording Blind Ali Dall, 1958. (Courtesy of School of Scottish Studies, University of Edinburgh.)

piper and a very good singer, was working in a firm, also in Edinburgh. So we had these fantastic singers available.

So anyway, in that flat in Queen Street which Sorley had at that time, we recorded not only Flora McNeill and several others but also the fine piping of the piper, later pipe major, John Burgess. And they are in the early Lomax recordings, too. So that one day we recorded this incredible collection of things; recorded a bit of Sorley himself talking, but he was very nervous talking. He'd got more used to it since then, but he was very unused to this thing, so you can almost hear the tremors in his voice, you know. Got used to it later on.

So anyway, Lomax and I had this tour up the Northeast; he also did a tour with me of the Hebrides. He got a number of names and addresses from me, but many more for the Hebrides, I mean, from Sorley and Calum. And later on, when he was in South Uist from Alistair MacLean, who was another of the same family. He was a doctor there in South Uist. So you can see how a certain amount of synchronic luck played into our hands at that time.

So I wondered, then, what was going to happen now, because you see, I wasn't sure of my own moves at that time. Obviously I had to get a job and earn money. On the other hand, the sight of Lomax and the tour we had done gave me the idea: "…is it possible for me to get a job in this School of

Scottish Studies?"— as you might say, a ghost department; it has no build-ing. All that it had was tapes at that particular time! [laughs] The copies of the tapes that Lomax had made. That was strictly all that it had! Seeing we had no building, the copies of all of our tapes went to the Phonetics Depart-ment, down there in Chamber Street; they were lodged for the time being in the Phonetics Department. This up to a point was lucky as well, because the boss of the Phonetics Department was a chap who's dead now named David Abercrombie. And he was a friend of mine. I believe I first met him in Egypt, because he had a lecturing post in the Fuad Al-Awwal University in Cairo.

Anyway, that's when I met David Abercrombie first. So naturally when we were both back in Scotland, I got to know him better. And luckily, he was able, seeing that he was boss of the phonetics department, not only to offer harborage to our tapes but to speak up for me. And at that time, there-fore, the big question was who were they going to hire. So Calum MacLean and Francis Collinson and me, we were the first three scholars, or whatever you would call us, hired by the School of Scottish Studies.

This brings us up to the point where the School gets a building, which was in 1954. First of all, this building here, and then the two adjacent, these beautiful Georgian buildings, all of which were tenanted at one time by quite famous Scots. So I also enjoyed working in this building. The room that I have upstairs, that was Calum Maclean's room. I inherited it from him. I quite literally feel his presence in it. So I'm a lucky bloke. I had to retire in '88. Although retired, I still have a room here, so basically though techni-cally retired I'm still on the job.

It is noteworthy and perhaps not entirely accidental that the establish-ment of the School of Scottish Studies coincided with the rise of the postwar Scottish revival. Like his American mentor Alan Lomax, Hamish's musical tastes and activist political philosophy encompassed traditional folk music and topical protest songs. Nationalistic feelings were stirring once again in Scotland. In 1949 millions of Scots signed The National Covenant, a decla-ration of Scotland's desire for political and cultural autonomy. The crown-ing of the current Queen set off a wave of protest, which resulted in Scottish nationalists purloining the famous Stone of Scone, the Stone of Destiny upon which Scotland's kings had been enthroned until Edward I carried it down to London where it rested for nearly seven centuries in Westminster Abbey, and also prompted the composition of topical songs commemorating the event. It was in this volatile cultural and political atmosphere that Hamish Hender-son emerged as a prime mover of the Scottish folk revival:

Well, you've probably heard of People's Festival — this was a kind of anti–Festival — well, it was a kindred but different Festival. The big Edin-burgh Festival was not going to occupy itself very much with traditional folk culture, so the leftwing parties, the trades unions, the Labour Party, the

Communist Party and so on got together to found what was called the People's Festival. And I was in charge of the folk side of this.

We laid on this fantastic ceilidh in the middle of '51 including some of the singers that we'd been recording with Alan Lomax. And, the music critics at the *Times* actually said that our festival from the musical point of view was the only really interesting thing in the Edinburgh setup at that time. The big festival had gotten a lot of big names like Maria Callas, Sir Thomas Beecham and all that; that was quite a compliment.

But the *ceilidh* was the big event which presented traditional musicians and singers to the public. Ewan McColl had one of his plays. Which one was it, the first one? You know, it might have been *Operation Olive Branch*, which was his version of the *Lysistrata* of Aristophanes. It was either that year or the following year, I can't remember which. No, that year it was *Uranium 235*; Sean O'Casey and Bernard Shaw both praised *Uranium 235* a lot. Ewan really had got good critics on his side.

So anyway, that was our contribution to Edinburgh culture at that time. Needless to say, this was very much disliked by the very same person I told you about. Part of our *ceilidh* was done when Lomax got a programme, but in London of course.

So, the People's Festival. We succeeded in keeping it going for three or four years, but money problems finally knocked it in the head. You see, all sorts of internecine intrigues took place. It was partly regarded, you know, as too Communist for the liking of the right-wingers in the Labour party. So finally the Labour Party, very, very stupidly and shortsightedly, withdrew its support and succeeded in getting quite a number of the unions to withdraw their support as well. Oh, that was our problem from the other side of the fence, as you might say. Still we kept it going for some time.

The Scottish folk revival was in full swing by the end of the nineteen fifties. By the early sixties, Henderson and Grieve/MacDiarmid, who had abandoned his earlier use of literary Scots in favor of a highly stylized form of polysyllabic "scientific" English, had become embroiled in a bitter controversy over the use of vernacular Scots by the Scottish folksong revival. In retrospect, the extended debate between these two major twentieth century Scottish cultural leaders is a textbook illustration of conflict between elitist and populist interpretations of vernacular language in particular and folk culture in general.

So while Grieve/MacDiarmid saw the Scottish folk revival as an insidious reincarnation of the tartan music hall and the Kailyard, Henderson argued that the older man's rejection of the folk revival was nothing more than elitist rejection of the revolutionary potential of a popular cultural movement to radicalize the Scottish masses, especially the youth. When I asked him to comment on the connections between the folk revival and the use of vernacular language in contemporary Scottish creative writing, Hamish responded:

Hamish Henderson (top, center) with participants in Scottish Folk Music Festival, Edinburgh, 1959. (Courtesy of School of Scottish Studies, University of Edinburgh.)

Well, I'm prejudiced, naturally, but I think that the Scottish folk revival, the general interest in traditional music and song, is at the core of all this. It woke many young people, woke them up to the beauty of this vernacular heritage. And to that extent, it is very ironical that MacDiarmid [laughs] turned against me completely in this. MacDiarmid affected to view the folk revival as a kind of new Kailyard, you know.

It seemed to me that one of the great beauties of Scottish history has been this amazing vitality of the folk tradition, which, at all times, has remained very close to the cultivated art tradition. The thing that distinguishes Scottish poetic tradition has been exactly this close kinship of the often anonymous vernacular tradition and the art tradition. That's what makes our ballads so good.

You know, MacDiarmid, to that extent, as the saying goes, was cutting off his nose to spite his face. Because basically, or putting it another way, he was kicking from under him the ladder from which he rose to greatness. Because in the twenties, it was exactly this movement that he took through the vernacular tradition, through dictionaries, for example; he found that he had an access through words to this old tradition. So it was a very, very curious sensation for me to have to, eh, knock him in the mug. [laughs].

But it was necessary. I mean, these particular developments would not have been possible without what you might call a big flyting at that time. And that naturally took the shape of a flyting, for that is a fine Scottish word in the vernacular tradition; this particular pleasure in rummies or argy-bargy, or whatever you want to call them —conflict.

So MacDiarmid and I went at it hammer and tongs for weeks; they just went on printing our letters in *The Scotsman*. I was always thinking after one of MacDiarmid's or after one of mine, you'd see a little rather tight-lipped one, "this correspondence is now at an end."[laughs] No, it went on and on. And consequently, I suppose on one level it caused a lot of amuse-ment in Scotland, but also it served to clear the air. And of course I think I won, but MacDiarmid obviously thinks he won. It's like the Battle of Sher-rifmuir, you know: "There's some say that we won, and some say that they won, and some say that nane won at all, but of this I'm sure, a flyting there was," etcetera. Anyway, that is going back to 1964.

While MacDiarmid viewed the eclecticism of the folk revival with alarm and disdain, Hamish reveled in it. Instead of pursuing the lofty, lonely path of avant garde poetry as Grieve/MacDiarmid did, Hamish devoted himself to increasing popular awareness and appreciation of traditional and topical songs not only as a composer and collector but also as a performer and pro-moter. He was particularly proud of the role he played in making Scots con-scious of the great heritage of traditional music preserved by the marginal wandering pariahs formerly known as "tinkers" but now more respectfully referred to "travelling people." As it turned out, his old hometown, Blair-gowrie, located in one of Scotland's most productive agricultural districts, attracted a transient population of farm workers, including travelling folk with vast stores of songs and ballads. Not only did he record their music, he also featured them at festivals and folk clubs. Hamish's concern with tradi-tional music helped to inspire the formation of the Traditional Music and Song Association of Scotland in 1966, which held its first festival of tradi-tional Scottish music in Blairgowrie. Reflecting back on the evolution of the Scottish folk revival, Hamish comments:

The folk revival really gave a lift to many of the Travellers, who were and in many cases still are the outcasts of Scottish society.
The whole Scottish cultural scene has been a gradual climb upwards

since the time at the end of the war. There have been occasional jolts backwards and there have been antagonists as I have been saying. I mean, young folk in Scottish schools now to my certain knowledge are much more alive to Scottish cultural traditions than they were. I'm very sanguine about the whole Scottish situation.

The great majority of the Scottish people do think that it is inevitable that within the next year or two, that some form of devolution will take place. But I would guess myself that once there is a certain degree of devolution in place it will be inevitable that we will gradually get independence. That is my own guess. Also my hope, I must say because I think Scotland would be a cracking small country on its own feet, you know.

I mean, people like Joy Hendry, the lassie that edits *Chapman* and Ray Ross, the editor of *Cencrastus,* and people working in the cultural field have got a reception which they couldn't have got when I came home to Scotland at the end of the war.

And it's partly due — in some cases I think it's almost completely due to the folk revival. The folk revival has spread out, as you might say, in all directions. This same characteristic of Scottish culture you mentioned earlier — the way in which so-called "art" culture and "folk" culture intertwine in Scottish history; this has been one of the main agents.

When I asked him to assess the current Scottish folk scene, Hamish replied:

Well, of course, to a very large extent, the folk revival gradually became more and more organized; to that extent, commercialized of course. But, well, this was just bound to happen. But the grassroots folk revival is still a reality, you know. If you go out to the folk festivals, you will find plenty of people who have become, as you might say, new aficionados of the whole thing, who are not sort of commercial singers but are keeping The People's Festival going on that level; that still exists. Although of course there's the other side to it as well. The commercialism has been a drawback in Scotland. Some of the people gradually became more attracted to money than to art. But in the main I think we've been pretty lucky in that respect. Even some of the very successful folksingers have kept the common touch, whatever you want, and don't sort of shut themselves away from the rest of the folk scene. That's my experience, anyway.

A man of many interests and many talents, Hamish believed his original songs were probably his most enduring contribution to Scottish culture, and what thrilled him most is that several of them, including his stirring anti-imperialist anthem voiced in braid Scots, "Freedom Come-All-Ye," actually entered oral tradition during his own lifetime:

The thing that naturally pleases me personally is that some of my songs like "The Freedom Come-All-Ye" have spread with amazing rapidity. I get them sung to me. Originally, when I wrote "The Highlanders Farewell to Sicily," I found when I got back collecting with Lomax up in the northeast that people would occasionally bring it out, buried amongst some of the other things, you know. [laughs] I could tell you a lot about this naturally, but [laughs] Lomax was always very amused when this happened, because they would sing the song quite oblivious of the fact that the author of the song was sitting right there next to them.

And the reason for this is that the Highlanders got back to Scotland before I did; it was sent back after Sicily, so it moved very quickly even there, you see. I first sang that song, "The Banks of Sicily" in a Gordon's Officers' Mess the same night I'd written it. But it began to spread, and I found myself scribbling it out in pencil for all ranks. In war things move with tremendous quickness because people's emotions are heightened. I didn't need to hum or write down the tune because it was a familiar pipe tune, "Farewell to the Creeks." It was composed during the First War by James Robertson of Banff. So it was the Northeast, the late Arthur Argo, the great grandson of Gavin Greig used to say, it was the Gordon Highlanders that put that song on the map. And indeed so it was ... it arrived back two years in Scotland before I did. I was very pleased, naturally. Delighted, in fact, because it had obviously pleased folk, and to that extent, it was doing the job.

The same has been true more recently of the "Freedom Come-All-Ye," of course. It's been passed around; it's been on a number of records, and of course, sung quite a lot by people who've just heard it orally.

About two weeks ago Nan Middleton, John MacLean's daughter, died. At Stirling Crematorium, there was a little farewell service in memory of Nan Middleton, who was an amazing woman. And they actually printed for the use of people at this service my song, "Freedom Come-All-Ye."

Hamish Henderson and his dog Sandy in The Meadows, Edinburgh, late 1980s. (Courtesy of Ian MacKenzie, School of Scottish Studies, University of Edinburgh.)

FREEDOM COME-ALL-YE
(to the tune of "The Bloody Fields of Flanders")

Roch the win i the clear day's dawin
Blaws the clouds heilster-gowdie owre the bay
But there's mair nor a roch win blawin
Thro the Great Glen o the warl the day
It's a thocht that wad gar our rottans
Aa thae rogues that gang gallus fresh an gay
Tak the road an seek ither loanins
Wi thair ill-ploys tae sport an play
Nae mair will our bonnie callants
Merch tae war whan our braggarts crousely craw
Nor wee weans frae pitheid an clachan
Murn the ships sailin doun the Broomielaw
Broken faimilies in launs we've hairriet
Will curse 'Scotlan the Brave' nae mair, nae mair
Black an white ane-til-ither mairriet
Mak the vile barracks o thair maisters bare
Sae come aa ye at hame wi freedom
Never heed whit the houdies croak for Doom
In yer hous aa the bairns o Aidam
Will fin breid, barley-bree an paintit room
Whan MacLean meets wi's friens in Springburn
Aa thae roses an geeans will turn tae blume
An a black laud frae yont Nyanga
dings the fell gallows o the burghers doun.

©Hamish Henderson

As a postscript, it is worth noting that one of the songs the Scottish Parliament considered adopting as Scotland's new national anthem along with Robert Burns' "Scots Wha Hae (Wi' Wallace Bled)" was Hamish Henderson's "Freedom Come-All-Ye," though in the end they chose Ray Williamson's plaintive "Flower of Scotland," made popular by The Corries.

Hamish Henderson died on March 8, 2002, in Edinburgh. Hamish's long and productive career as a folklorist, poet, songwriter, performer, and progressive political activist stands as a refutation to deconstructionist cultural critics who contend, like his old adversary, the author of "A Drunk Man Looks at the Thistle," that the idea of the folk is an exhausted, tainted construct, evoking a falsified past without a future.

8

Folk-Bashing and Cultural Self-Determination in Scotland, Nova Scotia and Appalachia: Looking for Constructive Alternatives to Deconstructionism

*C*ultural critics including Tom Nairn in Scotland (1977), David Whisnant (1983) and Allen Batteau (1990) in Appalachia, and more recently Ian McKay in Nova Scotia (1994) have done their best to debunk cultural nationalism (and regionalism) including folk revivalism, portraying it as bourgeois romantic myth-making obscuring class conflict and perpetuating false consciousness. Heavily influenced by David Whisnant's *All Things Native and Fine: The Politics of Culture in an American Region* (1983), Ian McKay contends in *The Quest of the Folk: Anti-Modernism and Cultural Selection in Twentieth Century Nova Scotia* (1994) that urban middleclass romantics have appropriated and exploited the common cultural property of marginal working class people designated as The Folk to suit their own purposes. Allen Batteau begins *The Invention of Appalachia* (1990) with the claim that "Appalachia is a product of the urban imagination" and then proceeds to assert that the folk of Appalachia and their lore have no independent existence outside of the selective interpretations of their culture by outsiders. Like Batteau, McKay endeavors to expose the spurious premises underlying the bourgeois myth of the Folk and their Good and Simple Life: "The concept of the Folk is a form of 'essentialism'—the reification of a construct stemming from conservative anti-modernism: *There never were any Folk.* There were only the categories and vigourously described if not invented traditions that enabled us to think there were." (page 302). The Quest of the Folk destroys the purity and integrity of the object of its search, imposing alien categories and desires upon the people labeled Folk. McKay concludes that The Folk and folklore are exhausted constructs that serve no positive progressive political purpose.

But is this really the case? Bringing to mind the widespread folktale motif of the corpse that sits up at its wake, if the idea of the folk is dead, then we are looking at an extraordinarily lively cadaver. Yet it is undeniable that concepts of the folk and their lore have come under fire for various reasons, some more valid than others. Firstly, we must understand that Fascist and Nazi rhetoric linking Folk, Blood and the sacred Earth of the homeland (*Volk, Blut und Erde*) brought the term Folk into grave disrepute. This prompted European folklorists after World War II to rename their field of study *ethnology*, the Greek equivalent (*ethnos* = "peoples, nationalities"+ *logos* = "knowledge, study"*) of the emphatically Germanic/Anglo-Saxon *folk-lore*, which the pseudonymous Englishman William J. Thoms invented in 1846 to replace the outmoded 18th century Latinate term *popular antiquities.*

The more recent ascendancy of deconstructionism and poststructuralism in the academic world during the last three decades of the twentieth century has also called the idea of the folk into question, along with all sorts of other so-called "artificial constructs." Consequently, many folklorists in Europe and North America have been critically scrutinizing the basic assumptions underlying the lexicon of their professional discourse, casting about for new appellations for a field of study whose outlines have become increasingly fuzzy and problematic. Nevertheless, scholarly and popular interest in folk life and folk culture continues unabated in various parts of the world including Appalachia, Nova Scotia, and Scotland. This consequential social and cultural phenomenon should not be automatically dismissed as individualistic escapism or reactionary myth making. Special interest groups focusing on folklife and folklore have often expressed the desire for cultural self-determination, which may or may not be the same as "counter-hegemonic opposition," a term that David Whisnant, among others, borrowed from Antonio Gramsci. Gramsci's *Letters from Prison*, written during his incarceration by the Fascist regime in pre–World War II Italy have greatly influenced latter-day Marxist cultural criticism, particularly in Scotland. As Angus Calder comments in *Revolving Culture: Notes from the Scottish Republic* (1994):

> Gramsci had no time for the liberal-idealist tradition, which conceived of culture as having nothing to do with politics, as a spiritual matter. But he was equally critical of fellow-Marxists who saw culture as merely "reflecting"— that word again- the economic base. He anticipated the tendency which finally emerged on the British New Left to discard the base/superstructure dichotomy of orthodox Marxism [Calder 1994: 240].

Reviving subordinated and suppressed regional and national languages and diverse genres of folk culture enables subordinated people to "cast off the internalized dominative mode," thereby rejecting an established elite's presumed cultural superiority and right to govern. Cultural nationalism thus becomes a pragmatic means toward the end of destabilizing the status quo, creating the basis of a reconstituted communal identity. There is always the possibility, admittedly, that cultural nationalism can become an end in itself, resulting in folk romanticism, idyllic middle-class escapism which tacitly condones the established order. Again we need to remember that in Nazi Germany and Fascist Italy propagandists and ideologues deliberately exploited and falsified folklore and folk culture to advance reactionary political agendas.

Is there a sustainable future for folklore, or has the concept been permanently tainted and compromised, as some critics would contend? The idea of the folk may be wounded, as far as some intellectuals may be concerned, but it is far from dead, judging from the vitality of folk revivalism in various parts of the world. Deconstructing nationalist and regionalist symbols does not help us understand why people continue to find meaning and value in them, even though those meanings and values may vary from person to person, as University of Edinburgh social anthropologist Anthony P. Cohen suggests in "Personal Nationalism: A Scottish View of Some Rites, Rights and Wrongs" (1996). Acknowledging the co-existence of competing visions of Scottishness, Cohen nonetheless asserts that the basis of Scottish nationalism is a common body of traditions, symbols and reference points comprising the shared heritage of the nation: "Even though these items may be interpreted differently, it is on the sharing of them that the sentiment of and attachment to the nation is predicated" (Cohen 1996: 805).

David McCrone and other Scottish sociologists have commented upon the lively interest in diverse aspects of Scottish culture, including folklore and the folk arts, throughout this century. McCrone believes that this cultural movement has played an instrumental role in raising Scottish national consciousness, culminating in the recent re-establishment of a Scottish Parliament. Cultural nationalism can inspire and sustain movements towards political autonomy as well as create new social contexts for the active expression of personal and communal identity. "…identity is the result of a process of claim and acknowledgement, a process whereby who we are and who we claim to be is dependent on the social and political situation around us, and our participation in it" (Brown, McCrone and Paterson 1996: 197).

Like McCrone, the late Hamish Henderson saw clear ties between cultural and political nationalism in twentieth century Scotland. As he commented at the very beginning of my interview with him recorded at the School of Scottish Studies in Edinburgh on June 13, 1996: "It's been a gradual upward movement. If by upward, one means successful and integrated movement since the 1940s. There's no doubt in my mind that there is an interest in a very large swath of the population in Scottish literature, for example, and in the folk revival — all the things connected with it. Art is to a certain extent the cultural product of the political movement itself."

Though it is convenient to talk about a single Scottish cultural revival, there are numerous special interest groups centered around diverse genres of Scottish culture. Within the broad category of folk and traditional arts, there are flourishing revivals of folksong, various types of instrumental music including fiddling, accordion playing, the Scottish harp or *clarsach*, also the Scottish small pipes; *ceilidh* dancing, an informal style of Scottish country dancing, has gained many devotees, along with Scottish step-dancing which has been reintroduced to Scotland from Cape Breton, Nova Scotia.

Cape Breton has seemingly emerged as a late twentieth century counterpart to Appalachia, widely reputed as a haven of traditions which have disappeared from the homeland but have been preserved, ostensibly because of isolation from the main currents of cultural fashion and social change. An active Scottish-Gaelic revival movement has been taking place in Nova Scotia, and Cape Breton in particular, at least since the 1920s, which has directly contributed to the Gaelic revival at home in Scotland. Cape Breton artists, traditionalists and eclectic innovators, are prominent in the current trans–Atlantic Scottish cultural revival, which extends far beyond Scotland itself. McKay's deconstruction of the Nova Scotia folk revival only serves to obscure its actual international scope and impact.

Two major linguistic revivals are currently taking place in Scotland. While many outsiders have some vague awareness of Gaelic, few of us understand that Scotland also has another language, a submerged, problematic language known as Scots. Proponents of Scots have been actively promoting its elevation from dependent dialect to autonomous national language distinct from Standard English, working towards the creation of a Standard Scots language primarily drawn from the dialects of the central Lowlands. The revival of Scots has been a continual element of modern Scottish cultural nationalism for most of this century. As of the 1990s, Scots is increasingly heard in everyday communication and in various genres of creative expression. As for the mass media, Billy Kay reports in *Scots: The Mither Tongue* (1993) that the hegemony of Received English in British broadcasting had largely given way to a diversity of local, regional and national accents by the mid-80s, a trend which continues to the present. The official recognition given to Scots and Gaelic by the European Community's Commission on Minority Languages has encouraged ongoing efforts to promote Scotland's minority tongues. Proponents of both Scottish languages have succeeded in getting these languages into the educational curriculum. Naturally, this has not taken place without considerable resistance from educators who, like their counterparts in the United States, firmly believe that local vernacular languages detract from what they perceive to be the primary mission of education: to put their students in touch with what are presented as "the universals," "the great tradition."

Local vernacular languages, mother tongues, are possibly the most important media of expression through which we give voice to our desire for communion with those significant others with whom we identify most deeply. Raising vernacular languages to the status of literary languages elevates the subordinated region or nation.

Attempts to invalidate cultural identity symbols such as vernacular language and literature and folk arts have come from various points of the political compass. Basically their intent is the same: to deprive people who are seeking to define themselves in their own terms of the very symbolic means through which a coherent sense of identity is expressed and sustained. Though the young Scottish highlander may have been derided as a fraud in his own day, it is undeniable that James Macpherson's *Ossian* poems (1760–63) helped to shape the course of modern history, inspiring the Romantic Nationalist movements that spread through Europe from the mid 18th century, revived by the neonationalists and neoregionalists of the latter 20th century. (See Calder 1994: 26–27.) Latter-day folk-bashers like Tom Nairn in Scotland, Allen Batteau and David Whisnant in Appalachia and Ian McKay in Nova Scotia rationalize their efforts to invalidate these lively, tenacious popular cultural movements in neo–Marxist terms, contending that bourgeois romantics have expropriated and falsified working class culture beyond recognition. Ironically, no less a highly regarded neo–Marxist theorist than Antonio Gramsci himself maintained that regionalist and nationalist cultural revivals can break down internalized beliefs in the innate superiority of dominant elites which sustain their hegemony in the minds of their subordinates.

However, we need to understand that affinity for particular cultural forms may not signify anything more revolutionary than the ostensibly non-political desire to participate in an appealing social/cultural activity which provides a desirable release from everyday life. Belonging to a socially and esthetically satisfying special-interest group may be the primary attraction for devotees of *ceilidh* dancing or Appalachian clogging. The thing in itself can be an end in itself or not, depending upon the feelings and desires of the individual. Personal cultural choices are fashion statements and sometimes more than that. Whether we are talking about bagpipe reeds or banjo strings, popular interest in folk culture has concrete economic consequences. Even the least overtly commercial of these anti-mainstream cultural movements creates business opportunities for entrepreneurs who cater to these special interests. Overtly non-political movements may have latent political significance, enabling their advocates to "cast off the internalized dominative mode" and maintain a semblance of cultural autonomy and distinctive identity, if only periodically and symbolically.

Currently diverse groups of alienated, marginal people around the world are redefining and empowering themselves through the articulation of new forms of cultural expression or the reformulation of older ones. Traditions once associated with particular groups and regions have been globalized. We should not be surprised to find native-born Scots wearing blue denim and playing bluegrass or country music and natives of Appalachia wearing tartans and playing bagpipes.

In *Vested Interests: Cross-Dressing and Cultural Anxiety* (1992), Marjorie Garber argues that transvestitism collapses prevalent binary oppositions, resulting in cognitive and emotional dissonance, which Garber terms "crises of categorization." According to Garber, transvestitism is an expression of "gender dysphoria," dissatisfaction with the roles and symbols of gender assigned by the dominant ("hegemonic") social order. Gender divisions represent idealized types; their violation produces anxiety in those who believe that cultural rules are naturally or supernaturally ordained. Cross-dressing is inherently an act of cultural rebellion with powerful political implications.

If we can compare transculturalism and transnationalism with transvestitism, then these conditions can be said to stem from "cultural dysphoria," dissatisfaction with one's ascribed cultural status and associated modes of symbolic expression. Assuming the emblematic appurtenances of some other idealized group liquidates this sense of cultural lack. While appropriating the identity of idealized may satisfy the emotional needs of individuals experiencing various types of dysphoria, it may also generate anxiety and hostility in others.

In the conventional discourse of the folklore profession, the organic community based in biological kinship has been the functional equivalent of anatomically determined gender. Folkloric authenticity rests upon a qualitative distinction between the organic and imagined community. Overt displays of transnationalism and transculturalism violate these categorical distinctions. The folkloristic purist perceives transnationals and transculturals as posers, imposters, inauthentic, perpetrators of fakelore. (The postmodern perspective would contend that all communities are imagined.)

The purist notion of the organic folk community explicitly denies the possibility or the validity of adoptive cultural affiliations. While some individuals or groups may be wary of outsiders and guard their esoteric knowledge jealously, others may be willing to share what they know with friendly foreigners and newcomers and actually create adoptive roles for them. These adoptive roles may be intentionally humorous in character, as in the case of the Wannabe initiation ceremony described by Barre Toelken in his illuminating study of present-day Native American powwows. (See Stern and Cicala 1991: 149.)

But even if *some* outsiders are acceptable to *some* members of *some* established communities in *some* contexts, this still begs the question of the legitimacy of transculturalism, transnationalism and folk romanticism. Are folkies and citybillies simply transcultural cross-dressers? Are so-called folk revivalists and other species of Wannabes simply to be dismissed as marginal misfits or romantic escapists, or are they expressing a widespread human need to periodically divest themselves of unsatisfying ascribed identities and assume other personae that are more appealing to them? Whether unsympathetic cultural critics choose to ignore or discount transculturalism or take it seriously, it is nonetheless a meaningful expressive outlet for many people living today.

In his essay "Defining Identity Through Folklore "in *Folklore Matters* (1989), Alan Dundes emphasizes the contrastive character of personal and collective identity: "There can be no self without other, no identity of group A without group B" (1989: 6). Folklore, broadly defined, provides the symbolic basis for the articulation of a communal identity (1989: 8–9). Traditional concepts of folkloric authenticity would restrict us to studying groups defined by shared ancestry. However, we must now also take account of affinity groups as well, defined by their shared attachments to particular modes of cultural expression, which may be adopted or assumed rather than inherited. Cultural anthropologist George DeVos has stated that "...the ethnic identity of a group of people consists of their subjective symbolic or emblematic use of any aspect of culture in order to differentiate themselves from other groups" (Devos 1975: 116 in Dundes 1989: 9). In the end, it really does not matter whether these symbols are ancient or recently invented, handed down over generations or newly adopted from other groups. What does matter is that a particular set of identity symbols generates a sense of communion with significant others, who may be an extended kinship group or a special interest group sharing affinity for particular forms of cultural expression, such as old-time Appalachian banjo music or the Scottish bagpipes.

Folklorist Linda Dégh has described the identity symbols of immigrants as "cultural umbrellas," constituting the lowest common denominator of national, ethnic, or regional identity. The cultural umbrella needs to be as wide and as simply constructed as possible to accommodate all the disparate personalities and constituencies gathered beneath it. It almost goes without saying that there will always be debunkers and deconstructionists tearing holes in its fabric on the grounds that it is an artificial construct and therefore without value or meaning, except, of course, to the people who have found meaning and value in the very process of fabricating it. As Angus Calder says: "The search for 'identity' is valid, in persons and nations, I am suggesting, so long as we realise it's something made and examined, not 'rediscovered' and therefore granite, inert, or iron bladed" (1994: 2).

From the vantage point of Southern Appalachia, it seems very clear that partisans of Scottish cultural autonomy have been grappling with local variations on universal themes of cultural domination and subordination.

What are the salient points of convergence between the Scottish and Appalachian situations?

1) A sense of internal division, manifested in a gap between the official culture and language of the greater nation-state and the non-official culture and language of the subordinated region or nation.

2) Resolution of ambiguous feelings concerning the hegemony (internalized belief in the innate superiority) of the dominant language and culture and the presumed inferiority and irrelevance of the subordinated language and culture.

3) The emergence of cultural leaders, conspicuously teachers, performing folklorists, and poets, who have struggled with internal division and resolved it by reviving and reinventing cultural and linguistic patterns formerly considered inferior and degraded. These leaders seek in very practical ways to convert stigmata into emblems of cultural pride and distinctiveness.

Though deconstructionists may choose to trash the folk and bash folklore and folklorists, people of diverse backgrounds and interests in Scotland, Appalachia and elsewhere continue to make creative use of folk culture, along with vernacular language and literature, to express themselves in their own terms. Studying these movements in comparative perspective helps us better appreciate the complexities of identity politics in a world that is becoming more and not less culturally diverse.

Dinna Say Dinna:
Teachers as Agents
of Linguistic Colonialism
in Scotland and Appalachia

I was painfully, tentatively roughing out the first draft of *The Thistle and the Brier* in the early summer of 1997 when my old friend Jerry Williamson, longtime editor of *The Appalachian Journal*, invited me to review Bill Best's anthology *One Hundred Years of Appalachian Visions* (1997), an offer I'm now glad I didn't refuse for at least two very good reasons.

Talk about good timing! Reading the first section of Best's anthology, I suddenly became aware of recurring allusions to Scotland in the writings of early influential commentators beginning with William Goodell Frost which I have documented in detail in the first chapter of this book.

Reading the second section of *One Hundred Years of Appalachian Visions* made me realize that perhaps the single most important point of convergence between Scotland and Appalachia is the shared experience of subjection to linguistic colonialism. I can relate to linguistic colonialism on a very personal level as a native of the urban hinterlands of Brooklyn, New York, which has more in common with Appalachia (and Scotland) than most people might imagine. (More about that later.)

Bill Best, the compiler of this ground-breaking Appalachian anthology, has been actively engaged in Appalachian Studies since the mid-sixties, developing the very first Appalachian Studies course for the Berea Upward Bound program for disadvantaged youth in 1968. Born and raised in rural Haywood County, North Carolina, Best received a B.A. from Berea College and a doctorate from the University of Massachusetts focusing on Appalachian education in 1973. As a graduate student he organized and convened the very first Appalachian Studies conference in 1971. Reflecting on the flourishing scholarship and literature in the field after attending an Appalachian Studies Conference with his wife Irmgard several years ago, Bill was inspired to compile *One Hundred Years of Appalachian Visions*. To Bill Best's eternal credit, he does not exclude non-natives like myself from this discourse but rather challenges all of his readers to think "ocean-to-ocean" as Jim Wayne Miller put it in "The Brier Sermon" instead of "ridge-to-ridge."

Reading *One Hundred Years of Appalachian Visions* confirmed my long-held personal conviction that the Borough of Brooklyn is to the City of New York what Appalachia is to the United States. Marginal, subordinate, and popularly portrayed as uncouth, Brooklyn was still home to the Dodgers during my boyhood, affectionately dubbed "the Bums" in those happy secure days before baseball magnate Walter O' Malley violated our collective innocence and took away a key element of our communal identity when he shipped the Dodgers three thousand miles across the continent to Los Angeles.

Back then, the mass media tended to typecast Brooklynites as urban counterparts of rednecks and hillbillies, either as barbaric thugs or comical mugs with colorful vocabularies and uncouth accents. I have already alluded to Thomas Wolfe's short story, "Only the Dead Know Brooklyn" (1936), in which an out-of-towner with a map of Brooklyn in his hand asks a nervous little subway rider for directions. Wolfe's nameless stranger with a map has been wandering around different sections of the borough including Red Hook, a sinister neighborhood down by the docks where thugs reputedly dumped the corpses of gangland murder victims. The narrator, a generic comical mug with a broad Brooklynese accent, is even more incredulous when he learns that this alien being didn't have any particular reason for going there; he just wants to *explore* Brooklyn: "So den duh guy begins to ast me all kinds of nutty questions: how big was Brooklyn an' could I find my way around it, an' how long would it take a guy to know duh place. It'd take a guy a lifetime to know Brooklyn t'roo an' t'roo. An' even den, yuh wouldn't know it all."

Thomas Wolfe may have *thought* he heard Brooklynites talk like that, but I never did, and I actually had next-door neighbors who had moved out of the dockside slums of Red Hook, comparable to The Gorbals in Glasgow. We were all familiar with the stereotyped comic Brooklyn accent, but like most Americans, we mostly encountered it through the media rather than on the street. Our neighborhood, Gravesend, was a multi-ethnic, multi-lingual melting pot with a substantial population of first generation immigrants like my grandparents who had more or less successfully assimilated a limited amount of some variety of English which they spoke sometimes but necessarily not all of the time. Consequently I didn't hear any one single accent, dialect or language growing up in Brooklyn. Nonetheless, that burlesque Brooklynese dialect presented by popular television comedians like Jackie Gleason and Art Carney had very real effects on our lives, how we perceived ourselves and how we believed ourselves to be perceived by others.

Before lobbying by Hispanics and African-Americans brought about policy changes in the wake of the passage of the Civil Rights Act of 1965, prospective school teachers in New York City were required to take a practical speech examination designed to screen out people whose accents included too many so-called "substandard speech variables." Both of my parents became teachers in the New York school system in the early 1950s. I still vividly remember the two of them, both educated from elementary school through college in New York, struggling to reduce the stigmatized features in their speech to a passable minimum, in order to meet an external artificial standard mandated by the upper echelons of the NYC Board of Education. My sister Carole had to take the same speech examination when she was licensed to teach in the city school system in 1959. She had no trouble passing the exam, mainly because our parents, unlike our immigrant grandparents, were fluent English-speakers born and raised in New York City.

Even so, my parents and sister couldn't totally eliminate the "substandard" localisms from their speech, nor could I. Despite more than thirty years of living and working in the mountains of Northeast Tennessee, my Brooklyn origins come out every time I insert substandard glottal stops into words like "mountain" and "bottle," sociolinguistic links between the docks of my home town and Glasgow, Scotland's premier commercial port.

(Not only is Brooklyn New York City's Appalachia, but it is also America's Glasgow. In its turn, Glasgow is to Edinburgh and to Scotland as a whole what all of Scotland has been to an English-dominated Great Britain and what Appalachia still is to the United States.)

Reading *One Hundred Years of Appalachian Visions* helped me better understand why the recovery of native voices has been such a pivotal concern of cultural activists in Scotland and Appalachia up to the present. The theme of the muting and recovery of native voices is central to Burley Creech's poem, "Newground," which Bill Best included in his pioneering 1973 doctoral dissertation and reprinted in *One Hundred Years of Appalachian Visions*. Creech was a returned World War II veteran studying at Berea College on the GI Bill when he published his poem "New-Ground" in *Mountain Life and Work*, 1948, reflecting on the rediscovery of the identity of a self-proclaimed "corn-shucking hillbilly farm boy" (page 42). Stanza V clearly expresses the author's desire to come to terms with nettlesome feelings of shame and insecurity that have left him feeling internally divided:

> Now fading, mirrored mountain boy,
> You traitor to your memory!

Step out, confess, you hypocrite,
And quit your city-slicking ways!
Cut out that stuck-up school-larnt talk
With all those dictionary words.
Come clean, you see now what you are
And what you've always been
Beneath your two-faced head
Tell it to the whole blamed world,
Your shame of being ashamed
of being a backwoods boy
Talk, son. Tell your pap and maw [in Best 1997: 43].

I cannot help wondering if reading Burley Creech's "Newground" in *Mountain Life and Work* might have possibly germinated the seed of Jim Wayne Miller's "Brier Sermon: You Must Be Born Again," especially these particular lines:

But never let me lose the image
Of the ridge-runner, briar-hopper, squirrel-hunter
Of a mountaineer, a pioneer, a farmer ...
...And now I reclaim my birthright and liferight
I am reborn out of college and war...." [in Best 1999: 40].

Like Jim Wayne Miller's "Brier Sermon," Burley Creech's poem follows the classic sequence of separation, marginality and return common to rites of passage, heroic quests, healing ceremonies and cultural revitalization movements. Ronald Eller, director of the Appalachian Studies program of the University of Kentucky, has described Cratis Williams' lifelong advocacy of Appalachian Studies as

an odyssey from the happy innocence of a secure childhood in the cultural and social context of an Appalachian valley through troubling adventures of doubt, challenges to selfhood, denial, shame, and rejection, to understanding, acceptance, and affirmation of self as an Appalachian person who embraces his culture, searches out its history and is proud of his identity as an Appalachian person without feeling that he is something less of an American for being an Appalachian [Eller 1991: 26].

Carefully examining the autobiographies and poems Bill Best includes in *One Hundred Years of Appalachian Visions* shows that innocence, shame, denial/rejection, identity crisis, and reaffirmation are in fact the typical phases of the life histories of the leaders and participants in the Appalachian Studies Movement represented in Best's anthology. Crises of identity stemming from a sense of cultural inferiority, resulting from conflict between received standard and local vernacular language, have been resolved through personal contact with a mentor, like Cratis Williams himself, as well as encountering the creative works of other regional scholars, artists and performers who have been up and down that same lonesome road, arriving at what Rodger Cunningham, reflecting R.D. Laing's influence, terms "healing of the divided self."

The personal testimonies included in this Appalachian anthology shed light on what Best describes as "the emotionally crippling role that miseducation plays in deforming people's self-images." Expressions of intense primal attachments to family, homeplace and community, tied to love of the mountains, are juxtaposed with confessions of shame and denial of identification with the mountains, most often resulting from traumatic encounters with teachers who have themselves internalized the urban American elite's contempt for marginal groups including country dwellers, lower-class Southerners, and mountain people, who ironically think of themselves as Americans first and foremost until others choose to make them feel different and inferior, particularly by deriding their native speech ways.

After reading and comparing these revealing personal narratives, one can better appreciate why Appalachian intellectuals and their counterparts in Scotland have seen relevance in the works of anti-colonialists like Frantz Fanon, Antonio Gramsci and Edward Said, and why activist teachers striving to make a place for local languages and cultures in public education are challenging deeply engrained assumptions that anything or anybody native or local is by definition inherently inferior and deficient. Even if Appalachia and Scotland haven't been colonies in the most literal sense of that term, even if intellectuals in both places have found fault with the concept of internal colonialism, nonetheless what we have here is clear-cut evidence of the internalization of colonialistic attitudes by teachers who abuse students whose speech patterns deviate from an externally imposed elite standard.

Perhaps the single most painful reading in Best's collection is Judy K. Miller's "Only Ignorant People," a harrowing first-hand recollection of witnessing a teacher beat and humiliate a male classmate before their rural Appalachian first grade class for using old fashioned mountain speech ways in school, specifically for saying "hit" instead of "it." Here is her vivid description of that traumatic experience:

> One day in the middle of the winter when the snow had shut out much of the light from the windows and we were supposed to be practicing our "g's," Bob said, "Hit's cold in here. Hain't the old man got sense enough to put more coal in the stove?"
> I was pressing down hard on my pencil, half way through making a perfect curved back for my letter. My hand dropped into a squiggle that dropped below the green broken line. I wanted to cry because the big red

pencils had no erasers, and I noticed how the teacher eyed my mistake when she came to stand between Bob and me, her ruler tapping the palm of her hand.

"No more outbursts from you, young man," she said. She tapped the ruler for each word. "First we must learn manners. Though we may yell whenever we want to at home, we will not do that sort of thing here at school."

"Secondly," she said, "we must work on the way we speak so that we can be understood. No 'hits.' No 'hits.' No 'hits!'" Each time she said the word, she hit Bob on top of his head with her ruler.

"Only ignorant, stupid people say words such as 'hit' and 'hain't.' Repeat after me. And she made the whole class say it: "Only ignorant people who don't know any better say "hit."

We all said it three times. I whispered as softly as I could to get by with. These words, forced upon me as they were, made me cry in school for the first time [Best 1997: 71–72].

Judy Miller says that she learned the meaning of shame that day. This was by no means an isolated or unique incident. Reading Miller's narrative sharply reminded me of the time about ten years ago when I gave a presentation on collecting family folklore to a group of senior citizens in Unicoi County in the mountainous northeastern corner of Tennessee. After my talk, one of the members of the audience gently scolded me for having said "hit" for "it," remarking, "when I was teaching in this county, we would always hit students if they said 'hit' for 'it.'" Though I laughed off her remark at the time, I could not help wondering how many generations of mountain kids had been punished for similar offenses and whether this pattern of abuse stemmed from capricious informal prejudice or systematic official policy. I had no idea at that time that such an incident might have possibly contributed to the rise of the Appalachian Studies movement.

In his recently republished 1973 doctoral dissertation in Appalachian Studies, Bill Best records that a high school teacher humiliated fourteen year old Cratis Williams before his classmates during an oral presentation in a freshman English class. In their introduction *to The Cratis Williams Chronicles: I Come to Boone,* David Cratis Williams and Patricia Beaver reproduce Cratis' first-hand account of this emotionally devastating incident in his own words:

But as he began his story Miss Roberts interrupted and requested that he repeat the sentence he had just spoken:

"Hit was a-gittin' 'way up in the day," I responded.

The town girls restrained giggles.

"Say it again," Miss Roberts commanded.

"Hit was getting way up in the day," I repeated. The town girls, now unrestrained, laughed outright. I could feel my face flaming as Miss Roberts asked me to say it again.

"Hit was getting away up in the day," I almost shouted.

The town girls, now joined by many of the country children, laughed louder and longer.

"It, not hit," Miss Roberts corrected.

At that, "the country children laughed uproariously while the town girls merely smiled at Miss Roberts as she looked in their direction" [Williams and Beaver 1999: v–vi]

As Bill Best comments in his recently republished 1973 doctoral dissertation, "Unfortunately such degrading experiences rarely inspire a youngster to go forward in his own self-development" [1999: 14–15]. One of Best's friends took elocution lessons from a private tutor for eight years, only to discover that "he had traded a Kentucky accent for an Ohio accent. Such experiences probably inspired him to become a leader in the newly emerging field of Appalachian Studies" (1999: 15).

Fourteen year old Cratis Williams. (Courtesy of David Cratis Williams.)

Students of Scottish cultural history will immediately grasp the dismal parallel to the Appalachian situation and cringe in sympathy. Suppression and elimination of Gaelic and Scots was official educational policy within living memory. In *Scots: The Mither Tongue* (1993), Billy Kay includes an excerpt from William McIllvaney's novel *Docherty* (1983) describing the headmaster of a Scottish school beating and humiliating a schoolboy who inadvertently uses the Scots term "sheuch" in place of the English "gutter." Gordon Williams' novel *From Scenes Like These* also excerpted in *Scots: The Mither Tongue* vividly represents the reflections of an Ayrshire boy concerning official and vernacular language:

> It was very strange how the old man changed accents. Sometimes he spoke to you in broad Scots, sometimes in what the school teachers called proper English. They were very hot on proper English in the school. Once he'd gotten right showing up in the class for accidentally pronouncing butter "bu'er." Miss Fitzgerald had gone on (him having to stand in front of the

class) about the glottal stop being dead common and very low-class, something that would damn you if you wanted a decent job. A decent job—like a bank! His mother spoke proper English, but then she was hellish keen on proving that they were respectable. His father spoke common Kilcaldie which he knew his mother didn't like.

* * *

He remembered Nicol the English teacher saying that broad Scots was pronounced very much like Anglo-Saxon or middle English or some such expression. If that was so why did they try and belt you into speaking like some English nancy boy on the wireless? ... Why teach kids that Burns was the great national poet and then tell you his old Scots words were dead common? [Quoted by Kay 1993: 126–27.]

What we have here is a classic example of what anthropologist Gregory Bateson termed a double bind, generated by a mixed message that produces internal conflict and division within the individual who attempts to assimilate it. Scottish teacher and songwriter Nancy Nicolson's "Listen tae the Teacher" graphically presents the double binds of linguistic colonialism from the viewpoint of a young Scottish farmboy.

Listen tae the Teacher (used by permission of the author)

He's five year auld, he's aff tae school,
fairmer's bairn, wi' a pencil and a rule,
His teacher scoffs when he says "Hoose,"
"The word is 'House,' you silly little goose."
    He tells his Ma when he gets back
    He saw a "mouse" in an auld cairt track.
    His faither lauchs fae the stack-yard dyke,
    "Yon's a "Moose," ye daft wee tyke."

Listen tae the teacher, dinna say dinna
Listen tae the teacher, dinna say hoose
Listen tae the teacher, ye canna say munna
Listen tae the teacher, ye munna say moose

He bit his lip and shut his mouth
Which wan could he trust for truth?
He took his burden ower the hill
Tae auld grey Geordie o the mill
    And they did mock they for thy tongue,
    Wi them sae auld and thoo sae young?
    They werena makkin a fuil of ye,
    Makkin a fuil o themsels, ye see.

Listen tae the teacher....

Like Helen Lewis and Jim Wayne Miller in Appalachia, Nancy Nicolson proposes code-switching as a practical solution to the dilemma of divided identity:

> Say "Hoose" tae the faither, "House" tae the teacher
> "Moose" tae the fairmer, "Mouse" to the preacher,
> When ye're young, it's weel for you,
> tae dae in Rome as Romans do.
> > But when you growe and when ye are auld
> > Ye needna dae as ye are tauld
> > Nor trim your tongue to please yon dame
> > Scorns the language o her hame
> *Listen tae the teacher....*
> Then teacher thought that he was fine,
> He kept in step, he kept in line,
> And faither said that he was gran,
> Spak his ain tongue like a man.
> > And when he grew and made his choice,
> > He chose his Scots, his native voice.
> > And I charge ye tae dae likewise
> > An spurn yon poor misguided cries.
> *Listen tae the teacher....*

In August of 1999, just as she was preparing to perform at the Royal Oak, a long-established folk pub in Edinburgh, I asked Nancy Nicholson what had inspired her to compose "Listen tae the Teacher." She told me that when she was a little girl in Caithness, her teacher had corrected her before the entire class for having said "hoose" instead of "house." Though she stressed the point that her teacher had corrected her gently rather than cruelly, nonetheless a deep unspoken hurt and self-doubt remained with her, the same sense of divided identity that troubled Cratis Williams after his teacher humiliated him for saying "hit" for "it." Only years later, after she had become a mother and a teacher herself and had composed a prize-winning song in a contest sponsored by the Edinburgh Folk Club, did Nancy Nicolson come to terms with this prickly wound to her self-esteem through the healing process of composing, performing and eventually recording this song. Today she promotes appreciation of Scottish languages and traditional arts as a representative of the Traditional Music and Song Association of Scotland, singing and playing for Glasgow school children, working to undo the cumulative impact of generations of colonialistic teachers and culturally depriving schools.

In his essay "On Reclaiming the Local, or the Theory of the Magic Thing," in *Reports from the Present* (1995), Glasgow poet and critic Tom Leonard describes the suppression of indigenous languages and dialects in terms that apply equally well to Scotland, Appalachia and Brooklyn:

> A dominant value-system has been allowed to marginalise that which does not correspond to it, declaring it deviant and therefore invalid. It has been able to do so by the method of making these dominant values literally synonymous with "objectivity." It is the mode of expression that counts: that device by which the persona is given the status of being detached, impersonal, above the battle. In speech it has been achieved through the fee-paying Received Pronunciation, buttressed by the Classics-based prescriptive grammar hammered into the pupils [1995: 36].

Nancy Nicolson singing and playing accordion.

Leonard concludes, "It's in the reification of linguistic codes and their possession by dominant and powerful classes wherein lies real danger, now literally for the whole world.... In dismissing the language, one dismisses the existence of its users—or rather, one chooses to believe that they have dismissed themselves" (1995: 41).

Appalachian poet and teacher Rita Quillen's contribution to Best's anthology, "I AM A RUBE? The Question of Self-Image in Appalachia" supports Leonard's assertions concerning linguistic colonialism. Growing up in rural Hiltons, Virginia, the home of country music's original Carter Family, Quillen offers vivid, pungent recollections of country life: "...life was good, overall, and until the sixth grade, I didn't know that we were 'hillbillies,' pitied and laughed at by others" (Best 1997: 131). A Northern journalist's newspaper article depicting Kingsport Press strikers as shiftless, barefoot hillbillies offended Quillen, inspiring her, like the young Cratis Williams, to write a letter to the editor of the Kingsport, Tennessee, paper in protest.

Quillen was an outstanding student from grade school in Hiltons, Virginia, through graduate school at East Tennessee State University. Nonetheless she encountered teachers intent on bringing local students up to mainstream American speech standards: "...my supervising teacher for my

Undergraduate Practice Teaching Project informed me that I would have to get a tape recorder and practice until I lost my strong mountain accent. ' No one is going to take you seriously as an English teacher,' she said coolly, 'as long as you talk like you do'" (Best 1997: 132). One senses real bitterness here, especially when Quillen's poetry is dismissed for being "too Appalachian." Says Quillen, "This seems symptomatic to me of a dangerous self-loathing with which we've replaced the sneering outsiders" (Best 1997: 133). In Appalachia as in Scotland, self-hatred is the ultimate expression of divided identity.

University of Edinburgh literary historian and cultural critic Cairns Craig virtually echoes Rita Quillen when he says: "…the consequence of accepting ourselves as parochial has been profound self-hatred" (1996: 12). As Craig notes in his essay, "Peripheries," in *Out of History* (1996), "the troubling question of the Parochial haunts discussions of Scottish literature and culture, implying Scotland lacks an integrated, organic culture in its own right distinct from English culture" (1995: 11). Once again, here we have indicators of what Frantz Fanon termed "inferiorism." This generic sense of cultural inferiority undermines the self-esteem of colonial people, who automatically assume that truly great artists will naturally gravitate to the metropolis and surrender their marginal identity as the price of their success and celebrity: "If they were good enough, they wouldn't want to stay here."

If vernacular poets and writers in Scotland and Appalachia have tended to be dismissed as parochial and provincial, it is because their language, imagery and sentiments violate, even subvert, elite metropolitan sensibilities, which Rodger Cunningham, inspired by Raymond Williams, calls the "internalized dominative mode" and Tom Leonard terms "the diction of governance." Struggles against the hegemony of received linguistic standards are obviously not restricted to Scotland and Appalachia, but can be found wherever subordinated people are striving for self-determination.

As dramatist-social scientist Eberhard Bort, fellow of the University of Edinburgh's International Social Sciences Institute, states in his article, "It's a Darlin' Story: A Decade of Irish Drama in Tübingen" in "*Standing in their shifts itself…*": *Irish Drama from Farquhar to Friel*, a major goal of twentieth century Irish nationalist writers has been the "decolonisation of the mind" through the abandonment of standard Received English as a literary medium and the elevation of the vernacular to a literary language (Bort 1993: 15).

Vernacular language and literature have seemingly become trendy in post-imperial, devolving Britain in the 1990s. Following the critical and popular success of Scottish novelist James Kelman and his Irish counterpart Roddy Doyle, who both won Britain's Booker Prize for gritty urban novels employing street language in first person, a new populist school has emerged, fusing orality and print, rejecting elite diction and orthography along with the emotionally distancing device of third person narrative. The opening five minutes of the soundtrack of the film of Irvine Welsh's mordant novel *Trainspotting*, an instant trans–Atlantic Generation X cult classic, had to be redubbed for anglophone audiences who couldn't fathom the unadulterated underworld Edinburgh argot in the original Scottish version.

Can such language ever be of more than merely regional interest? Is the vernacular an impediment or an asset? Can the peripheral people who are the typical victims of linguistic colonialism learn official language to avoid being labeled in disadvantageous and degrading ways and still preserve distinctive local speech patterns, not only in ordinary communication but also as an expressive medium? Appalachian scholars have understandably tended to address these questions in local terms but clearly these issues are of more than parochial significance. Viewed as part of a global rejection of elite linguistic conventions, contemporary Appalachian literature isn't peripheral at all; instead, it's on the cutting edge of emerging postcolonial vernacular anglophone literatures. To quote Cairns Craig once again, "the imposed unity of the single language generates accents that assert difference as the inheritance of not one but several histories. The condition of 'being between' is not the degeneration of a culture but the essential means of its generation" (1996: 203).

Where must the regeneration of cultural identity begin? In his essay, "Appalachian Education: A Critique and Suggestions for Reform" (1977), Jim Wayne Miller described a disjunction between the official national culture promulgated by formal education and the informally perpetuated, non-official local and regional cultures that shape Appalachian personalities and communities. This gap between official and non-official cultures generates status anxiety in some Appalachian students and total alienation from the formal educational process in many others, contributing to one of the nation's highest drop-out rates: "We are actually running culturally depriving schools, schools that deprive students of the opportunity to see their lives reflected in the school, their experiences and knowledge legitimated in the school setting." Like his Berea College classmate and close friend Bill Best, another native of Western North Carolina, Jim Wayne Miller observed that the most zealous and unforgiving agents of mainstream hegemony have been teachers who are themselves pervaded with status anxiety. Insecure within themselves, such teachers transmit destructive mixed messages to their students that only reinforce low self-esteem and alienation from formal education. Breaking this self-defeating cycle is one of the primary goals of the Appalachian Studies movement itself: "the schools should provide students an opportunity for self-definition."

Teachers play critical roles in forming (and deforming) the cultural and personal identities of their students. Converting teachers from colonialist agents of ethnocide and linguicide to proponents of diversity and self-definition is the single most crucial mission of the artistic and educational movements that have flourished in Scotland and Appalachia since the seventies.

Editor of *Chapman*, a major Scottish literary journal, since 1976, Joy Hendry is deeply involved in the varied realms of contemporary Scottish cultural nationalism: "I was once dubbed an '*east coastie cult-nat*' by none other than Alan Bold!!"

Like Helen Lewis in Appalachia, Hendry's mission is basically to teach subordinated people how to unlearn the lessons they have learned in culturally depriving schools so that they can define themselves and take control of their own lives: "That compulsion of mine runs through absolutely everything — and teaching is just one of these things. Curiously, when actually teaching, I am very careful not to 'thrape' my enthusiasms too much down students' throats, but rather to entice them with hints, and the smell of my enthusiasms."

Like Helen Lewis, Hendry was a classroom teacher during an early stage of her career, shortly after she became editor of *Chapman*. She found herself battling entrenched resistance to making Scottish language and literature part of the educational experience of her students. Even her students could not accept the idea of a teacher of English speaking in broad Scots, deliberately breaking the rules of linguistic colonialism beaten into them by teachers who had suffered or witnessed similar abuse as schoolchildren and transmitting the same confidence-destroying mixed messages and double binds to their pupils: "I had to witness teachers (mostly scientists, as it happens) punishing children for speaking Scots to them, regarding it as impertinence, when those teachers themselves spoke broad Scots!!"

Hendry has carried her mission as a cultural activist from writing and working on *Chapman* into the classroom and from there into much larger public arenas. She was a member of the committee which produced the historic *Claim of Right for Scotland*, (1988), an all-party and non-party group laying the foundations for the Constitutional Convention out of which eventually emerged the Scottish Parliament. Hendry has also agitated for a National Theatre ("now almost a reality") — and generally stirred things up through the magazine and beyond as much as she can.

In addition to editing one of Scotland's premier contemporary literary magazines, she is also a newspaper arts reviewer and radio commentator, a playwright, a university lecturer and above all, a vocal advocate of cultural and linguistic pluralism in a democratic, autonomous Scotland.

In June of 1996, when excitement and anxiety were mounting concerning the vote to re-establish a Scottish Parliament in 1997, Hamish Henderson introduced me to Joy Hendry at a party in the flat of another major Scottish nationalist thinker and writer, Angus Calder. ("I spent years trying to convince him of my arguments, and to wean him away from the Labour Party!")

The next chapter of this book presents Joy Hendry's insights into the interconnections between language, literature and the folk revival in a Scotland caught up in the process of reclaiming its national identity:

> Basically, I started working to develop a literary magazine in Scotland, knowing nothing about Scottish literature, initially quite secure in the appalling assumption that it could only be inferior to the great canon of English literature, which I'd dutifully been taught in school and at university. When I realised I'd been cheated of my native language (Scots) by a mother ambitious for my 'social progress' and 'linguistic purity', and of my native literature by Scottish education, ironically lauded world-wide as exemplary — I became angry, very angry, and decided, by whatever means at my disposal — *Chapman,* teaching, dabbling on the fringes of politics — to do whatever I could to ensure that succeeding generations of Scots were not so cruelly treated. *Chapman* has never been explicitly nationalistic, but has always argued for greater political autonomy on the grounds that it was necessary for cultural and linguistic progress, to restore the Scot back into his or her own Scotland. Personally, I've only occasionally been a member of the SNP, believing that I can achieve more by maintaining a detached and 'impartial', or non-partisan stance.

Joy Hendry is not intellectually detached from the issues of poetics and politics she discusses so eloquently. Like her old friend Hamish Henderson, she is a genuine cultural activist passionately engaged in a personal mission to awaken her fellow Scots to their distinctive cultural and linguistic heritage, a heritage that an educational establishment devoted to converting Scots into North Britons had systematically dismissed and ignored.

Her mission began when she awoke to that fact, got angry, and decided to do something about it.

10

Poems Make the People:
A Conversation with Joy Hendry, Edinburgh, 1 July 1996

Joy Hendry recalls how she became a Scottish cultural activist:

> I went to school in the 1960s, and at that point the perspective with which we were indoctrinated was entirely an English — or British one, though it was really English. We were taught about English literature, English culture, English music — that whole scheme of things. Oh, I loved it; it was fine. I'm a great lover of English poetry and remain so to this day. But, when I came to university, I began to meet Scottish poets and began to understand for the first time that there was such a thing as Scottish poetry, which wasn't an inferior branch of English literature but something which was distinctive and had its own rules— and its own strengths.
>
> Gradually I came to discover also our Scottish traditions, in music, philosophy, science — and, perhaps most excitingly of all, our long-ingrained tradition of international intellectual trade. This discovery, that there was an enormous scheme of things which, despite having a good Scottish education, I knew nothing about was an enormous catharsis in my life. And I became incensed and very angry about how this could possibly happen to anybody anywhere in the world; that you grew up totally denied of your own culture in the process of education — ironic in a country praised for its education the world over!
>
> On my mother's side there were teachers, notably my grandfather, also doctors and ministers, including two great uncles, twins, one of whom became Moderator of the General Assembly of the Church of Scotland, the other the Moderator of the Free Church of Scotland — in the same year!!!! On my father's side were Dundee working class folk, my grannie being a spinner in the mills of Dundee —considered the lowest of the low, and my

grandfather at various times a hammerman, orra man, sanitary inspector, etc. It's from that side I think the creative spirit comes—and the crazy life I've led from the impossible cocktail of these genes!!

As I said, my grandfather was a great teacher (teacher, amongst other things, of Angus Calder's father in primary school in Forfar!). Being, I think, a natural teacher in some respects (I have a huge and almost irrepressible compulsion to help other people! Wish in some ways I didn't!) I became determined that I wanted to change the situation, so that Scottish people of whatever age, but particularly the younger generation, could have access to the culture I was denied as a matter of right—to knowledge about it, how to use it and how to participate in it and so on. There wasn't a single point at which I said, "This is what I am going to do with my life" but certainly I became very passionate about it and determined to do whatever small things I could do to bring about change. And indeed, to learn myself; the rest of my life has been a learning process, discovering all that. (Patricia Oxley, editor of *Acumen*, an English poetry magazine, described editing as "educating yourself in public." I have to concur!)

As a student at Edinburgh in the early 1970s, Joy Hendry began studying English literature but gave it up because she did not like the attitude towards Scottish culture:

> I found this enormous gulf—I mean, two things really, this kind of enormous attitude between the attitude of the academics towards Scottish literature: "keep the Jocks out!" as far as the English Department was concerned. No Hugh MacDiarmid; he's a radical Communist. We don't want anything to do with anything like that! But I really got to the point where I felt that if I was going to study English literature as an academic study, it was going to stifle any kind of creative spark that I had.

Before she graduated from Edinburgh University with a degree in philosophy, Joy Hendry found the creative outlet she was seeking in a newly established literary magazine that would become a major outlet for contemporary Scottish creative writers:

> Well, when I started working on the magazine, I was nineteen at the time. *Chapman* has been in existence twenty-five-ish years. The first six issues were little tiny pamphlets; eight page things. The very first issue, which I had nothing to do with. appeared in 1969. And then it transmogrified: the first big issue, twenty-eight pages, appeared in 1971 or '72, I forget which. And I had some poems in that; that was my first involvement with it.
>
> The magazine was started by a man named George Hardie and my first husband Walter Perrie; they started the magazine because they felt the literary scene was too cliquish and that a radical, independent and irreverent

voice was needed. The two of them produced those early issues, six of eight pages. George Hardie dropped out, and I got involved when I got involve with Walter, so it spiralled from that. We attempted to make a sparkling literary debut with our next number on ancient Chinese literature, art and culture (!!). We did this just as we were getting married, on student grants. We printed 3,000 copies, at 30p each. Almost single-handed, I managed to sell enough copies to pay the £600 printer's bill. I became joint editor with Walter at this point.

The mission of *Chapman* evolved over the years, reflecting the diverging personal visions of its three successive editors. Its first editor, George Hardie was primarily concerned with expanding what was then a primarily Scottish literary magazine. ("Élitist" is quite wrong!) His co-editor, Joy Hendry's first husband Walter Perrie, envisioned *Chapman* as an ambitious élitist international literary journal publishing issues on Rainer Maria Rilke, ancient Chinese writing and literature and philosophy and art, and only incidentally focusing upon contemporary Scottish creative writing. ("This approach evoked quite a lot of bad feeling amongst Scottish writers.")

That editorial policy would change radically when Walter Perrie and Joy Hendry were divorced and she became sole editor of *Chapman* in 1976:

> When I really got involved in it, I began to realize that so many people were like me, totally ignorant of Scottish writing, Scottish poetry, and so on, and there still isn't, even to this day, the right degree of access to Scottish literature amonst the public at large, or anything like its rightful presence in the media, Scottish or UK. People at that time were not aware of the quantity and quality of Scottish writing. When I got my hands on the controls of the magazine, I thought "What's the point of having issues on Rainer Maria Rilke when you could actually be looking at Tom Scott, Norman MacCaig, and Hugh MacDiarmid and actually try to follow through the questions they were asking." So I began to make the magazine much more narrow-focused for a long time, trying quite deliberately to use the magazine, quite self-consciously, to develop the infrastructure of Scottish literature and culture. There has been a huge improvement over the intervening 20 years, 76–96, in almost every respect, partly because of the political ground swelling in favour of devolution/independence — which was quite positively and explicitly stimulated by writers and artists in particular.

> With my first solo issue, No. 16, I had the idea of asking six Scottish poets three questions: What started you writing, what keeps you writing, and what's your relationship with poetry and the Muse? The essays in that issue have become absolutely seminal. Sorley MacLean, Norman MacCaig, Iain Crichton Smith, Kathleen Raine and George Mackay Brown gave their fundamental aesthetic credo: whether there is a distinctive Scottish aesthetic; whether the languages of Scotland have any real future; whether Scotland has a future as a semi or totally autonomous nation; whether there

is a kind of Scottish landscape or accent of the mind which can actually make a unique contribution to world literature, world thinking, and world culture; those sorts of things were touched on, though often obliquely. Above all, they discussed their own personal springs of creativity. (I am about to reprint these essays in *Chapman* 100!)

It seemed to me that the answer to all those questions was "Yes." I happened to be in the right place at the right time and they wrote those unique pieces for me. That made me think, "Yeah, wait a minute; I can actually do this." And as a youngster then in my early twenties, this was a real bombshell, because it was new territory. It was something that had been there for thousands of years but it was new to me. And my passion and commitment was to say, "Okay, now how do we make this stick? How can we get Scottish writing reviewed in the London media? How can we make sure that good works of Scottish literature actually get published? How can we make sure that these voices have access to the radio? How can we make sure that everyone has access to that way of thinking, to that rich philosophic tradition, to that genuine internationality?" So much for "narrow nationalism!"

Because it seemed to me such an essentially rich and vibrant, different and unique way of thinking (of interacting with the world at large), I wanted it to be fully enjoyed, not just by myself, but everybody else in the community, and *particularly* everybody coming up behind me. And it's still what I want to do; I want to light the bonfires all over the hills, if you like, so "there's a good heather burning" to quote Sorley MacLean. [laughs]

When I asked Joy Hendry to enumerate some of the major accomplishments in Scottish culture and politics since the late 1960s, she replied:

> It's been a very slow ongoing movement, and sometimes the progress has been relatively imperceptible. In 1979, when I was working on the Scots Language issue of *Chapman,* I think perhaps more than fifty percent of the Scottish people had decided that it was important for whatever reason to have a Scottish Assembly. The SNP's [Scottish Nationalist Party] vote had gone up to above 30% in the October 1974 election, and so Labour took up the cause of devolution; many said, "Yes, that's fine." But when it was decided to have a referendum with a forty percent rule — namely, that forty percent of the registered voting population had to vote "yes"— people began to have doubts: "Ah goodness, will we ever get there?" (The legislation, confusing and inadequate to start with, was endlessly and even more confusingly revised.)
>
> There was also a very, very strong "no" campaign from within Scotland. And because the reasons for wanting devolution, independence, or whatever were not grounded in sufficient knowledge of what Scotland is and where it comes from and why it should be independent anyway, because you were talking about a population totally ignorant about Scottish literature, Scottish culture, Scottish history, you name it, people lost confidence, they

became afraid. They'd nothing to ground it on, this "yes" vote on a parliament, an assembly. It was coming out of an emotional impulse which was only shakily grounded, the reasons for the existence of which they barely understood. It was like trying to face the world at large dressed only in a coat of dreams.

Now, that's changed. In the past twenty years, people know more about Scotland and what Scotland and Scottish culture is, so they're not coming from nowhere any more. People are more secure in their ability to make a decision, to assess reality for themselves.

When I asked her what accounted for this dramatic change in consciousness and interest in Scottish culture, Joy Hendry answered:

Knowledge — a lot of hard work has gone on in the background. There have been a number of significant successes. When I began to teach in 1977, the only teachers who taught Scottish Literature were regarded as fanatics; they met together once a year to exchange fanaticisms [laughs], which I thought was pretty useless. We needed to get at the decision-makers, and most of all, at the students and pupils. Taking this message "on board" myself, I organised the first ever conference for school pupils which was a dramatic success. We were turning the pupils away in their hundreds, and those who got in came away from it very stirred up, and, like I had been, very, very angry. It was dynamite!

I didn't intend to be a teacher, but did it only because my marriage to Walter was breaking up, and I wanted to lay something of a secure foundation to my life before casting off all securities to work on literature full time. But it would seem, from my teaching career, and judging from the responses of my pupils and students, that I may, almost against my will, be a "natural teacher." The cultural compulsion comes out of working in the literary field, through *Chapman*, but finding myself, rather reluctantly, a teacher, I threw myself into campaigning for more Scottish literature and Scots language in schools, becoming a cultural nationalist through the realisation that for Scottish languages, literature and culture to survive and prosper, public support for them, both financial and otherwise would have to be forthcoming, which could only happen if we had at least partial autonomy. It is not a matter of patriotism, which I rather despise, or sentiment.

Linguistic colonialism was still very much alive in Scotland's schools when Joy Hendry began her stint as a classroom teacher. As she recollects:

You would get the ridiculous spectacle of teachers who themselves spoke broad Scots actually administering the belt to children who had used "nuh!" or "na" instead of "no" in the classroom.

When I started to teach, I obviously wanted to teach Scots anyway. For the first couple of years the kids were incensed about it: "You're no alloo'ed tae speak like that; you're an English teacher!" they would say to me in broad Scots. And I would say, "who are ye tae tell me I cannae speak as I want tae?" [laughs] (They regarded this on my part as almost an infringement or an invasion of their underground *samizdat* language.)

And eventually the word got round the school that this was what I did, so nobody questioned it any more. But I still find teachers who will say, "We can't possibly do the best for our children if we're not giving them access to the best, and the best is English."

Well, bollocks to that! It's not. I took a decision quite early on that I would never teach an English text if a Scots one would do just as well or better, and I found it was almost always possible to find something Scottish comparable in quality, content and style to the standard English item on the syllabus. So it was a political decision to teach Scottish literature rather than English. My headmaster (ex public school, English) would have loved to try to stop me, but didn't dare.

I immediately became involved in the campaign to get more Scottish literature into the schools. The Canongate Classic Series, and the Canongate Kelpie Series in particular, came in part out of a meeting I organised between Scottish teachers and publishers where the teachers said to the publishers, "Look, give us the texts; we'll teach them" and the publishers said, "We don't really believe you." But five years later, the Kelpie Series began, and was a huge success.

Wee things like that, very much on the fringes, but you find that now Scottish literature is much more found in schools; everybody reads Lewis Grassic Gibbon (author of the trilogy of novels, *A Scots Quair*); everybody reads Norman MacCaig, whereas twenty years ago that simply wasn't happening. So when people are talking about Scotland now, they've got icons to focus on. There's a much more systematic teaching of Scottish history. A number of Scottish novels have been spectacularly successful, things like James Kelman's *How Late It Was, How Late*. It was a great victory for a book like that to be awarded the Booker Prize.

There have been different waves which have brought different aspects of the Scottish cultural scene to prominence. The musical aspect has been very important. There has been an ongoing process since the Scottish traditional folk revival started post-war. There is the factor that you now have the resurgence of Gaelic, although Scots still trails behind. While Scottish literature may now be more widely taught, Scots language is still a thistle not sufficiently grasped in the classroom.

One of the most important things I've been involved in is "The Scots Kist." "Kist" is Lowland Scots for "chest," as in treasure chest. The basic idea of this project is to introduce elementary school children in Scotland to the beauties of a language and literature that had largely been ignored and even suppressed by Scottish educators, except for perfunctory, parroted readings and recitations of the poetry of Robert Burns.

Joy Hendry told me how she became involved in this project:

Well, the way the Kist evolved, I was asked in 1992 to do a three-part report on Scots language for Radio Scotland, on the situation of Scots in the media, arts and education.

I mean, the Scots language is a thousand years old. It has a very respectable literature which goes through John Barber to James Kelman and Irvine Welsh. It has a tremendously earthy, anarchic feel to it; it's enormous fun to have access to.

Partly because it hasn't had to adapt to modern social and scientific purposes, it retains a strong grip on reality in the words themselves, through the strong onomatopoetic element in the language. "Wag-at-the-waa" is the Scots word for "clock."

When I'm asked about Scots and English and so on, I say, "Well, you know that people say that Scots is just a dialect of English (or merely an accent, or worse, slang or bad English), but you might as well as say it the other way around, because the only difference between the two is that England has the power, the army, navy and the air force. And so it has political power. You cannot divorce political power, the matter of politics, from the matter, the substance and the fate of a language. Now, in terms of politics, Scots has been extremely unlucky, and the Scots themselves don't have a clear understanding of the language they speak and where it comes from.

You only need to walk down the street to hear that people are talking a language which has, of course, many connections with English and a lot of similarities with it, but it is a different language with its own grammar, its own vocabulary, and its own history with independent borrowings from different languages; there's a totally different emotional feel to it altogether.

The great thing that Hugh MacDiarmid did in the twentieth century was to try to establish that language as a kind of poetic language which could actually carry even the most abstruse and difficult and intellectual of poetic discourse. And he succeeded. "The Drunk Man Looks at the Thistle" is the Scottish "Waste Land." I mean, it's a masterpiece, and it's written in a language which English speakers don't recognize the legitimate and independent existence of and one which Scots themselves have great trouble with. [laughs]

But to come back to the Kist; I was commissioned to investigate the state of Scots in the arts, the media and education for a series of broadcasts on Radio Scotland. I "discovered" what I knew anyway, because I'm in schools a lot doing creative writing classes, that in 1992 virtually no Scots [knew Scots]. I interviewed teachers and people in teacher training colleges in universities and pupils as well, and it became clear that it just wasn't there.

But, somebody said to me — I promised I wouldn't say who it was — "I'm sorry; Scots is a low priority. We have standard grade, we have new developments in exams, we have new aspects of assessment and workloads, and teachers can't cope. And for us to bother about Scots is quite honestly unreasonable!" And I thought, "You've actually got a point there." The problem is resources: there aren't the resources; there aren't the textbooks; there isn't the know-how. I mean, teachers of English don't know how to teach Scots, unless they have an enthusiasm for it themselves. What are you going to do about this?

So I went to the Scottish Office [laughs] and found the right person [laughs], stuck a microphone under his nose and said, "What are you going to do about this?" The obvious thing to do is not to wag the finger at teachers and say, "You ought to be teaching Scots!" "Why?" they will say. And they're quite entitled to say "why?" But if you present them with the wherewithal, if you give them the knowledge which will make them actually want to do it, then it will happen. And this person agreed on air to make the promise to create this resource, and that's the Kist. One of the wee things I managed to pull off [laughs], or light the fuse of!

The Kist was great. Robbie Robertson, who was the official I spoke to, said, "Yes, I agree with you; that's absolutely right. So I'll do it! He agreed to make a statement to that effect on the air. And did it. Fortunately I was able to be involved right through to the end, sat on a committee and advised, having to take a back seat because it was no longer my baby. And he took it forward, and I think it's the most revolutionary thing in education that's happened in twentieth century Scotland. It really is transforming things. (Well, currently rather more in limbo than one might like.)

And going to the launch and seeing these kids from Dundee and Falkirk and Edinburgh standing up with obvious pleasure — now they weren't just doing their party piece with their hands clasped like this in front of them — they were really doing something which connected with their own personal language. And you could see that they were emotionally involved with it in a way which they couldn't have been if they had been speaking English. Suddenly their own language was given legitimacy in a public place in front of a government minister. That was big stuff.

Our conversation then shifted to points of convergence between folklore, vernacular language and creative literature, a topic I had previously discussed with Hamish Henderson. Joy Hendry offered her interpretation of the great "flyting" or argument between Henderson and MacDiarmid concerning the value of folklore and vernacular language:

Oh, absolutely! I think that's where Hamish is such an important figure. I mean, MacDiarmid rejected the whole folk movement, and you can understand why; the Kailyard, the couthy folk arts, the heedrums hodrums, had dragged Scottish culture down to a level of discourse which he found intellectually unacceptable. So he was trying to do a big heave-up number where he was trying to assert, and I think quite rightly, that it is possible to use Scots language, Scottish idiom, Scottish aesthetic, if you like, to discuss anything at all, like, from nuclear physics to hoovering the floor, and that was important for him to establish.

But having said that, with MacDiarmid the baby to some extent was being thrown out with the bath water. Hypocritically, because on one hand he was using traditional songs and rejecting traditional songs at the same time! " Jenny Nettles" is a good example of that. [Look at his poem, a] lovely thing, "Empty Vessel":

I met ayont the cairney
A lass wi' tousie hair
Singin' till a bairnie
That was nae langer there.
Wunds wi' warlds to swing
Dinna sing sae sweet,
The licht that bends owre a' thing
Is less ta'en up wi't [in Riach and Grieve: 1992: 19].

Now that's a folksong. The first verse is pinched from the folksong "Jenny Nettles." But while he was doing that, on the one hand he said, "There have been too many folksongs! This is all sentimental rubbish!," he was also fervently exploiting the tradition in other respects. And that was the great source of the conflict between Hamish and MacDiarmid. And the reason Hamish is so important is because he asserts what's always been true, that poetry and song go together. And that's one of the very strong things about Scottish literature and its own system of literary values. In England they've lost contact with songs completely. Alright, you have the high art songs, the song cycles, the Britton this and the Britton that and German lieder and what not, but there is a real gulf between high literature and folksong, the latter being regarded as intrinsically inferior. Now that prejudice doesn't exist here. There's a real feeling that poetry is song and song is poetry, and that goes back — it's not a new thing — it goes back centuries.

This is something we ought to hold onto, because it's so strong, powerful and natural. It keeps us grounded, if you like, in the lyrical impulse on one hand, and it also keeps us grounded in the fact that poetry, however intellectually difficult it may become, somehow has to make the connection with ordinary people. That's a very Scottish principle. So you see a principle of Scottish thought and one of Scottish aesthetics coming together and being sustained in the present. You see it sustained in the work of James Kelman, for example, where he insists that his discourse is the discourse of the ordinary working class punter in, like, Bellshill or some place like that. It's a very important principle, whether people can articulate it to themselves or not, and it's somehow being carried through to the future. It's such a healthy principle; I'm delighted to be part of a culture that thinks like that.

I asked her to comment upon the emphasis in Scottish literature on erasing the gap between the written word and oral narrative:

Well, you can look at that historically, because so much of the work of Burns, for example, is intended to be recited or sung; it doesn't really matter which. That's a continuing strand. The great female contribution, the Scottish songwriters like Lady Nairn and all these other women, they have this idea that the language — the language of the people — was the important thing to keep going, even if it wasn't the language *they* spoke, though it was. And they tended to celebrate it in song rather than poetry. The Gaelic tradition is the same; the distinction between song and poetry is blurred.

When you come into the twentieth century, you see the same thing operating. If you take Violet Jacob's wonderful poem, "The Wild Geese" — it's set to an incredibly beautiful melody by Jim Reid — but so many Scottish songs are now being created by contemporary musicians lifting the poems and putting them to melodies, often with a traditional basis even if in a classical or avant garde musical idiom: William Soutar's poems — James MacMillan has set them; Benjamin Britton has set 'em — lots of others. I was singing last night some of my settings of Sydney Goodsir Smith. We refuse to dissociate song and poetry in any absolute terms.

One of the reasons Burns has suffered is because he is regarded as "just" the writer of "Ye Banks and Braes" and "My Love is Like a Red, Red Rose." Well, that's nonsense: it's beautiful poetry and beautiful song as well And we won't let go of it, and that's why Hamish is so important — because he's someone who here and now insists that these two things can and do go together.

Another rejection of that dichotomy is the use of subjective first person narrative in contemporary Scottish literature. According to Hendry, political as well as aesthetic principles are involved in refusing to allow the intellectual and emotional detachment and separation generated by the objective voice of the third person:

> Well, it's a kind of implicit rejection of the bourgeois values of the English novel. [laughs] Jim Kelman is quite explicit about it.
>
> If you look back to Grassic Gibbon in *Sunset Song,* he's doing the same thing in the way he turns his dialogue into a stream of consciousness. There are no inverted commas, only an uninterrupted flow between narrative in Roman and dialogue in Italic and back to Roman again. Sometimes it's hard to tell the difference between the two — because it's all really coming from inside, inside the character her/himself. And that's the whole point. And his use, for example, of the second person: "You felt like this ... you were the English Chris then, back to the English words so sharp and clear and true. And then you were the Scots Chris.." And it's all a matter of trying to make real, meaningful contact with the individual at the feeling level.
>
> And I suppose, to be perhaps a little melodramatic about it, it's the democratic intellect, the Presbyterian idea that the feeling of ordinary people is important, that we're all equal before God. Ordinary people's thoughts

and their stories must be important, so you've got to find a narrative that actually reflects that, so you develop a narrative which exemplifies that literary value, and this impulse in fiction remains operative to this day.

You have to remember, too, that the native voice is *samizdat.* Okay, you have people like Stevenson and Scott who had access to the world's publishers and the world's readers, but apart from them, the vast corpus of Scottish writing and Scottish cultural expression was *samizdat.* It wasn't recognized by the English establishment, the English publishers, and so on. So there's a deep sense that whatever we have to say has got to come from "underground."

The great thing we have achieved — and I think we have achieved it, maybe not completely but to some extent at least — is to show the world how important your toes are: extremities matter. And your extremities feel the cold and the heat first, and are the most sensitive part of your body, like your nose and ears. Now, we've been the nose and ears of the British Empire for a long time [laughs]; we've felt a lot of things other parts haven't felt.

I really do believe that's true. When you are essentially oppressed, which Scots have been — you have to develop several extra senses and, amongst other things, get to "know your enemy." There's an interesting parallel between the oppression of Scots and Scottishness and the situation of women. If you talk to women about men, they often know more about men than men do, because you have to know and understand, very well, the forces ranged against you; you have to know what it is you're fighting against, why and what for. That's been very true of Scotland; we've had to acquire a degree of self-knowledge that a nation in power or a community in power simply doesn't have to acquire, because it is in power. They can take so much for granted that they don't have to know or understand anybody — not even themselves, because their power, influence and money protects them from reality.

When I started publishing *Chapman,* many Scottish writers who were very worthwhile simply couldn't get a book published! Talk about the voice! Where was the poetry to go? It had to exist somehow. That's been the case for quite some time; there's a problem about publication, there's a problem about audience, there's a problem about publicity and so on. So it becomes *samizdat,* and the voice, in that context, becomes absolutely crucial. The oral tradition was greatly needed.

Since she is a radio commentator herself, I was particularly interested in hearing what Joy Hendry had to say concerning the increasing prevalence of Scottish voices on Scottish radio and television:

I think people are much more comfortable now hearing a Scots voice. It's come into fashion and almost gone out of fashion again. The media still tends to be controlled by people with fairly plummy accents. Three years ago, it was the flavour of the month to have a Scottish or a regional voice.

In London, that perception has shifted now; they've shifted away from the concept of "we must have regional voices" to "we must have personalities." So unless they happen to be regional voices, Scottish or whatever, and personalities, they're now not getting through. In fact, *some* Scottish voices are being suppressed because they don't seem to carry with them the right kind of stupid personality the controllers of radio programming are wanting. What's that got to do with anything? Those are the rather arbitrary principles by which cultural change is impeded or advanced, and that's what makes everything, cultural advance especially, more difficult.

It's still true that people from public school backgrounds with plummy voices, who are well educated and have good degrees and good backgrounds and so on have a much easier access to positions of power than someone like me coming from nowhere. Of course, the other side is that we have got a kind of understanding, an impulse, and an anger and an agenda which they don't have, which can carry us further — simply because you're not just fighting for yourself; you're not just trying to advance a career. You're actually trying to do something which has wider implications: liberation.

Scotland could be a wonderful place. Of course there are bad things about Scots, Scottish history and the Scottish character, but essentially Scots people are very warm, hospitable, lively, very cosmopolitan, energetic and sociable. And it depresses me to see people who could be like that in a public arena, with just a little more education, a little bit of the right possibilities, being denied access to that public arena. Now that happens in every country, but I think this happens particularly in Scotland, where people have been divided from themselves, their essential natures denied and devalued, often through abuse and stereotyping.

In the *5 to 14 Report*, which the Scots Kist emerges out of, it's emphasized that the teacher has to respect the language children bring to school. Now that was framed not for the Scots or the Gaels but for the immigrants — the Pakistanis and the Bengalis and the Chinese — not for the indigenous population. But this Kist has managed to exploit that. (If the authorities had realised that they were creating such an opportunity, for Scots language in particular, they might have thought twice about using that slogan.)

But if you're going to make that your principle, that, you cannot *possibly* deny the native languages. They simply can't argue against it. So there's a gradual relaxation; people in Scotland are coming to know more who they are, where they come from and where they might go to. And it's gradually coming together. There's a long way to go with Scots language. People are *still* filled with ignorant, derisory notions about it. I want to see that disappear. The only future is bi- or tri-lingualism.

I've just come back from the International Declaration of Linguistic Rights in Barcelona. I've been working on this for three years at various conferences. This Declaration is going to be presented via UNESCO to the United Nations, maintaining that every language has certain linguistic

rights. The implications for Scots and Gaelic of the assertion of those linguistic rights, educationally and socially and so on, are huge and exciting. It
makes you realize how backward a country this is; what would have to be
done to achieve the principles that we've set out in that document here
would cost a lot of money. And you would see the British government kicking and screaming and refusing to do it. I want to see all that in place, so
that people in Scotland have easy access to the three languages.

Joy Hendry is hopeful that the new Scottish Parliament will enable the
Scottish nation to reclaim its own distinctive identity and cultural values:

So much work needs to be done in the Scottish arts. I would hope that
a Scottish Parliament would be willing to put up the money needed for all
that to happen. I'm actually in favour of independence rather than devolution of the United Kingdom, because in practice I think that's what people
really want, although they might not have got round to thinking like that
yet. I'm a democrat, I believe in leaving people to go along at whatever
speed they're at, and I feel confident that any kind of devolved assembly is
going to lead to more powers here rather than less. And that can only be a
good thing in the long term, although in the short term, I'm sure there will
be difficulties.

Just as I was about to conclude my conversation with her, I remembered
that she had told me that she was in the midst of writing an essay titled
"Poems Make the People." The title and topic intrigued me, so I asked her
to tell me about them:

The poems there are a metaphor for culture generally. I'm going to try
to trace back at least to Burns's "Parcel o' Rogues in a Nation," "Tree of
Liberty" and coming up, of course, into the twentieth century to MacDiarmid and Soutar; to trace how in their persistent articulation, our poets,
our singers, our artists, and our novelists have been the ones who have
made it their business to retain that grasp of the Scottish thistle, its roots
and its shoots.

The poets and the artists are the ones who have to have their fingers in
the soil, who teach us how to *unlearn* things we've been taught at school and
at university and through what's in the air through society. The job of the
poet — it sounds like an awfully pretentious cliche — is to try to grab hold of
what is true and fundamental to the people you are speaking for. You can't
speak for the world's people; you can only speak for your own people. It's
like "Auchtermuchty stood as pairt o' an eternal mood" [quoting from Mac-
Diarmid's "Drunk Man"]. If you know Auchtermuchty well enough, you
will know the world well enough, and what you say about your own people,
your own situation, your own village will be to some extent extendable and
transferable to the situation in Bangladesh or Australia or Appalachia.

So, in Scotland, it has been the poets and artists who, because of that basic need to be the root and branch, the continuing vein of communication, have carried us forward. It has come down to the poets and the artists to maintain this running stream of memory. So what you have is a situation where the current political upsurge has been created and "funded" [in several senses of the word] by the refusal of our artists and our poets to desert that "running stream" in favour of international fame. It's to their eternal credit that people like MacDiarmid and William Soutar and even Robert Burns have kept that carrying stream flowing, and kept it as pure as they can, often to the extreme detriment of their own lives. And it's thanks to their success and their commitment and their vision that we will soon have a Scottish Parliament and a nation which begins to know itself again.

The Beginning of a New Song: Some Reflections Upon the Opening of the New Scottish Parliament

*W*hen the last independent Scottish Parliament was dissolved following the passage of the Act of Union of the Parliaments in 1707 establishing the modern United Kingdom of Great Britain, the Earl of Seafield, the Scottish chancellor who officially recorded the act of dissolution ruefully commented, "that's ane end of ane auld sang."

Roughly two hundred and ninety-two years later, the newly elected Scottish Parliament convened for the first time on the first of July, 1999, in Edinburgh. Accompanied by her husband Prince Phillip, the Duke of Edinburgh, and her eldest son and heir-apparent Prince Charles, who bears the Scottish title of Duke of Rothesay, Queen Elizabeth, direct descendant of Mary, Queen of Scots and daughter of a venerable Scottish Queen Mother, conferred upon the new Scottish Parliament a ceremonial mace upon which were engraved, among other things, the words, "there will be a Scottish Parliament" and the emblem of the thistle. In keeping with the studied semi-informality typifying this pivotal day in contemporary Scottish history, the Queen was not robed and crowned in traditional regalia but wore instead an elegant dress and plumed hat in subtle shades of purple and green, also evoking the shape and colors of the thistle.

The Queen and her party, led by the Lord Lyon of Arms, the principal overseer of the crown and other regalia, followed by attendants bearing the ancient Crown of Scotland and the newly crafted Scottish parliamentary mace, entered the General Assembly hall of the Church of Scotland to the accompaniment of an orchestral fanfare conducted by its composer James Macmillan.

Scottish broadcast journalist Tom Fleming read a poem by the late Iain Crichton Smith, "The Beginning of a New Song," which concludes with the declaration that the restoration of a Scottish Parliament will enable the Scottish people to "esteem themselves" once again. "How to Create a Great Country," a prize-winning poem written by Amy Linekar, a Scottish school girl, and recited by Victoria Joffe received a warm response. Sheena Wellington, a great Scottish folksinger who is executive director of the Traditional Music and Song Association, sang a profoundly moving rendition of Robert Burns' democratic anthem, "A Man's a Man for a' That" which prompted the entire Scottish Parliament to join in on the last verse and chorus, underscoring the democratic spontaneity pervading this event.

From Robert Burns to Iain Crichton Smith and their living successors, nationalist poets have continuously voiced the aspirations of the Scottish people for political and cultural autonomy. In his welcoming remarks to the queen, the First Minister of the Scottish Parliament, the late Donald Dewar, eloquently expounded upon the power of poets as expressive leaders to inspire and sustain the popular movement which recently came to fruition in the establishment of the new Scottish Parliament.

Iain Crichton Smith's wish that the Scottish people might esteem themselves again brings to mind Emma Bell Miles' hope that a counterpart of Burns would emerge from the Southern Highlands to awaken the dormant self-awareness of the people of Appalachia, poetically transmuting their devalued native speech from a prickly badge of shame into an emblem of blossoming self-esteem.

Transmutation of flawed identity symbols not only heals the divided self, it regenerates the subordinated community as well.

Conclusion:
Thinking Ocean to Ocean

*W*hat final conclusions can we draw from this exploration of points of convergence between Scotland and Appalachia ?

"Our past has a future," Jim Wayne Miller concludes in his 1995 essay, "Nostalgia for the Future":

> The Appalachian people, Cratis Williams tells us, have migrated at least four times. Many moved to the border country between England and Scotland during the time of the Roman Empire. Many migrated to Northern Ireland in the seventeenth century, to the American colonies and into Appalachia in the eighteenth and early nineteenth. Several millions migrated from the region to urban industrial centers in the Midwest in this century [Higgs, Manning and Miller 1995: 718].

Jim Wayne Miller goes on to say:

> I believe a knowledge of our history and heritage, of our common interest and problems, is capable of giving the Appalachian people — many of whom are descended from these Scots who later came to be known as Scots-Irish — something to think about, seriously and deeply. And I believe people will respond warmly to it. They are already doing so.
>
> Our literature is one of the resources we have for providing something to think about. The nostalgia for the future found in it can be used as a means of possessing the future. Our imaginative literature can enable people all over the region to say "I have a place."

Miller's ideas converge with those of Angus Calder when he declares, "all culture is derived from place" (1994: 1).

Sense of place is the spatial extension of selfhood, intertwined with sense of community; the vocal extension of place is local accent and idiom, along with other modes of voicing cultural distinctiveness, such as song and poetry and folk arts.

Points of convergence between Scotland and Appalachia are concrete and meaningful. The Thistle and the Brier are not merely abstract metaphors. Thistles and briers actually do thrive on rocky slopes, and between the cracks of sidewalks. Literally and figuratively, marginal spaces are seedbeds of creative regeneration.

The poets who wrote "A Drunk Man Looks at the Thistle" and "The Brier Sermon" lived in different places and spoke in different accents, yet in the end, the message of their best loved poems is the same.

As Hugh MacDiarmid demonstrated so brilliantly in "A Drunk Man Looks at the Thistle," it is possible to voice universal concerns in local idioms, to bring together the best of now and then, as Jim Wayne Miller said in "The Brier Sermon," by "thinking ocean to ocean." In a fragmented twenty-first century world torn by religious, ethnic, national and regional strife, we desperately need constructive alternatives to xenophobic, self-glorifying provincialism and rootless, nay-saying cosmopolitan cynicism.

We cannot afford to succumb to parochial tunnel vision or urbane intellectual nihilism. All of us need to think ocean to ocean.

Bibliography

Alburger, Mary Ann. 1986. *Scottish Fiddlers and Their Music*. London: Gollancz.

Batteau, Allen. 1981. "An Agenda for Irrelevance: Malcolm Chapman's The Gaelic Vision in Scottish Culture." *Appalachian Journal (AppalJ)* vol. 8, no. 3: 212–215.

_____. 1990. *The Invention of Appalachia*. Tucson: University of Arizona Press.

Beaver, Patricia Duane, and David Cratis Williams, eds. 1999. Introduction to Cratis Williams' *The Cratis Williams Chronicles: I Come to Boone*. Boone, NC: Appalachian Consortium Press.

Best, Bill, ed. 1997. *One Hundred Years of Appalachian Visions*. Berea, KY: Appalachian Imprints.

_____. 1999. *From Existence to Essence: A Conceptual and Mythological Model for an Appalachian Studies Curriculum*. Berea, KY: Appalachian Imprints (reprint of 1973 dissertation).

Blaustein, Richard. 1996. "Scottish Americans." In Jan Harold Brunvand (ed.) *American Folklore: An Encyclopedia*. New York and London: Garland Publishing Company, 652–655.

Blethen, H. Tylor, and Curtis W. Wood, Jr., eds. 1997. *Ulster and North America: Transatlantuc Perspectives on the Scotch-Irish*. Tuscaloosa and London: University of Alabama Press.

Bold, Alan. 1983. "Healing Scotland's Divided Self." *The Weekly Scotsman* (Edinburgh), Saturday, May 7 n.p.

Bort, Eberhard. 1993. "It's a Darlin' Story: A Decade of Irish Drama in Tübingen." In *"Standing in their shifts itself...": Irish Drama from Farquhar to Friel*. Bremen: European Society for Irish Studies, 15–21.

Boyd, Clifford C., Jr. 1989. "Prehistoric and Historic Human Adaptation in Appalachia: An Archaeological Perspective." *Journal of the Appalachian Studies Association (JASA)*, vol. 1: 15–27.

Brown, Alice, David McCrone and Lindsay Paterson. 1996. *Politics and Society in Scotland*. New York: St. Martin's Press.

Calder, Angus. 1994. *Revolving Culture: Notes from the Scottish Republic*. London & New York: I. B. Taurus Publishers.

Campbell, John C. 1969. *The Southern Highlander and His Homeland*. Foreword by

Rupert Vance. Lexington: University Press of Kentucky [1921], Introduction by Henry D. Shapiro.

Campbell, Olive Dame. 1968. "The Life and Work of John Charles Campbell," Berea Archives, copyright Lois Bacon, Trustee. Madison, Wisconsin: College Printing and Typing Company, Inc., 104–105.

Caudill, Harry M. 1962. *Night Comes to the Cumberlands: A Biography of a Depressed Area.* Foreword by Stewart L. Udall. Boston and Toronto: Atlantic–Little, Brown and Co.

Chapman, Malcolm. 1978. *The Gaelic Vision in Scottish Culture.* London and Montreal: Croom Helm and McGill–Queen's University.

_____. 1992. *The Celts: The Making of a Myth.* London: Routledge.

Cohen, Anthony P. 1996a. "Personal Nationalism: A Scottish View of Some Rites, Rights and Wrongs." *American Ethnologist* vol. 23, no. 4, 802–818.

_____. 1996b. "Owning the Nation, and the Personal Nature of Nationalism: Locality and the Rhetoric of Nationhood in Scotland." In Vered Amit-Talai and Caroline Knowles (eds.), *Re-situating Identity: The Politics of Race, Ethnicity, Culture.* Ontario, Canada: Broadview, 267–281.

Cowan, Edward J. 1980. *The People's Past.* Edinburgh: Polygon.

Craig, Cairns. 1996. *Out of History: Narrative Paradigms in Scottish and British Culture.* Determinations Series. Edinburgh: Polygon.

Cunningham, Rodger. 1987. *Apples on the Flood: The Southern Mountain Experience.* Knoxville: University of Tennessee Press.

_____. 1990. "Eat Grits and Die: Or, Cracker, Your Breed Ain't Hermeneutical," *Appalachian Journal* vol. 17, no. 2: 135–182.

_____. 1997. "Meeting The First Time Again," in Best 1997: 135–139.

Donaldson, Emily Ann. 1986. *The Scottish Highland Games in America.* Gretna, LA: Pelican Publishing Company.

Donaldson, Gordon. 1966. *The Scots Overseas.* Westport, CT: Greenwood [1976].

_____. 1980. "Scots." *Encyclopedia of American Ethnic Groups.* Cambridge, Mass., and London: Harvard University Press; 908–16.

Doran, Paul E. "The Backgrounds of The Mountain People." *Mountain Life & Work,* January 1936. Reprinted in Best 1997: 29–38.

Dunaway, Wilma A. 1996. *The First American Frontier: Transition to Capitalism in Southern Appalachia, 1700–1860.* Chapel Hill and London: University of North Carolina Press.

Dunbar, John Telfer. 1989. *The Costume of Scotland,* London: Batsford.

Dundes, Alan. 1989. "Defining Identity through Folklore" and "Fabricating Folklore." In *Folklore Matters.* Knoxville: University of Tennessee Press.

Dykeman, Wilma. 1977. "Appalachia in Context." *An Appalachian Symposium: Essays in Honor of Cratis D. Williams.* Boone, NC: Appalachian State University Press.

Edwards, Owen Dudley, ed. 1989. *A Claim of Right for Scotland.* Edinburgh: Polygon.

Einstein, Frank. 1980. "The Politics of Nostalgia: Uses of the Past in Recent Appalachian Poetry." *AppalJ* vol. 8, no. 1: 32–39.

Eller, Ronald D. 1977. "Finding Ourselves: Reclaiming the Appalachian Past," *An Appalachian Symposium: Essays in Honor of Cratis D. Williams.* Boone, NC: Appalachian State University Press; 35–46. Reprinted in Kuhre and Ergood 1991.

  167

Ellis, Peter Berresford. 1993. *The Celtic Dawn: A History of Pan Celticism*. London: Constable and Company, Ltd.

Ergood, Bruce, and Bruce E. Kuhre. 1991 [1976]. *Appalachia: Social Context Past and Present*, 3rd edition. Foreword by Loyal Jones. Dubuque, IA: Kendall-Hunt Publishing Co.

Farmer, Henry George. 1970 [1947]. *A History of Music in Scotland*. New York: Da Capo.

Ferguson, William. 1998. *The Identity of the Scottish Nation: An Historic Quest*. Edinburgh: Edinburgh University Press.

Fischer, David Hackett. 1989. *Albion's Seed: Four British Folkways in America*. Oxford and New York: Oxford University Press.

Frost, William Goodell. 1899. "Our Contemporary Ancestors in the Southern Mountains." *Atlantic Monthly*. In W.K. McNeil, 1995 [1989]. *Appalachian Images in Folk and Popular Culture*, 2nd edition. Knoxville: University of Tennessee Press; 91–106.

Garber, Marjorie. 1992. *Vested Interests: Cross-Dressing and Cultural Anxiety*. New York and London: Routledge.

Hamilton, Clive [C. S. Lewis]. 1919. Excerpt from poem "World's Desire." In Mike W. Perry, ed. 1999 [1919], *Spirits in Bondage*. London: William Heineman; 102–04.

Harrington, Michael. 1981 [1962]. *The Other America: Poverty in the United States*. Harmondsworth, Middlesex and New York: Penguin.

Harvie, Christopher. 1994 [1977]. *Scotland and Nationalism*. 2nd edition. London and New York: Routledge.

Hechter, Michael. 1975. *Internal Colonialism: The Celtic Fringe in British National Development, 1536–1966*. London: Routledge and Kegan Paul.

Henderson, Hamish. 1992. *Alias MacAlias: Writings on Songs, Folk and Literature*. Edinburgh: Polygon.

Henley, William Ernest, ed. 1966 [1894]. *The Complete Poetical Works of Burns*. Cambridge Edition. Boston: Houghton Mifflin.

Hewitson, Jim. 1993. *Tam Blake & Co.: The Story of the Scots in America*. Edinburgh: Canongate.

Higgs, Robert J., Ambrose N. Manning and Jim Wayne Miller. 1995. *Appalachia Inside Out*. 2 vols. Knoxville: University of Tennessee Press.

Jackson, Clayton. 1993. *A Social History of the Scotch Irish*. Lanham, MD: Madison Books.

Kay, Billy. 1993. *Scots: The Mither Tongue*. Alloway: Darvel.

Keller, Kenneth W. 1991. "How Distinctive Are the Scotch-Irish?" In Robert D. Mitchell, ed., *Appalachian Frontiers*. Lexington: University Press of Kentucky, 1991; 69–86.

Kephart, Horace. 1976. *Our Southern Highlanders: A Narrative of Adventure in the Southern Appalachians and a Study of Life among the Mountaineers*. Knoxville: University of Tennessee Press. Originally published New York: Macmillan, 1922 [1913].

King, Duane H. 1979. *The Cherokee Indian Nation: A Troubled History*. Knoxville: University of Tennessee Press.

Laing, R.D. 1991 [1959]. *The Divided Self: An Existential Study in Sanity and Madness*. New York: Penguin Books.

_____. 1967. *The Politics of Experience*. New York: Penguin Books.

Leonard, Tom. 1995. "On Reclaiming the Local, or The Theory of the Magic Thing," In *Reports from the Present*. London: Jonathan Cape: 31–43.

Lewis, Helen M. 1982. "Appalachian Studies: The Next Step." *AppalJ* vol. 9, nos. 2–3: 162–171.

_____, Linda Johnson and Donald Askins, eds. 1978. *Colonialism in America: The Appalachian Case*. Boone: Appalachian Consortium Press.

Macafee, Caroline. 1985. "Nationalism and the Scots Renaissance Now." In Manfred Görlach, ed., *Focus On: Scotland* (vol. 5, *Varieties of English Around the World*). Amsterdam/Philadelphia: John Benjamins Publishing Company, 1–15.

MacDiarmid, Hugh (pseud. Christopher Murray Grieve). 1926. "A Drunk Man Looks at the Thistle." In Michael Grieve and Alan Riach, eds., *Hugh MacDiarmid: Selected Poems*. London: Penguin Books, 1994; 25–113.

McIllvaney, William. 1983. *Docherty*. Edinburgh: Mainstream Books.

McKay, Ian. 1994. *The Quest of the Folk: Anti-Modernism and Cultural Selection in Twentieth Century Nova Scotia*. Montreal and Kingston: McGill-Queen's University Press.

MacLaren, Ian (pseud. Rev. John Watson). 1894. *Beside the Bonnie Brier Bush*. New York: Dodd, Mead and Company.

MacNaughtan, Adam. 1991. "Hamish Henderson." *Tocher* no. 43. Edinburgh: School of Scottish Studies; 2–4.

McCrone, David. 1992. *Understanding Scotland: The Sociology of a Stateless Nation*. London and New York: Routledge.

McKenzie, Roberta. 1991. "Appalachian Culture as Reaction to Uneven Development: A World Systems Approach to Regionalism." Originally published in *JASA*, vol. 1, 1989; reprinted in Kuhre and Ergood 1991: 284–289.

McWhiney, Grady, and Forrest MacDonald. 1988. *Cracker Culture: Celtic Ways in the Old South*. Tuscaloosa: University of Alabama Press.

_____. 1989. "Celtic South." In Charles Reagan Wilson and William Ferris, eds., *Encyclopedia of Southern Culture*. Chapel Hill and London: University of North Carolina Press; 1131–32.

Miles, Emma Bell. 1975 (1905). *The Spirit of the Mountains*. Knoxville: University of Tennessee Press.

Miller, Jim Wayne. 1977a. "Appalachian Literature." *AppalJ* vol. 5, no. 1: 82–91.

_____. 1977b. "Appalachian Education: A Critique and Suggestions for Reform." *AppalJ* vol. 5, no. 1: 13–22.

_____. 1980. "The Brier Sermon — You Must Be Born Again." In *The Mountains Have Come Closer*. Boone, NC: Appalachian Consortium Press; reprinted in Higgs, Manning and Miller 1995.

_____. 1982. "Appalachian Studies Hard and Soft: The Action Folk and the Creative People." *AppalJ* vol. 9, nos. 2–3: 105–113.

Miller, Judy K. 1997. "Only Ignorant People." In Best 1997: 71–2.

Montgomery, Michael B. 1997. "The Scotch-Irish Element in Appalachian English: How Broad? How Deep?" In Blethen and Woods 1997: 189–212.

Mooney, James. 1900. *Sacred Myths and Formulas of the Cherokee*. Washington, D.C.: Smithsonian Institution Bureau of American Ethnology.

Munro, Ailie. 1996 [1984]. *The Democratic Muse: Folk Music Revivals in Scotland*. Edinburgh: Scottish Cultural Press.

Murdock, George Peter. 1972. *Outline of World Cultures.* New Haven: Human Relations Area Files, Inc.

Nairn, Tom. 1977. *The Break-Up of Britain.* London: Verso.

Neely, Sharlotte. 1991. *Snowbird Cherokees: People of Persistence.* Athens and London: University of Georgia Press.

Prebble, John. 1963. *The Highland Clearances.* London: Secker & Warburg.

Quillen, Rita Sams. 1989. *Looking for Native Ground: Contemporary Appalachian Poetry.* Boone, NC: Appalachian Consortium Press.

_____. 1997. "I AM A RUBE? The Question of Self-Image in Appalachia." In Best 1997: 131–133.

Redmond, Gerald. 1971. *The Caledonian Games in Nineteenth Century America.* Rutherford, NJ: Fairleigh Dickinson University Press.

Reed, John Shelton. 1983. *Southerners: The Social Psychology of Sectionalism.* Chapel Hill and London: University of North Carolina Press.

_____. 1986. *Southern Folk, Plain and Fancy: Native White Social Types.* Athens: University of Georgia Press.

Riach, Alan. 1992. "Reading Hugh MacDiarmid." In Riach and Grieve 1992: xiii–xxi.

Roosevelt, Theodore. 1904. *The Winning of the West.* New York: Current Literature Pub. Co.

Shapiro, Henry D. 1978. *Appalachia on Our Mind.* New Brunswick, NJ: Rutgers University Press.

_____. 1977. "Appalachia and the Idea of America: The Problem of the Persisting Frontier." In *An Appalachian Symposium: Essays in Honor of Cratis D. Williams.* Boone, NC: Appalachian State University Press; 42–55.

Skipp, Francis E., ed. 1989. *The Complete Short Stories of Thomas Wolfe.* New York: Collier Books.

Smith, Anthony D. 1979. *Nationalism in the Twentieth Century.* New York: New York University Press.

Smith, C. Gregory. 1978 [1919]. *Scottish Literature.* Folcroft, PA: Folcroft Library Editions.

Snyder, Bob. 1982. "Image and Identity in Appalachia." *AppalJ* vol. 9, nos. 2–3: 124–33.

Stern, Stephen, and John Allan Cicala, eds. 1991. *Creative Ethnicity.* Logan: Utah State University Press.

Trevor-Roper, Hugh. 1983. "The Invention of Tradition: The Highland Tradition of Scotland." In Eric Hobsbawm and Terence Ranger, eds., *The Invention of Tradition.* Cambridge, England: Cambridge University Press, 1983; 15–41.

Turnbull, Ronald, and Craig Beveridge. 1987. "Recent Scottish Thought." In Cairns Craig, ed., *The History of Scottish Literature,* Vol. 4. Aberdeen University Press, 1987; 61–74.

Wagner, Melinda B., Allen Batteau and Archie Green. 1983. "Images of Appalachia: A Critical Discussion." In Barry M. Buxton, ed., *The Appalachian Experience: Proceedings of the 6th Annual Appalachian Studies Conference.* Boone: Appalachian Consortium Press; 3–9.

Walls, David. 1977. "On the Naming of Appalachia." In *An Appalachian Symposium: Essays in Honor of Cratis D. Williams.* Boone, NC: Appalachian State University Press; 56–76.

Weller, Jack. 1995 [1965]. *Yesterday's People*. Lexington: University Press of Kentucky.

Whisnant, David. 1980a. "Developments in the Appalachian Identity Movement: All Is Process." *AppalJ* vol. 8, no. 1: 41–47.

_____. 1980b. *Modernizing the Mountaineer: People, Power and Planning in Appalachia*. New York: Burt Franklin (Second edition: University of Tennessee Press, 1994).

_____. 1983. *All Things Native and Fine: The Politics of Culture in an American Region*. Chapel Hill: University of North Carolina Press.

Williams, Cratis. 1972. "Who Are the Southern Mountaineers?" *Appalachian Journal* vol. 1, no. 1; reprinted in Robert J. Higgs and Ambrose N. Manning, *Voices from the Hills*. New York: Frederic Ungar Publishing Company, 1975; 493–506.

_____. 1961. *The Southern Mountaineer in Fact and Fiction*. Unpublished Ph.D. dissertation, New York University.

_____. 1999. *The Cratis Williams Chronicles: I Come to Boone*, Patricia Beaver and David Cratis Williams (eds.). Boone, NC: Appalachian Consortium Press.

White, Kenneth. 1998. *On Scottish Ground*. Edinburgh: Polygon.

Williams, Gordon. 1986. *From Scenes Like These*. Edinburgh: Magna Print Books; reprinted 1989 in paperback by B&W Books, Edinburgh.

Wertenbaker, Thomas Jefferson. 1963. *Old South: The Founding of American Civilization*. New York: Cooper Square.

Personal Communications
(Letters, notes of conversations and transcripts of recorded interviews)

Eberhard Bort, Edinburgh, 13 May 1996 (notes of conversation).

Anthony P. Cohen, Edinburgh, May through July 1996 (notes of conversations).

Peter Cooke, Edinburgh, 11 June 1996 (notes of conversation).

Rodger Cunningham, 13 August 1998 (letter).

Owen Dudley Edwards, Edinburgh, 31 May 1996 (notes of conversation).

Flora MacDonald Gammon, Waynesville, North Carolina, 17 January 1994 (taped interview).

Hamish Henderson, Edinburgh, 13 June 1996 (taped interview).

Joy Hendry, Edinburgh, 1 July 1996 (taped interview).

David McCrone, Edinburgh, 16 May 1996, 25 July 1996 (notes of conversations).

Ailie Munro, Edinburgh, 10 June 1996 (notes of conversation).

Index

Apalachen 21
Apalatchi 21; etymology of Appalachia 21
Appalachia: economic exploitation 20, 42, 52; etymology and pronunciation 20–21; geology 12, 19; history of human habitation 20; out-migration 11, 47; stereotypes 47
Appalachian Consortium 4, 61
Appalachian Journal (AppalJ) 52, 55, 57, 69
Appalachian Regional Commission (ARC) 13, 48
Appalachian State University 49, 51
Appalachian Studies: history of movement 1, 11, 13, 46, 47, 49, 98
Appalachian Studies Association 1, 2, 48, 49
Appalachian Studies Conference 1, 2, 12, 49
Appalshop, Whitesburg, KY 49

ballads 34, 35, 51
banjo 9–10
Batteau, Allen 2, 26, 54, 58 63–64, 99, 107, 124
Beaver, Patricia 50, 137
Berea College, Berea, Ky. 27, 28, 29, 143
Beside the Bonnie Brier Bush 29
Best, Bill 2, 3, 12, 132–33, 135, 143
Billy Boys 46
Blethen, H. Tylor 31
Bold, Alan 67–69, 144
"border thesis" (cultural pre-adaptation of Ulster Scots to Appalachian frontier) 31
Bort, Eberhard 142
Boyd, Clifford C., Jr. 23
"The Brier Sermon: You Must Be Born Again" 8, 11, 104–6; *see also* Miller, Jim Wayne
Brooklyn, NY 10, 11, 133
Bruford, Alan 61
Burns, Robert 26, 28, 29, 37, 38, 68, 108, 153, 158, 159

Caledonian anti-syzygy 58–61, 67, 107
Caledonian Games (19th century precursor of modern Highland Games) 74
Campbell, John C. 12, 27, 40–44; *see also* John C. Campbell Folk School
Campbell, Olive Dame 40
Caudill, Harry 10, 48
Ceilidh 79, 83, 90, 92–95, 118
Celtic Twilight 12, 54, 68–69
Center for Appalachian Studies and Services (CASS), East Tennessee State University 3
Chapman, Malcolm 14, 66, 69, 70, 99
Chapman (literary journal) 144, 147–50, 156
Cherokee 22–25; aboriginal name (Ani Yun Wiya) 22–23; origin of name (Tsalagi) 22
Choctaw 22
Civil War, American 48, 53
Clinch Valley College, Wise, VA 9, 48
Cohen, Anthony P. 16, 98, 126

Colonialism in Modern America 65; *see also* Lewis, Helen
colonialists and colonialism 53; and linguistic colonialism 50, 56, 68, 102, 131, 136–45
Council of the Southern Mountains (CSM) 40, 48
Covenanters 45
Cowan, Edward J. 67
Craig, Cairns 30, 103
Creech, Burley 134–35
cultural revitalization movements 59, 71, 72, 98, 135
cultural revivals 1, 9, 13–14, 26, 56, 63, 71, 72–75, 100, 124–31
Cunningham, Rodger 12, 13, 14, 15, 20, 25, 65, 69, 108, 136

Dall, John 77
deconstructionism 62, 124; cultural criticism 63, 100, 124
De Soto, Hernando 21
Doak, the Rev. Samuel 43
Doran, Paul 13, 44–45, 52
Dorson, Richard M. 10
double otherness 64, 107; Caledonian anti-syzygy 107; inferiorism 69, 143; *see also* "healing the divided self"
"A Drunk Man Looks at the Thistle" 8, 11, 106–9
Dunaway, Wilma A. 24
Dundes, Alan 71, 75, 130
Dykeman, Wilma 2, 13, 53, 56

East Tennessee State University, Johnson City, TN 1, 14, 140; Scottish Appalachian Program 14
Edwards, Owen Dudley 68
Einstein, Frank 2, 56
Eller, Ronald 135
Emory and Henry College, Emory, VA 9

Ferguson, Col. Patrick 43; *see also* Kings Mountain, Battle of
fiddle tunes 35, 87–88
Fischer, David Hackett 30, 38, 69
folk revivals 3, 9, 71, 81, 117–19, 134–31, 145
folk speech 27, 37, 128
Folklore Institute, Indiana U. 10
Fox, John, Jr. 12, 27, 28, 30–33, 56

Franklin, State of 43
Frost, William Goodell 12, 27–29, 38

Gaelic, revival of language 127
Gammon, Flora MacDonald 1, 2, 15, 76–97
Garber, Marjorie (*Vested Interests*) 129
Gatlinburg (TN) Highland Games 91, 93
Gaventa, John 57
George, Franklin 85, 88, 90
Germans in Appalachia 28, 42, 52
Gramsci, Antonio 113–14, 115, 125, 128
Grandfather Mountain (NC) Highland Games 15, 16, 90–97
Green, Archie 2, 64
Greig, John 15
Grose, Captain Francis 37
Gunn, Neil M. 64

Hamilton, Clive (C.S. Lewis) 7
handicrafts, revival of 28
Haring, Lee 10
Harrington, Michael 48
Harvie, Christopher 11, 106
"healing the divided self" 15, 25, 69, 71, 104, 107–8, 136
Hechter, Michael 102
Henderson, Hamish 1, 2, 110–23, 144, 153, 155
Hendry, Joy 1, 17, 144, 146–59
Higgs, Robert J. 52
Highland Clearances 25, 74
Highlander Center, New Market, TN 48–49
Highlanders, Scottish 13, 25, 30, 34, 39, 40
hillbillies 25, 30, 59, 113

identity politics 13, 57, 64, 72, 98, 100, 104, 105, 107, 131, 136, 156
identity reformulation 67, 71, 129, 150–59
indigenous language and literature, revivals of 13, 26, 35, 71, 72, 125–27, 145–51, 161
Irving, Washington (first published reference to Appalachia [1839]) 26

John C. Campbell Folk School 40
Jones, Loyal 49–50

Kailyard 29, 51, 54, 62, 100
Kay, Billy 138
Keller, Kenneth W. 33
Kephart, Horace 12, 27, 36–40
kilt: history of development 59–62; symbol of Scottish identity 59–62
King, Duane H. 22
"King Billy" (William of Orange) 46
Kings Mountain, Battle of 43

Laing, R.D. 25, 67, 136
Leonard, Tom 140–41
Lewis, Helen 9, 13, 48, 57
linguistic colonialism 3, 50–51, 131, 132–45, 150–51
Linton, Ralph 72
local color literature 29, 54
Lomax, Alan 114–16
Lunsford, Bascom Lamar 10

Macaulay, Thomas Babington 39
MacDiarmid, Hugh (Christopher Murray Grieve) 8, 16, 106–9, 110–12, 118–20, 147, 153–59
MacDonald, Donald 77, 78–80
MacDonald, Forrest 38, 59, 69
MacLaren, Ian (the Rev. John Watson) 29; *see also* Kailyard
MacLean, Sorley 149
MacNaughtan, Adam 112–13
Macpherson, James 73–75
Manning, Ambrose 52
McCrone, David 16, 29, 100, 126
McGowan, Thomas 57
McKay, Ian 16, 124
McKenzie, Roberta 16, 101–3
McNeil, W.K. 30
McWhiney, Grady 38, 59, 69
Miles, Emma Bell 12, 27, 33–35, 161
Miller, Jim Wayne 7, 11, 12, 16, 55, 104–6, 135, 143, 162–63
Montgomery, Michael 32
Mooney, James 22
Morris, David 76, 85, 88–90
Morton, Agnes McCrae 80–82
mountain boomers 36
Mountain Life and Work 9, 44
"mountain whites" 41, 44
Muskogean languages 21

Nairn, Tom 26, 100–2, 124
Neely, Sharlotte 22

Nicholson, Nancy 139–40
Norman, Gurney *(Divine Right's Trip)* 56
nostalgia 29, 56, 60, 68; *see also* cultural revitalization movements; folk revivals; romantic nationalism

Over Mountain Men 43; *see also* Kings Mountain
"Over the Water to Charlie" 34

poetics and identity politics 8, 12, 26, 134–36, 146, 154–55, 160–63
Prebble, John 58, 61–62
Presbyterians 33, 43–44, 78, 83

Quillen, Rita 141–42

Reed, John Shelton 69–70
Regulators (Battle of Alamance) 44
Riach, Alan 26
Ritchie, Jean 10
romantic nationalism 60, 64
Roosevelt, Theodore 43
Ross, John 24–25

Sandy Bell's 15
School of Scottish Studies, Edinburgh University 1, 2, 14, 25, 107
Scot, origin of name 22
Scotch-Irish 13, 20, 31–33, 35, 28, 40, 52, 99
Scots language 127 156–57
Scott, Sir Walter 30
Scottish organizations 73
Scottish Parliament 144, 158–59, 160–61
Scottish settlers in colonial America 20, 24, 36, 52
Shapiro, Henry D. 27, 54
singing games 34
Smith, Anthony D. 70
Smith, C. Gregory 67
Smoky Mountains 35
Snyder, Bob 57
social activism in Appalachia 99
Southern Back Country 20, 31, 38, 43, 52
Southern Highlanders 36–40
The Southern Mountaineer in Fact and Fiction 9, 51, 55; *see also* Williams, Cratis
Sprung, Roger 10
stereotypes 25, 69

Teuchter 22
Thoms, W.J. 8, 37
Toelken, Barrhy 129
Toynbee, Arnold 39
"The Trail of Tears" (Cherokee Removal of 1839) 25
Trevor-Roper, Hugh 59, 60–62
Turner, Frederick Jackson 43, 52

Ulster 43
Union of the Parliaments, 1707 72, 108, 169

Wagner, Melinda Bollar 3, 64
Wallace, Anthony F.C. 72
Wallerstein, Immanuel 57, 65; internal colonialism 57, 65; world systems theory 65, 101–3
Walls, David S. 20–21, 57
war on poverty 13, 48

Watauga settler see Over Mountain Men
Watson, Doc and Merle 51
Weatherford, W.D. (The Southern Appalachian Region: A Survey [1962]) 48, 50
Weller, Jack 48
Welsh, Irvine 43
Wertenbaker, Thomas Jefferson (The Old South [1961]) 28
Whiskey Rebellion 36
Whisnant, David 26, 57–62, 63–65, 124
Williams, Cratis 2, 8, 9, 11, 13, 42, 45, 49, 55, 58–59, 135–36, 137–38, 162
Williams, David Cratis 50
Williamson, J.W. ("Jerry") 52, 57
Wolfe, Thomas ("Only The Dead Know Brooklyn") 20–21, 105, 133
world systems theory 101–3; Hechter, Michael 15, 102; Wallerstein, Immanuel 101–2
Wovoka 8